A BIBLIOGRAPHY OF THE WRITINGS OF
JEREMY TAYLOR TO 1700

JEREMY TAYLOR

Drawn from the original in the possession of the Reverend Dr. Barrett of Lambeth, by G. F. Harding. Courtesy of Robert Gathorne-Hardy.

A BIBLIOGRAPHY OF THE WRITINGS OF

JEREMY TAYLOR

TO 1700

With a Section of Tayloriana

By

Robert Gathorne-Hardy

and

William Proctor Williams

NORTHERN ILLINOIS UNIVERSITY PRESS

DEKALB, ILLINOIS

Contents

Preface

This bibliography of Jeremy Taylor's writings is an expansion and revision of Robert Gathorne-Hardy's original bibliography which appeared in 1930 as part of Logan Pearsall Smith's *The Golden Grove: Selected Passages from the Sermons and Writings of Jeremy Taylor* (Oxford: The Clarendon Press). We have included all editions, printings, and issues of works by Taylor which appeared before 1700, with the sole exception of *On the Reverence Due to the Altar,* first published in 1848, which has been included. All works in this section of the bibliography, which is arranged in order of date of first publication, have been assigned an arabic number and each appearance of the work has been assigned a capital letter. For appearances of a work before approximately 1667, a quasi-facsimile transcription of the title-page, collation and pagination statement, and full description of the contents have been provided. For appearances after 1667, where little or no intervention from authorial material has occurred, a shortened title and statement of format only have been supplied. For all appearances notes on variants and general notes appear when appropriate. For editions and issues, locations of copies are included.

In general, the method of bibliographical description is that set forth by Professor Fredson Bowers, but modifications have been made. No attempt has been made to transcribe parts of the title-page in lower case non-Roman alphabets, nor have we tried to describe completely printers' devices and ornaments which are of no particular significance. In the collational formula we have allowed ourselves an occasional total of leaves which is an odd number when this is certainly the way the book was to be offered for sale to the public, and we have devised a statement of pagination which deals only with the leaves bearing page numbers, or which are part of a series of leaves bearing page numbers. When a particular page is not part of our pagination statement it indicates that the page is not part of such a series. In the statement of contents, the lack of recto or verso signs indicates that the entire leaf is meant. The heading of each entry lists the title of the work, if this is its first appearance, the nature of the appearance (edition, issue, or printing), the date, and the number assigned by the STC or Wing, if any.

However, a word about our use of the term "printing" is needed. A printing of a work in this bibliography means the production of a new edition of a single work as an integral part of another one. Thus, when *The Liberty of Prophesying* (No. 6) is reset in type for its occurrence as an integral part of the 1657 *Polemical Discourses* (No. 28 A), such an appearance is called a printing, and is bibliographically described under the latter work, though the transmission of the text involved is discussed under the former work. Since this situation occurs with many of Taylor's books, such a method for dealing with it was demanded.

The list of copies for each entry very greatly supplements the locations provided by Wing. Although we have seen nearly all of the copies listed, we do not mean to imply that we have examined every one, and the additional locations have been included as an aid to other scholars.

Three additional sections of this bibliography list the printings of Taylor's contributions to the works of other authors (the shortened form of description is employed), the printings of Taylor's letters and the locations of the originals of these letters, if known, and a section of Tayloriana which records significant contemporary biographical comments, spurious works, and attacks on Taylor during the seventeenth century. Items in the Contributions section are designated by an upper case C and an arabic numeral, in the Letters section by an upper case L and an arabic numeral, and in the Tayloriana section by an upper case T and an arabic numeral. No locations are given, but Wing numbers are provided throughout.

The compilation of this bibliography has been spread over so many years that it is simply impossible to thank personally all those librarians and scholars who have aided us in this work. Our thanks are therefore extended, broadcast, as it were, to the staffs of all those libraries listed in the Table of Library Abbreviations and to the individuals listed there. Mr. Williams would like to express his appreciation to Misses Diane Haack and Dona Ruby for their diligence in the preparation of the final manuscript of this bibliography.

ROBERT GATHORNE-HARDY
WILLIAM PROCTOR WILLIAMS

Table of Library Abbreviations

See also: Library. 5th Ser. 28(3) Sept. 1973. p.243-44 for holding of St. David's University College, Lampeter.

BRITISH

Ab	Aberdeen University
AC	St. Asaph's Cathedral
AO	All Souls' College, Oxford
AS	Advocates' Library, Scotland
BC	Bury St. Edmunds Cathedral
BM	British Museum
BO	Balliol College, Oxford
Bod	Bodleian Library, Oxford
CCC	Gonville and Caius College, Cambridge
CCO	Corpus Christi College, Oxford
CD	Cashel Diocesan Library
CHW	C. H. Wilkinson
CM	Chetham Library, Manchester
CO	Christ Church, Oxford
Con	Congregational Library, London
CUL	Cambridge University Library
D	Durham
DC	Dulwich College, London
Dro	Dromore Cathedral, Ireland
DW	Dr. Williams's Library, Dublin
E	Edinburgh University Library
EC	Ely Cathedral
ECM	E. C. Malden
EmC	Emmanuel College, Cambridge
Et	Eton College
Ex	Exeter Cathedral
FL	Friends Library, London
GK	Geoffrey Keynes
H	Robert Gathorne-Hardy
Hai	Haigh Hall (Crawford Library), Wigan
HM	Hugh Macdonald
IT	Inner Temple, London
J	St. John's College, Cambridge
JC	Jesus College, Cambridge
JR	John Rylands Library, Manchester
KCC	King's College, Cambridge
LI	Lincoln's Inn, London
Linc	Lincoln Cathedral
LS	Law Society, London
LSE	University of London, School of Economics
MC	Magdalen College, Cambridge
ML	Marsh's Library, London
MeO	Merton College, Oxford
MO	Magdalen College, Oxford
NC	Norwich Cathedral
NCE	New College, Edinburgh
NI	National Library of Ireland, Dublin

NLW National Library of Wales
NPL Norwich Public Library
P   Logan Pearsall Smith collection
PC   Peterborough Cathedral
PCC Pembroke College, Cambridge
PCD St. Patrick's Cathedral, Dublin
QC   Queen's College, Cambridge
R   Hugh Trevor-Roper
RIA Royal Irish Academy, Dublin
RLH Royal Library, Hague
RS   Roger Senhouse
SE   Signet Library, Edinburgh
TCC Trinity College, Cambridge
TCD Trinity College, Dublin
Th   Thomason Collection, BM
VA   Victoria and Albert Museum
WO   Worcester College, Oxford

AMERICAN

Bow Bowdoin College
BP   Boston Public Library
C   Colgate
Cla Clark Library, Los Angeles
Col Columbia University, New York
CU   Colorado University
CW   Chapin Library, Williams College
F   Folger Library, Washington, D.C.

FU   Fordham University
Har Harvard University
Hav Haverford College
HH   Henry Huntington Library, San Marino, Calif.
I   University of Illinois
KS   Kansas State University
KU   University of Kansas
LC   Library of Congress, Washington, D.C.
MU   University of Michigan
NIU Northern Illinois University
NL   Newberry Library, Chicago
NW   Northwestern University
NYP New York Public Library
Pb   Peabody Library, New York
PH   Pennsylvania Historical Society
PU   Princeton University
RB   Carleton R. Richmond, Boston
RU   Rutgers University
S   Stanford University
SC   Swarthmore College
Tex University of Texas
UC   University of Chicago
US   Union Seminary, New York
V   University of Virginia
W   William Proctor Williams
Wat Watkins Library, Hartford, Calif.
Wi   Donald Wing
WSC Washington State College
Y   Yale University

Works Frequently Cited

Arber, Edward. *The Term Catalogues, 1668–1709.* . . . 3 vols. London, 1903–1906.

Gosse, Edmund. *Jeremy Taylor.* London, 1904.

Johnson, Alfred Forbes. *A Catalogue of Engraved and Etched English Title-Pages Down to the Death of William Faithorne, 1691.* Oxford, 1934.

Lowndes, William T. *The Bibliographer's Manual of English Literature.* new ed. Henry G. Bohn. 6 vols. London, 1857–64.

The Poems and Verse Translations of Jeremy Taylor. ed. Alexander B. Grosart. London, 1870.

Pollard, A. W., and G. R. Redgrave. *A Short-Title Catalogue . . . 1475–1640.* London, 1926.

A Transcript of the Registers of the Worshipful Company of Stationers; From 1640–1708 A.D. ed. G. E. B. Eyre. 3 vols. London, 1913–14.

The Whole Works of Jeremy Taylor. ed. Reginald Heber. 15 vols. London, 1822; revised by Charles Page Eden. 10 vols. London, 1847–52.

Willmott, Robert Aris. *Bishop Jeremy Taylor: His Predecessors, Contemporaries and Successors.* London, 1847.

Wing, Donald. *Short-Title Catalogue of Books . . . 1640–1700.* 3 vols. New York, 1945–51.

Wood, Anthony. *Athenae Oxonienses.* 2 vols. London, 1691–92; second edition, 1721.

Sources for letters quoted can be found in the "Letters" section of this bibliography.

I

Works by Jeremy Taylor to 1700

1 A. *Gunpowder Sermon.* First Edition. Oxford, 1638. STC 23724.

Title: [all within double rules] A | SERMON | PREACHED IN | SAINT MARIES | Church in OXFORD. | Vpon the Anniversary of the | GUNPOWDER-TREASON. | [rule] | By IEREMY TAYLOR, Fellow of | *Allsoules Colledge in* OXFORD. | [rule] | *Nolite tangere Christos meos* | [device] | OXFORD, | Printed by LEONARD LITCHFIELD | Printer to the Vniversity. | M. DC. XXXVIII.

Coll: Quarto: A-E⁴ F² G-K⁴ L², 40 leaves. Paged irregularly B2ʳ-L2ᵛ: pp. 1-34, 37-52, 45-64 [=70].

Contents: A1ʳ, title-page (verso blank); A2ʳ-B1ᵛ, dedication to Laud; B2ʳ-L2ᵛ, text.

Variants: On B1ᵛ, the last line of the dedication is a short one with only three words. This is followed below by "Your Graces | most observant | and obliged | Chaplaine | Ier. Taylor." In some copies "Your Graces" begins to the right of the last line, and the line "and obliged" reaches beyond the word "Chaplaine" below it. In other copies "Your Graces" begins within the limits of the preceding line, and "Chaplaine" extends to the right beyond "obliged."

On F2ʳ (p. 33), in some copies the first word of the last line is "refute," and the catchword is "of"; this is correct. In other copies the words are "efute" and "for." The first variant is most likely the result of a badly locked up chase, with perhaps too few quads. The second must be due to an accident. The r of "refute" must have come out, and probably, at the same time, the catchword; the three letters, happening to make up a word, were then put back inaccurately as "for." Any of these variants may occur with either from the other pair; since each was evidently the result of type being disturbed during the printing, no priority can possibly be assigned to any of them.

Notes: As in other such cases, the irregularity of paging is probably due to the employment of two or three compositors at once, and perhaps two presses. The paper used is not always uniform throughout, suggesting either haste or economy in the printing. The two half-sheets F and L are probably a whole sheet divided into two; this theory is perhaps borne out by the fact that, whereas

3

the normal full page has thirty lines to it, the seven full pages on these two half-sheets are of thirty-one lines each, the matter left over being compressed to save paper. We have not noticed any regular appearance of the watermark in these half-sheets; in one copy taken at random F has the watermark and L has none, while in another copy there is no watermark in either sheet.

Royston, Taylor's most regular publisher, eventually took over the Sermon but he did not enter it in the Stationers' Register until April 18, 1656, when he entered it together with *Episcopacy Asserted* (No. 2), and *An Apology for Liturgy* (No. 8), obviously for the purpose of establishing his rights, before reprinting these works in *Polemical Discourses, 1657* (No. 28 A). According to Anthony Wood, Taylor was at this time suspected of leanings toward Rome; and there is an improbable tradition that the Vice-Chancellor of Oxford forced Taylor to introduce anti-papal passages. Since the whole Sermon is anti-papal, it is difficult to see how this could have been necessary.

St. John's College, Cambridge, has a large paper copy. This copy measures $9\frac{7}{8} \times 6\frac{1}{8}$ inches (a normal cut copy measures about $7\frac{1}{4} \times 5\frac{1}{4}$ inches). It is bound up in a volume of tracts bequeathed to the college in 1638 by Francis Dee, the Laudian Bishop of Peterborough, who died in October of that year. Dee had, in 1638, inducted Taylor into the living of Uppingham.

A large paper presentation copy is in the BM. It is partly uncut, inscribed on the title-page, in what is almost certainly Taylor's hand, "ex dono authoris." A biographer of Taylor's, Robert Aris Willmott, in discussing this sermon, says, "I have had the gratification of reading his discourse in a copy rendered invaluable by the autograph inscription of the author" (p. 98), and he adds in a note "Ex dono authoris on the title-page." Since inscribed presentation copies of Taylor's works are extremely rare, it is probable that Willmott was referring to this particular one.

Copies: AC, BM, Bod, CUL, J, JR, Linc (2), LSE, PC, TCD; Col, CW, F, HH, LC, NYP, Wat, Y.

1 B-C. Second and Third Issues. 1648 and 1650.

See *Treatises,* 1648 and 1650 (Nos. 7 A and 10 A).

Notes: A large edition must have been printed of this, almost the dullest of all Taylor's works, for the book is by no means uncommon, and cannot have been sold out before 1650. Remainders of this edition made up a part in each of the two composite volumes of *Treatises.* It does not appear to have been separately reprinted.

1 D. Second Printing. 1657.

See *Polemical Discourses* 1657 (No. 28 A).

Notes: There appear to be no alterations in the text. This was the only reprint made during Taylor's lifetime. A heading to the second printing says that the sermon was preached in 1637. Gosse—and he was not alone in this—assumed that the year was 1638. The date is probably not significant. It seems to have been a not uncommon practice to date a book printed during the winter by the approaching year.

1 E. Third Printing. 1673.

See *Eniautos,* 1673 (No. 20 D), where it is added to the *Ten Sermons* (No. 44 B).

1 F. Fourth Printing. 1678.

See *Eniautos,* 1678 (No. 20 E).

2 A. *Of the Sacred Order.* First Edition. Oxford, 1642. Wing T353.

Title: [all within double rules] OF THE | SACRED ORDER, | *AND OFFICES OF* | EPISCOPACY, | BY DIVINE INSTITUTION, | Apostolicall Tradition, | *& Catholike practice.* | *TOGETHER* | With their titles of Honour, Secular | employment, manner of election, dele- | gation of their power, and other appen- | dant questions, asserted against the | *Aerians, and Acephali,* | *new and old.* | [rule] | By IER. TAYLOR late Fellow of | *All-Soules* in *Oxon.* | [rule] | Published by His MAIESTIES Command. | [rule] | *There is no Power but of God. The powers that be are or-* | *dained of God.* Rom. 13. 1. | Council Chalced. | [one line of Greek] | [rule] | OXFORD, | Printed by LEONARD LITCHFIELD, | *Printer to the Vniversity.* 1642.

Coll: Quarto: §⁴ ¶¶⁴ A-3B⁴ 3C², 202 leaves. Paged A1ʳ-3C3ᵛ: pp. 1-386.

Contents: §1ʳ, title-page (verso blank); §2ʳ-¶¶2ʳ, Dedication to Sir Christopher Hatton; ¶¶2ᵛ, blank; ¶¶3ʳ-¶¶4ᵛ, Syllabus Paragraphorum, followed by errata list; A1ʳ-3C1ᵛ, text; 3C2, blank.

Variants: The headlines in sheet A are *"Of the Sacred Order,* | *and Offices of Episcopacy &c."* In the rest of the book the headline to each page is simply *"Episcopacy asserted."* In some copies, the headline on A4ᵛ (p. 8) is *"Of the Sacred Order"* facing *"Episcopacy asserted"* (B1ʳ); in other copies, the heading to A4ᵛ has been corrected to *"Episcopacy asserted."* It is clear that the sheets were gathered indiscriminately. Examples of the heading in its earlier state can be found in the 1647 second issue (No. 2 B); copies with the corrected headline are often to be found with the 1642 title-page.

Notes: Of the Sacred Order was entered in the Stationers' Register by Richard Royston on April 18, 1656 (See No. 1 above). On November 1, 1642, Taylor was made Doctor of Divinity at Oxford probably as a reward for writing this book. Heylyn, in *Cyprianus Anglicus* (1671), says that the book, with the *Aeriomastrix* of John Theyer, was "backt . . . and encouraged by many Petitions to his Majesty and both Houses of Parliament, not only from the two Universities, whom it most concerned, but from several Counties of the Kingdom." It was, of course, a small particle in a huge controversy, and seems to have excited very little notice in the world, with the exceptions mentioned above, unless it aroused the reference to Taylor in *Mercurius Britannicus* (No. 69) as "a most spruce neat formalist, a very ginger-bread idol, an Arminian in print." By the time of its publication, even the great protagonists, Milton and Hall, had withdrawn from the battle. The book was referred to in advertisements, as in the headlines, and at least once by Taylor himself, as *Episcopacy Asserted*. This abbreviated title was evidently borrowed from Joseph Hall's *Episcopacie by Divine Right Asserted* (1640, STC 12661), which started off the Smectymnuus controversy.

BM and H possess large paper copies. H is 8½ × 6¼ inches (a normal cut copy is about 7¼ × 5¼ inches). The BM copy is in a handsome contemporary calf binding, now somewhat perished; the H copy is in a particularly beautiful contemporary morocco binding with gilt and gauffered edges. An unlocatable copy, formerly H2, is also in contemporary morocco, but its margins have been injured by damp. The first two copies, and perhaps the third also, have A4ᵛ (p. 8) in its corrected state; this indicates that the large paper copies were printed off when the rest of the edition had been completed. These large paper copies may have been for presentation, though none of those recorded is inscribed; but it is not unlikely that they were produced with an eye to the wealthy royalists who were then crowding into Oxford.

Copies: AS, BM, Bod, CUL, H, TCD; Har, I, US, W.

2 B. Second Issue. 1647. Wing T354.

Title: OF | THE SACRED ORDER | AND OFFICES OF | EPISCO-PACIE, | By *Divine Institution, Apostolicall Tradition,* | and *Catholique Practice* | *TOGETHER WITH* | Their Titles of Honour, Secular Employ- | ment, Manner of Election, Delega- | tion of their Power, and other ap- | pendant | questions, asserted against the | *Aerians, and Acephali,* | new and old. | [rule] | By Ier: Taylor, D. D. Chaplaine in | Ordinarie to His Maiestie | [rule] | Published by His Maiesties Command. | [rule] | Rom. 13. 1. | *There is no power but of God. The Powers that be, are ordained of God.* | [rule] | Concil. Chalced. | [one line of Greek] | [rule] | *LONDON,* | Printed for Richard Royston | at the Angel in Ivie-lane. 1647.

Coll and *Contents:* as in No. 2 A, except § 1 is a cancel.

Variants: The TCC copy of *Treatises,* 1650 (No. 10 A) has, as part of its contents, this issue showing the apparent stub of the 1642 title-page, and, between the stub and the 1647 title-page a blank page. It may be part of a half-sheet on which Royston's cancel title-page was printed.

Copies: BM, Bod, GK; Har, I, KS, US, Y.

2 C-D. Third and Fourth Issues. 1648 and 1650.

Of the Sacred Order was remaindered by Royston as part of *Treatises,* 1648 (No. 7 A) and *Treatises,* 1650 (No. 10 A). In these cases it usually, but not always, appears with the 1647 title-page.

2 E. Second Printing. 1657.

See *Polemical Discourses,* 1657 (No. 28 A).

2 F. Third Printing. 1674.

See *Polemical Discourses,* 1674 (No. 28 B).

Notes: A number of misprints are corrected in the list of errata at the end of this volume. Three in English, two in Latin, and one in Greek correct errors which first appeared in the second printing (1657, 2 E); one in Latin, and one in English correct errors which had escaped notice in both the first edition and second printing (1642, 2 A and 1657, 2 E). The small remainder is of errors which first appeared in this third printing. This pattern of correction demonstrates that the 1657 printing was set from a copy of 1642 and the 1674 printing from a copy of 1657. The subtlety of the corrections, involving slips in ancient tongues, and the fact that one such slip is first corrected here, hint at the dead author's hand. It seems not improbable that, after the printing of the text had been completed, it was collated with a copy of the 1657 printing corrected by Taylor. It will be found under other entries that the texts of most works reprinted in the 1674 edition of *Polemical Discourses* appear to have undergone the same meticulous treatment.

3 A. 1-2. *The Psalter of David* and *Devotions.* First Edition. Oxford, 1644. Wing B2402 and D1238.

Title of 1: [all within double rules] *THE* | PSALTER | OF | DAVID | WITH | Titles and Collects accor- | ding to the matter of each | Psalme | [row of four type orns.] | OXFORD, | Printed by *Leonard Lichfield,* Printer to | the *Vniversity.* 1644.

Title of 2: [all within double rules] DEVOTIONS | FOR THE | Helpe and assistance | OF ALL | *CHRISTIAN PEOPLE:* | In all occasions and necessities. | [rule] | [woodcut] | [rule] | Printed in the Yeare, | 1644.

Coll of 1: 8vo: *⁸ **² A-2A⁸ 2B⁴, 206 leaves; plates 1 (engraved title [Johnson: Vaughan #10] before *1). Paged A1ʳ-2B4ᵛ: pp. 1-392.

Contents of 1: *1ʳ, title-page (verso blank); *2ʳ-**2ᵛ, "The Preface"; A1ʳ-2B4ᵛ, text.

Coll of 2: 8vo: A-D⁸, 32 leaves. Paged A2ʳ-D8ʳ: pp. 3-63.

Contents of 2: A1ʳ, title-page (verso blank); A2ʳ-D8ʳ, text; D8ᵛ, blank.

Note: Numbers 1 and 2 always appear together but were apparently considered somewhat distinct in this edition. Hereafter they will be considered as one work.

Variants: In copy H, the title-page to the *Devotions* is a cancel; part of the cancelled leaf can be seen. The binding is of the seventeenth century, decorated and mended in the nineteenth; however, it does not appear that the original stitching has been interfered with. The cancel title-page is printed from exactly the same setting as those found in the other copies. It is possible that some alteration or damage took place while the sheet was being printed, and that the faulty variant was cancelled. It is also possible that the paper was defective in copy H and that a perfect leaf was used to replace the imperfect one.

Notes: This book was advertised for many years as by Christopher, Lord Hatton; yet, from a relatively early date, it was attributed to Taylor. The Bod copy belonged to Anthony Wood and is inscribed, "For my noble & much honored frend Sr John Culpeper Kt Master of the Roles from your affectionate & obliged servant Chr: Hatton." It is dated March 7, 1644, by Hatton. "Chr: Hatton" has been crossed out, and "Edward Wood" written in. Anthony Wood has added a note: "Sr Joh. Culpep. Kt. then lodging in my mothers house against Merton Coll. Christopher Ld. Hatton then in Oxon. sent him this book, wch. after Culpeps departure came into the hands of my brother Edw. Wood." Opposite the engraved title, Anthony Wood has written, "These psalmes with the devotions at the end were collected & published by Christopher. Ld. Hatton." Below, in different ink, he has added, "But written by Dr. jer Taylor of Alls Coll." For other opinions of Wood on this work see No. 3 E below. Every editor of Taylor, and almost every writer on him, has accepted the proposition that he had at least a very large hand in the work. For the present writers' belief about the division of authorship between Hatton and Taylor see *The Times Literary Supplement,* February 18, 1955, p. 1127.

Copies: BM, Bod, H.

3 B.   Second Edition. 1646. Wing B2419.

Title: THE | PSALTER | OF | *DAVID:* | WITH | Titles and Collects according | to the matter of each *Psalme.* | *Whereunto is added,* | DEVOTIONS | For the help and assistance | of all Christian People, in all | occasions and necessities. | [double rule] | *LONDON,* | Printed for R. ROYSTON, | at the Angel in *Ivie-Lane.* | 1646.

Coll: 12mo: A^{12} (a)^2 B-Q^{12} R^6, 200 leaves. Paged B1^r-R5^v: pp. 1-370.

Contents: A1, blank; A2^r, engraved title-page (verso blank); A3^r, title-page (verso blank); A4^r-A11^r, "The Preface"; A11^v, blank; A12^r, table of psalms (verso blank); (a)1^r-(a)2^v, index; B1^r-O9^v, text of the *Psalter*; O10, blank; O11^r, divisional title for *Devotions* (verso blank); O12^r-R5^v, text of *Devotions*; R6, blank.

Variants: Copy H is lacking O11 and O12.

Notes: The engraved title-page is the same as in the first edition but has now found its way inside the first gathering.

In this edition there is omitted from *Devotions* a prayer for the bishops; evidence of uncharacteristic timidity on Royston's part, comparable to his temporary substitution of "Ruler" for "King" in the second and third editions of *Holy Living* (Nos. 11 B and 11 C).

Copies: BM, Bod, H.

3 C.   Third Edition. 1647. Wing B2426.

Title: THE | PSALTER | OF | *DAVID:* | WITH | Titles and Collects according to | the matter of each PSALME. | *Whereunto is added,* | DEVO-

TIONS | For the help and assistance | of all Christian People, in all | occasions and necessities. | [rule] | The third EDITION. | [rule] | *LONDON,* | Printed for R. ROYSTON, at | the Angel in *Ivie-lane.* | 1647.

Coll: 12mo: A-Q^{12} R^6, 198 leaves. Paged B1^r-R6^r: pp. 1-371.

Contents: A1^r, blank; A1^v, engraved title; A2^r, title-page (verso blank); A3^r-A9^r, "The Preface"; A9^v, blank; A10^r, table of psalms (verso blank); A11^r-A12^v, index; B1^r-O9^v, text of *Psalmes*; O10, blank; O11^r, divisional title for *Devotions* (verso blank); O12^r-R6^r, text of *Devotions*; R6^v, blank.

Variants: Bod copy has the following prayer, in a contemporary hand, pasted on the last end-paper:

> For the mystery of thy holy Incar=
> =nation, for thy holy nativity and cir=
> = cumcision, for thy Baptism Fasting
> and Temptation
>   For thine Agony and bloudy sweat,
> For thy Cros and Passion. for thy-
> Pretious Death & Buriall, for thy
> Glorious Resurrection & Ascension,
> and for the Coming of the holy Ghost.

Notes: This edition is a fairly careful reprinting of the second edition (No. 3 B). In this edition the prayer for the bishops is re-inserted.

Copies: Bod.

3 D. Fourth Edition. 1650. Wing B2439.

Title: THE | PSALTER | OF | *DAVID:* | WITH | Titles and Collects according to | the matter of each PSALME. | *Whereunto is added,* | DEVO-TIONS | For the help and assistance | of all Christian People, in all | occasions and necessities. | [rule] | The fourth EDITION. | [rule] | *LONDON,* | Printed by *J. F.* for *R. Royston* at | the *Angel* in *Ivy-Lane.* | 1650.

Coll: 12mo: A-Q^{12} R^6, 198 leaves. Paged B1^r-R6^r: pp. 1-371.

Contents: A1^r, blank; A1^v, engraved title; A2^r, title-page (verso blank); A3^r-A9^r, "The Preface"; A9^v, blank; A10^r, table of psalms (verso blank); A11^r-A12^v, index; B1^r-O9^v, text of *Psalms*; O10, blank; O11, division title for *Devotions* (verso blank); O12^r-R6^r, text of *Devotions*; R6^v, blank.

Notes: This work is a very close reprinting of the previous edition; sometimes following not only page for page but line for line. However, comparison of the two editions indicates that the work was entirely re-set for this edition.

The engraved title is the same as in previous editions but badly worn.

Copies: BM, Bod.

3 E. Fifth Edition. 1655. Wing B2439.

Title: THE | PSALTER | OF | *DAVID:* | WITH | Titles and Collects according to | the matter of each PSALME. | *Whereunto is added,* | DEVO-

TIONS | for the help and assistance | of all Christian People, in all | occasions and necessities. | [rule] | The fifth | EDITION Enlarged. | [rule] | *LONDON,* | Printed by J. F. for *R. Royston* at | the *Angel* in *Ivy Lane.* | 1655.

Coll: 12mo: A-O¹², 178 leaves; plates 1(2 leaf plate between B11 & 12). Paged C3ʳ-O12ʳ: pp. 1-283.

Contents: A1ʳ, blank; A1ᵛ, engraved title; A2ʳ, title-page (verso blank); A3ʳ-A8ʳ, "The Preface"; A8ᵛ, blank; A9ʳ-B2ʳ, *"The Calendar"*; B2ᵛ-B11ᵛ, almanack & perpetual calendar; B12, "The use of the Circular INSTRUMENT"; C1ʳ-C2ᵛ, index; C3ʳ-M12ᵛ, text of *Psalter*; N1ʳ, divisional title for *Devotions* (verso blank); N2ʳ-O12ʳ, text of *Devotions*; O12ᵛ, blank.

Notes: For this edition the engraved title has been touched up and the border has been slightly cut down, not affecting the engraved part. Vaughan's name, removed in the process, is restored in the engraving in the pavement at the feet of King David.

The "Calendar" and tables for finding movable feasts (A9ʳ-B12ᵛ) were added to the work in this edition, as was the plate of the "Circular Instrument" which was to be used in computing religious dates.

In the Bod copy, which was Wood's, the following note appears on the fore end-paper in Wood's hand:

The I. edit. of this book
came out in Oxon. in
1644. Collected, written
& published by Christoph
Ld Hatton.

Copies: BM, Bod, TCC; Har.

3 F. Sixth Edition. 1661. Wing B2474.

Title: THE | PSALTER | OF | *DAVID*: | WITH | Titles and Collects according to | the matter of each PSALM. | *Whereunto is added* | DEVO-TIONS | For the help & assistance | of all Christian People, in | all occasions and necessities. | [rule] | The sixth EDITION Enlarged. | [rule] | *LONDON,* | Printed by *J. F.* for *R. Royston* at | the *Angel* in *Ivy-Lane.* | 1661.

Coll: 12mo: A¹² (-A1) B-Q¹² R⁶, 198 leaves; plates 2 (before A2; folding plate before A9). Paged C1ʳ-R4ᵛ: pp. 1-344.

Contents: A1, cancelled; A2ʳ, title-page (verso blank); A3ʳ-A8ᵛ, Preface; A9ʳ-B2ʳ, calendar; B2ᵛ-B11ʳ, almanack & perpetual calendar; B11ᵛ, "Place the Circular *Instrument* here"; B12, use of the circular instrument; C1ʳ-P1ᵛ, text of *Psalter*; P2ʳ, divisional title-page for *Devotions* (verso blank); P3ʳ-R4ᵛ, text of *Devotions*; R5ʳ-R6ᵛ, index.

Notes: In Bod copy the plate of the circular instrument is bound in between A8 and 9 but the verso of B11 still reads "Place the Circular *Instrument* here" and the instructions on its use follow on B12.

The usual engraved title-page appears.

This is listed by Madan in *Oxford Books* (May 2, 1644) as a 1657 edition. No such edition appeared and the Bodleian has now concluded their copy of Madan to read 1661.

Copies: Ab, Bod.

3 G. Seventh Edition. 1668. Wing B2495.

Title: THE | PSALTER | OF | *DAVID*: | WITH | Titles and Collects according to | the matter of each PSALM. | *Whereunto is added* | DEVO-TIONS | For the help & assistance | of all Christian People, in | all occasions and necessities. | [rule] | The seventh Edition Enlarged. | [rule] | *LONDON,* | Printed by *E. Tyler* for *R. Royston* | Book-seller to the Kings most | Excellent Majestie, 1668.

Coll: 12mo: B¹²(-B1) C-Q¹² R⁶, 186 leaves; plates 1 (before B2). Paged C1ʳ-R4ᵛ: pp. 1-344.

Contents: B2ʳ, title-page (verso blank); B3ʳ-B12ᵛ, preface; C1ʳ-P1ᵛ, text of *Psalter*; P2ʳ, divisional title-page for *Devotions* (verso blank); P3ʳ-R4ᵛ, text of *Devotions*; R5ʳ-R6ᵛ, index.

Notes: The plate of David is tipped in on the stub of B1.

This edition was advertised in the Term Catalogue for Michaelmas, 1668.

This edition omits from the *Devotions* the prayer for the Prince of Wales. There are added at the end "A Prayer wherewith S. Augustine began his Devotions" (R4), "A Prayer wherewith to conclude our Devotions" (R4ᵛ), and the "Blessing." We have not found these in Taylor's acknowledged works.

P3 is missigned P5.

Copies: BM.

3 H. Eighth Edition. 1672. Wing B2509.

The Psalter of David ... Devotions ... By *Jer. Taylor* D. D. Chaplain to King *Charles* I of Blessed Memory ... Eighth Edition Enlarged ... London, Printed by *E. T.* and *R. H.* for *R. Royston* Bookseller to the King's most Excellent Majesty. MDCLXXII. 12mo.

This edition has the same engraved title as previous editions. Taylor's name appears at the end of the Preface for the first and only time in any edition of this work.

The printers, whose names appear on the divisional title for *Devotions,* were E. Tyler and R. Holt.

There was perhaps a second issue of this edition, since an edition is advertised in the Michaelmas Term Catalogue for 1679. However, we know of no copies having a title-page bearing this date.

Copies: Bod, H.

3 I. Ninth Edition. 1683. Wing B2552.

The Psalter of David ... Devotions ... The Tenth Edition ... London, Printed by J. Macock for Richard Royston ... 1683. 12mo.

The final two leaves of the "Preface" signed a and a2, appear in the Bod copy between T2 and T3, in the "Index." T is a six-leaf signature and the last two leaves of "Preface" were printed with the "Index" as an octavo gathering and in the case of the Bod copy were not removed and placed in their proper location.

This edition has seven extra prayers, as well as the three extra which appeared in the seventh edition. The seven are reprinted with slight alterations from *A Collection of Offices,* 1658 (No. 30 A). In the following list they are given their original headings, and the new ones where there has been an alteration. The prayers are numbered in *Psalter,* and their number appears directly before the title of the prayer.

A Collection &c.	*The Psalter*
I 4. A General Confession	S 8^r, xvii. "A General Confession." The "we" of 1658 is altered to "I."
B 8^v-C1^r. A Prayer against Temptation	S 8^v, xviii. "A Prayer against Temptations."
O 4. A wife's prayer "if, from a vitious husband she have escaped any violence intended her by his malice or passion."	S 9^r, xix. "A Prayer for Thanksgiving for any great deliverance."
Q 8. A Prayer for all prisoners	S 9^v, xx. "A Prayer to be said by a Prisoner in behalf of himself."
R 6. The Prayer, under the general heading "A forme of prayer for Mariners."	S 10^r, xxi. A Prayer to be used by those that "are at Sea."
R 6^v-R 7^v. In a storme, or danger of Pirates or shipwrack, and a prayer headed III.	S 11^v-S 12^v, xxii and ii. The same title and prayers, but shortened from the 1658 version, and differently divided.

St. Augustine's Prayer, numbered XVII, precedes these additions, "A Prayer . . . to conclude . . . our Devotions," numbered XXIV, and "The Blessing," from the seventh edition (No. 3 G), follow at the end.
Copies: BM, Bod.
3 J. Tenth Edition ["Eleventh"]. 1691. Wing B2578.

The Psalter of David ... Devotions ... The Eleventh Edition ... Printed by
R. N. for Luke Meredith, at the Angel in Amen-corner, 1691. 12mo.

A new plate, before A2, was added to this edition. It replaces the old plate
of David. The David in the new plate is also playing the lyre, but is seated,
facing forward. The same passage from Mark 11.10. is at the foot. It is signed
"Sturt sc:".

This edition may have been issued again in 1696 for there is an advertisement in the Hilary Term Catalogue of that year for such a work to be "sold by
P. Moncton at the Star in St. Paul's Churchyard." However, we have never
seen a copy of the work bearing a title-page of that date.
Copies: BM.

4 A. *Prayer Ex tempore.* First Edition. Oxford, 1646. Wing T312.
Title: A | DISCOURSE | *concerning* | PRAYER *Ex tempore,* | or, | By pre-
tence of the Spirit. | *In Iustification of Authorized and* | *Set-formes of Lyt-*
urgie. | [rule] | I. Cor. 14. 32. | [two lines of Greek and two lines of translation]
| [rule] | [orn.] | [rule] | Printed in the Yeere, | CIƆ IƆC XLVI.
Coll: Quarto: A-E⁴, 20 leaves. Paged A2ʳ-E4ᵛ: pp. 1-38.
Contents: A1ʳ, title-page (verso blank); A2ʳ-E4ᵛ, text.
Copies: AS, Bod, CUL, H, TCD; Har, HH, I, US, Tex, Y.
4 B. Second Edition. Oxford, 1646. Wing T312.

Title, Coll, and *Contents* as in 4 A with the exception of L for *L* in "Lyt-
urgie" (line 8) of the title-page.
Notes: The text of the second edition is, with one or two exceptions, a line for
line reprinting of the first edition until E3ʳ. In the remaining two leaves (E3
and E4) the text is slightly compressed, so that on E4ᵛ (p. 38) there are twenty-
two lines, whereas on the corresponding page of the first edition there are
twenty-eight lines. In both the first and second editions, at the beginning of the
text (A2ʳ) the ornamental capital is printed from the same block, but it is
upside down in the second edition. These editions cannot, therefore, be simul-
taneous printings.

Although no place of publication is given in the imprint, the ornament on
the title-page, which also appears at the head of A2ʳ (p. 1) was used at Oxford
and is found in the first edition of *The Psalter of David* (No. 3 A) which was
printed at Oxford.

The correction of the title-page and the compression of the text on the last
two leaves of the second edition are both indications of the order of the printings, but there is other historical evidence which corroborates such an order.
The absence of any name—either the author's, publisher's, or printer's—argues
that the production was a somewhat dangerous affair, and was probably car-

ried out after the surrender of Oxford in June, 1646. The book, in either form, is not extremely rare which suggests it must have had a fair, if surreptitious, circulation, and probably a demand for copies came from London; for this purpose a second edition was printed. Thomason's copy, which was, of course, acquired in London, is dated December 6, 1646, and is a second edition. The author's name was not a mystery to Thomason for he has added to his copy, "By Dr Tailour."

This work is in the form of a letter to a friend, occasioned by *A Directory for the Publique Worship of God,* published early in 1644. *A Directory* was the replacement for the Book of Common Prayer. The guidance of this work was obligatory on all ministers. It may be surmised that this guidance was sometimes evaded, for in copy H, which evidently belonged to a conforming Anglican, there are written carefully composed prayers, by no means extempore, and extracts from the Book of Common Prayer.

Copies: Th, H.

4 C. Third Edition. 1647. Wing T313.

Title: A | DISCOURSE | *CONCERNING* | PRAYER *Ex tempore,* | OR, | By pretence of the Spirit, | *In justification of Authorized and Set-forms* | of LITURGIE. | [rule] | I COR. 14.32. | [two lines of Greek and three lines of translation] | [rule] | [orn.] | [rule] | Printed for *Richard Royston,* 1647.

Coll: Quarto: A-D⁴, 16 leaves. Paged A2ʳ-D4ᵛ: pp. 1-30.

Contents: A1ʳ, title-page (verso blank); A2ʳ-D4ᵛ, text.

Notes: This edition is set from the first edition (4 A). Taylor was gone from Oxford by 1645 when he was taken prisoner at the siege of Cardigan Castle, and after his release there is no evidence that he left Wales during the next two years. During this period (1646-47) Royston became the new publisher of Taylor's works and in his arrangements with Lichfield, Taylor's Oxford publisher, he no doubt received a copy of the first edition of this work.

The third edition must have been a large one, and sold slowly, for it was put into the *Treatises* of 1648 (No. 7 A), and was also used in *Two Discourses* of 1653 (No. 18 A). It is also found occasionally bound up with the 1647 *Liberty of Prophesying* (No. 6 A).

This was the last appearance of *Prayer Ex tempore* in its original form. In the process of rewriting and enlarging this work as *An Apology for Liturgy* (No. 8 A) paragraphs 15-20, 34, 36-37 and 39-41 were omitted, and they have never been reprinted since 1647.

Copies: Bod, H, Hag, Hai; Har, I, LC, NL, Y.

5 A. *New Institution of Grammar.* First Edition. 1647. Wing T352.

Title: [all within a border of fleur-de-lis] A new and easie | INSTITUTION | of | GRAMMAR. | IN | Which the Labor of many | yeares, usually spent in learning | the Latine Tongue, | is short- | ned and made easie. | In usum Juventutis Cambro-Britannicae. | [rule] | *Non obstant hae Disciplinae per illas eunti-* | *bus, sed circa illas haerentibus* Quint. | [rule] | [woodcut] | [rule] | *LONDON,* | Printed by *J. Young,* for *R. Royston,* and | are to be sold at the signe of the An- | gel in Ivie-Lane, 1647.

Coll: 8vo: A⁸(a)⁴ B-H⁸, 68 leaves; plates 1 (before A2). Paged B1ʳ-H7ʳ: pp. 1-109.

Contents: A1ʳ, blank; A1ᵛ, "Explicatio Emblematis"; A2ʳ, title-page (verso blank); A3ʳ-(a1)ᵛ, Latin epistle to Christopher Lord Hatton by William Wyat; (a2)-(a3)ᵛ, English epistle to Christopher, son of Lord Hatton, by Taylor; (a4), Latin verses to Taylor by F. Gregory and *imprimatur* signed by Jo Langley; B1ʳ-H7ʳ, text; H7ᵛ, Latin verses; H8, blank.

Variants: Lacking leaves A1 and H8, Bod; lacking H8, Har; lacking plate and H8, P.

Notes: The plate represents Apollo on a hill, holding a laurel over two laurel-crowned figures, Philonus and Musaeus, who are holding up a sheet with the title engraved on it: "A | New and Easy | Institution | of | Grammar. | *Expedire Grammatico* | *etiamsi quaedam nesciat.* | Quint." Below are four schoolboys reading, two on each side of the arms of the University of Oxford. The names of the artist and engraver are not given.

The *Grammar* was entered in the Stationers' Register on December 21, 1646, and was the joint effort of Taylor and Wyat. At this time they, with William Nicholson, later Bishop of Gloucester, had set up a small school for young gentlemen at the little village of Llanfihangel-Abergychych, in the Towey valley, a few miles above Carmarthen. They dignified the school with the name of Newton Hall. Across the valley from Llanfihangel is Golden Grove, where lived the Earl of Carbery, Taylor's second great patron.

The Latin poem to Taylor begins:

En ut Sacerdos, en ut Orator potens.

This, even allowing for the conventional fulsomeness of dedicatory poems, indicates that Taylor was already renowned for his preaching, although he had published nothing so far in that line except for the *Gunpowder Sermon.*

Heber says that the Grammar was probably in most part the work of Wyat; Gosse describes it as "apparently a joint production" (p. 36); and when one of the present writers said that it was a joint work (Gathorne-Hardy, "A Bibliography of Jeremy Taylor," *The Golden Grove,* ed. Logan Pearsall Smith, Oxford, 1930, p. 299) he spoke with no authority, as, we suspect, did his predecessors; however, we have little doubt that he spoke the truth. At least three times (the first and second editions of *The Golden Grove* [Nos. 22 A and B] and *The Real Presence* [No. 21 A]) Royston advertised the work as Taylor's; but it is possible that he omitted Wyat's name only because it would have added nothing to the sales of the book.

Wyat's introduction praises Lord Hatton and then explains the merits of this grammar. In these latter passages he speaks several times in the first person plural. Since he frequently, both before and after, uses the first person singular, this cannot be an example of the editorial "we," and it may be safely assumed that this is indeed a joint work.

Copies: Bod, CCC, CUL, ECM, H, P; Har.

6 A. *The Liberty of Prophesying.* First Edition. 1647. Wing T400.

Title: ΘΕΟΛΟΓΙΑ ΕΚΛΕΚΤΙΚΗ' | [rule] | A | DISCOURSE | OF | The Liberty of Prophesying. | *SHEWING* | THE UNREASONABLENESS | of prescribing to other mens Faith, and the | Iniquity of persecuting differing opinions. | [rule] | *By* IER: TAYLOR, *D. D.* Chaplaine in | Ordinarie to His MAJESTIE. | [rule] | [orn.] | [rule] | *LONDON,* | Printed for R. ROYSTON, at the Angel | in Ivie-lane. 1647.

Coll: Quarto: Π¹ a-f⁴ g² A-2K⁴ 2L² χ¹, 162 leaves. Plates 1 (engraved title [Johnson: Marshall #103] before Π1.). Paged a1ʳ-f4ᵛ: pp. 1-48; A1ʳ-2L2ʳ: pp. 1-267.

Contents: Π1ʳ, title-page (verso blank); a1ʳ-f4ᵛ, dedicatory epistle; g1ʳ-g2ᵛ, contents; A1ʳ-2L2ʳ, text; 2L2ᵛ, blank; χ1ʳ, "The Printer to the Reader" and errata (verso blank).

Variants: The errata list exists in two states. State I lists three errata immediately below "The Printer to the Reader" on χ1ʳ. This state is found in most copies. State II appears in the same location but lists forty errata including the three in state I. It is found in copies Bod, GK, H (1), and P (1). Leaf χ is found immediately after the title-page in the BM copy which is part of the 1648 *Treatises* (No. 7 A). This location of the leaf hints at Π and χ being parts of the same half sheet, at least in those copies with state I of the errata list, but not enough examples of such placement exist to make an absolute determination.

In some copies the inner forms of sheet a lack page numbers.

In two copies, H (1) and I, half-sheet g appears between the two leaves of half-sheet 2L. Since the location of the contents between the last two leaves of text can never be a standard format, it is clear that they were printed on a single sheet and that the two copies noted are accidents in cutting and binding.

Notes: Signatures X-2E are set from a different font of type than the remainder of the text and exhibit certain differences in compositorial style.

The engraved title, by Marshall, is a representation of the Pentecost. A Greek text (1 Corinthians 14.31) is engraved on the floor of the chamber. Below the panel is the name of the work.

Royston entered *The Liberty of Prophesying* in the Stationers' Register on March 8, 1647. Thomason acquired his copy on June 28, 1647.

Had Taylor died before writing this work, he might have been remembered, if at all, as the promising young disciple whom Laud imposed, with doubtful legality but happy results, on All Souls' College, Oxford. This was not, it is true, the first plea for toleration. It was probably from the circle around Falkland that Taylor conceived his liberal ideas. He must cerainly have read and been influenced by Chillingworth's *Religion of Protestants*, printed by Lichfield at Oxford in 1638. Taylor certainly knew its author and probably met other members of the latitudinarian circle around Falkland. He was evidently liked, though not always in all things approved of. "Mr Taylor," wrote Chillingworth to a friend, otherwise unnamed, whom he addresses as Harry, "did much confirm my opinion of his sufficience, but let me tell you in your ear—meethinks he wants much of the ethical part of a discourse, and slights too much many times the Arguments of those he discourses with; but this is a course he would quickly leave, if he had a friend that would discreetly tell him of it. If you and Mr Coventry would tell him, that you heard one that knowes him, magnifye him exceedingly for other thinges, but censure him for this, you might do him a very friendly office: . . . . but you must not give the least suspicion that I am the man, and therefore doe it not yet a good while." (Des Maizeaux, *Life and Writings of William Chillingworth*, 1725, p. 50).

It is evident, too, that he owed something to another member of that circle, John Hales, who had been a friend of Suckling's, and whose life Isaak Walton planned to write. In *The Liberty of Prophesying*, and also in later works, Taylor echoes phrases and images from sermons by Hales; and he must have studied Hales's *Tract concerning Schisme*, which was issued, with no author's or publisher's name, in London, in 1642.

The Liberty of Prophesying was for many years the bible of those who believed in toleration, and references to it are continually to be found during the seventeenth century. William Penn alluded to the book in chapter 6 of *The Great Case of Liberty of Conscience*, 1670. During the pamphlet war occasioned by James II's Declaration of Indulgence, section 16 of Taylor's book, *Whether it be lawful for a Prince to give Toleration to several Religions*, was reprinted in a single quarto sheet, with comments, as *Toleration tolerated: or a late learned Bishops opinion concerning Toleration of Religion* (this was listed by Lowndes as a separate work of Taylor's). There is a copy of it in the National Library of Scotland, where it is dated 1687 in the catalogue—a shrewd estimate which cannot be far wrong.

Before the nineteenth century, the most notable writer to use *The Liberty of Prophesying* was the third Earl of Shaftesbury. In his *Miscellaneous Reflections*, first published in 1711 as the third volume of *Characteristics*, he quotes extensively from the text. With artful irony, he puts the words into the mouth of an imaginary speaker discoursing in favor of free-thinking in matters of religion; at the end of the passage, Shaftesbury discloses the true author of the observations. Shaftesbury had an immense influence on European thought during the eighteenth century; liberal thinkers of the present day owe more than they know to Shaftesbury, and through Shaftesbury to Taylor.

Even a Roman Catholic writer of the late seventeenth century managed to make use of Taylor's book; in a tract called *The Doctrine of the Scriptures concerning the Middle State of Souls,* the author professes to find some support from Taylor, and quotes from *The Liberty of Prophesying.* The tract, at All Souls' College, Oxford, to judge by its neighbors in the same volume, was probably printed about 1699-1700; and its author was probably an Edward Stephens, who describes himself as "an English Catholic."

The body of people who drew most comfort from *The Liberty of Prophesying* were the anabaptists. In order to demonstrate that they should not be persecuted, Taylor devotes a chapter to showing that their opinions could be held by reasonable and pious men. He did the job rather too well, causing a certain amount of scandal. Much the same thing happened to Richard Baxter; in his *Plain Scripture Proof of Infant Church-membership and Baptism,* 1651, he wrote, on the unnumbered page (b 4^r) "Being at Gloucester when Mr. Winnels book against them came forth, I spoke so much in extenuation of their error, that my conscience hath since checked me for it; lest I should be a means thereby of drawing any from the truth, though I did discover my own judgement to be against them: As Doctor Taylors Arguments *de lib. Prophet.* have done by too many." Hammond answered these arguments in *A Letter of Resolution to Six Quaeres,* 1653 (No. T 15). Taylor himself answered them in *A Discourse of Baptism,* 1653 (No. 17 A), and in the enlarged version of the present book (see below). For a long time after this, anabaptists continued to quote Taylor's observations favorable to themselves, while uningenuously ignoring his own retorts against himself.

Apart even from little indiscretions like this defense of the anabaptists, Taylor met with disapproval of his main theme. The fieriest attack was by the Scotch writer Samuel Rutherfurd, in *A Free Disputation against Pretended Liberty of Conscience,* London, 1649 (No. T 14). Even loyal persecuted Anglicans objected. In Sir Philip Warwick's *Memories of the reigne of King Charles I,* 1701, he tells on page 301 how he visited the King at Caversham: "At Causham I had the honour to come into his presence, tho' I staid not there; but by all I could perceive either from himselfe or any other, he was very apprehensive, in what hands he was, but was not let it be discerned. Nor had he given that countenance unto Dr. Taylor's *liberty of prophesying* which some believed he had." From this anecdote Gosse conceived the idea that King Charles ordered the book answered by Hammond, an untenable supposition, as is demonstrated by the very description of Hammond's little book.

Orthodox disapproval seems to have started a legend that Taylor wrote the book in order to placate his enemies. This first appears in David Lloyd's *Memoirs of the Loyalists,* 1668. Under the section devoted to Taylor, he writes (pp. 702-703) of "unwary sentiments about . . . Liberty of Conscience. . . .

which he writ to weaken Presbytery by pleading for Liberty to all other Sects, as well as the undermine of it, as it had undermined Episcopacy." The most extreme form of the legend can be found in an unpublished manuscript note on the flyleaf of a copy of *The Liberty of Prophesying* at Queen's College, Cambridge. It records a story told by a Mr. Lewis of "Wronton-Holm" in Norfolk, a former chaplain of Taylor's. Lewis said that Taylor had written the book while he was in prison, and that "by it, he got his enlargement and liberty from the then Rulers of the rost." He goes on to say that Taylor, when Bishop of Down and Connor, sent him (Lewis) over to England to buy as many copies of the book as he could find, and to bring them over to Ireland. He then "set a day apart for solemn fasting and humiliation, and Offices of repentance for his past prevaricating with truth and his conscience in his composure of this tract; and after the day and its offices were at an end, he caused a fire to be made publicly for these books so brought to be burnt as a detestation &c of them &c." The improbability of this story is immeasurable. Taylor was fearless in all his comments on the usurping government and never gave any signs of sly submission; indeed he showed himself as reckless and obstinate in the promulgation of unpopular and dangerous opinions. His imprisonment after being taken at Cardigan was not long enough to compose a book of this size. It would have been impossible for Lewis to have collected enough copies for a fire sufficiently large to dignify Taylor's supposed penitence. Finally, had it been done so publicly, we may be quite certain of its having been indignantly reported by the Ulster presbyterians, who claimed to be persecuted by him.

Copies: Bod, CUL, EmC, H (2), P (3), QC, TCC, Th; CW, F, Har, HH, I, KS, NL, NW, US, W, Y.

6 B-C. Second and Third Issues. 1648 and 1650.

The Liberty of Prophesying (1647) was remaindered by Royston as part of *Treatises,* 1648 (No. 7 A) and *Treatises,* 1650 (No. 10 A). In both issues it appears with the 1647 title-page and engraved title.

6 D. Second Printing. 1657.

See *Polemical Discourses,* 1657 (No. 28 A).

Notes: Notable additions were made to this version. In Section XVIII Taylor had discussed the anabaptists; he here adds some twenty-three and a half folio pages refuting his hypothetical defense of them. He begins this part with an explanation: "because all men will not understand my purpose, or think my meaning innocent. . . . I will rather choose to offend the Rules of Art, then not to fulfill all the requisites of charity."

At the very end of the work a paragraph is added; it is a delightful tale, recounting how Abraham, having turned out into the night a fireworshipper who had sheltered with him, was reproved for it by God himself. The tale was included by Quiller-Couch in *The Oxford Book of English Prose,* where it is said to have been taken "from the sermons."

In the first edition, divisions of the sections were numbered with figures; here, they are expanded into words; thus "6" becomes "sixthly." All the errata in the lists have been corrected, except for two; curiously enough, one of these two occurs in both lists. In one case "cognsance" is directed to be read "cognesance"; in this printing it is put rightly as "cognisance." Since Taylor's written *e*, however small, is always exquisitely neat, it is likely that the errata list was not set up directly from his manuscript. The error which occurs in both lists and is not corrected is a marginal note in Section XI and was probably overlooked in the setting of this printing.

The engraved title of 6 A-C appears, touched up. The Greek text has below it an English translation. In the lower margin is inserted "The Second Edition enlarged. 1657."

6 E. Third Printing. 1674.
See *Polemical Discourses*, 1674 (No. 28 B).
Notes: On the internal title-page this printing is described as "The Third Edition Enlarged." The text does not substantially differ from that of 1657 (6 D). There is a plate containing oval representations of Daniel and St. John.

In the errata at the end of the volume, only five corrections are made in *The Liberty of Prophesying*. One corrects a mechanical misprint, three restore errors taken from the second printing, and one corrects an error which appears in both the first and second printings (6 A and D).

7 A. *Treatises.* First Edition. 1648. Wing T403.
General Title: Treatises | of | 1. *The Liberty of Prophesying.* | 2. *Prayer* Ex Tempore. | Together with | *A Sermon preached at* Oxon. *on the Anniversary of the* 5 *of* November. | [rule] | *By* Jer. Taylor, *D. D.* Chaplaine | in Ordinary to His Majesty. | [rule] | [device] | *London,* | Printed for R. Royston, at the | Angel in *Ivie-lane.* 1648.
Coll: Quarto. Π² Numbers 6 A, 4 B, 1 A, and 2 B. No accurate collation is possible since the make-up of the volume varies from copy to copy depending on accidents of binding.
Contents: Π1, blank; Π2ʳ, general title-page (verso blank); apart from *The Liberty of Prophesying* (1647), *Prayer Ex tempore* (1647), and the *Gunpowder Sermon* (1638), the volume normally contains *Episcopacy Asserted,* 1647 (No. 2 B).
Variants: Episcopacy Asserted with 1642 title-page (No. 2 A), PCC. *Apology for Liturgy* (1649, No. 8 A) replacing *Prayer Ex tempore,* Bod, GK.
Notes: The appearance of the 1649 *Apology for Liturgy* in a work dated 1648 indicates how slowly Royston remaindered these items and why the volume is found in so many different states. The Bod and GK copies represent a transitional phase between *Treatises* (1648) and *Treatises* (1650, No. 10 A), and

this has led some to speak of a 1649 issue of *Treatises*. To the best of our knowledge no copy exists with the general title-page dated 1649.
Copies: BM, Bod, CUL, GK, PCC; Har, MU, Y.

8 A. *Apology for Liturgy.* First Edition. 1649. Wing T289.
Title: [all within double rules] *AN* | APOLOGY | FOR | Authorised and Set Forms | *of* | Liturgie: | against | The Pretense | of | *The Spirit.* | 1. For *ex tempore* Prayer, | *And* | 2. Formes of Private composition. | [rule] | Hierocl. in Pythag. | [four-line Greek quotation] | [double rule] | *London,* | Printed for *R. Royston* in Ivie-lane, 1649.
Coll: Quarto: A-M⁴ N², 50 leaves. Paged B1ʳ-N2ᵛ: pp. 1-92.
Contents: A1, blank; A2ʳ, title-page (verso blank); A3ʳ-A4ᵛ, address to Charles I, signed "Taylor"; B1ʳ-N2ᵛ, text.
Variants: A1ʳ of the PCC copy bears the off-set impression of N2ᵛ. This probably came about from either the accidental stacking of still damp copies of the half-sheet N on A, or the pressing of stitched copies very tightly together in storage. In both cases, the blank leaf A would be quite susceptible to off-setting.
Notes: The only acknowledgement of Taylor's authorship is the signature to the epistle ("Taylor" A4ᵛ), a moving address to the imprisoned and soon to be beheaded king. To have published his name thus, in such dangerous times, is in itself almost sufficient answer to accusations that *The Liberty of Prophesying* (No. 6 A) was hypocritically written in order to gain the favor of his enemies.

Two books were published by Taylor in 1649, *Apology* and *The Great Exemplar* (No. 9 A). Since *Apology* was not entered in the Stationers' Register until April 18, 1656, when Royston was clearing up the question of ownership of copy before the second printing of this work (No. 8 B), this evidence is of no help in determining the order of appearance of the two works. However, since Charles I was beheaded on January 30, 1648/49, the internal evidence of the epistle indicates that it must have been written before that date. It is also probable that the text had been printed by then, and, had the printing of the preliminaries been long delayed surely some indignant allusion to the martyred king would have been inserted. It was not unusual in the seventeenth century for books printed before March 25 to bear the date of the approaching year. In the case of *The Great Exemplar* not only the title-page is dated 1649, but the fly title-page for the First Part (A1ʳ, part of the first gathering of text) also bears that date. Since the text would have been printed earlier and such a large volume could not have been completed early in the year, it may be assumed that *Apology* was published first.

Apology is a rewritten and very much enlarged version of *Prayer Ex Tempore* (No. 4). In an attempt to indicate the nature of the revision of the text by Taylor, the following record is given. In each book the paragraphs are numbered in the margin and the numbers in parentheses are those of *Prayer Ex Tempore,* those outside are of *Apology.*

2-4(2-4), 7(5), 10(7), 12-15(8-11), 30(14), 32(20), 34(23), 37(25), 44-47(27-30), 73(38), 85(35), 103(32), 104-105(33), 116(44), 117-120(45-48), 121-129(49-57), 131(59), 132(60), 133(61), 135-137(63-65).

The following paragraphs were altered, enlarged, or contain fragments from the earlier work and their relationships are noted as above.

1(1), 8-9(6), 16(12), 29(13), 31-32(21-22), 35(24), 43(26), 50(32), 73(38), 114(42), 130(58), 134(62), 140-141(65).

A rough estimate of the additions made by Taylor can be reckoned from the fact that the earlier work had 67 paragraphs and the later work 141.

Copies: BM, Bod, Con, CUL, PCC, TCC; Har, I, NL, US.

8 B. Second Issue. 1650.

See *Treatises.* 1650 (No. 10 A).

8 C. Second Printing. 1657.

See *Polemical Discourses.* 1657 (No. 28 A).

8 D. Third Printing. 1674.

See *Polemical Discourses.* 1674 (No. 28 B).

Notes: Among the errata relating to *An Apology,* at the end of the 1674 collection, six restore readings of the first edition and four amend errors found in all printings. Of these last, one is in Greek; the erratum corrects an error which appears in all printings, and restores part of a sentence which was omitted in the second printing.

9 A. *The Great Exemplar.* First Edition. 1649. Wing T342.

Title: THE | [all in red] GREAT EXEMPLAR | OF | SANCTITY and HOLY LIFE | [all in red] according to the Christian Institution. | [all in red] DE-SCRIBED | In the History of the LIFE and [in red] DEATH | of the ever Blessed | [in red] JESUS [in red] CHRIST the [in red] SAVIOUR of the WORLD. | WITH CONSIDERATIONS and DISCOURSES | upon several Parts of the Story, and Prayers | fitted to the several Mysteries. | [rule] | [all in red] IN THREE PARTS. | [rule] | By *Jer. Taylor,* D. D. Chaplain in Ordinary to His MAJ-ESTY | [orn.] | [in red] LONDON, | Printed by R. N. for [in red] *Francis* [in red] *Ash,* and are to be sold at the three Pigeons in | [in red] S. *Pauls* Church-yard. 1649.

Coll: Quarto, mostly in eights: Π^2 a-e^4, A-K^8 L$^4\chi^2$ 2A-2K^8 2L^4 ¶^{2} 3A-3L^8 3M-3O^4, 294 leaves. Paged A2^r-L3^v: pp. 1-166; 2A1^r-2L4^v: pp. 1-164; 3A1^r-3M3^r: pp. 1-181.

Contents: Π1, blank; Π2ʳ, title-page (verso blank); a1ʳ-b1ᵛ, dedication to Christopher Lord Hatton; b2ʳ-e4ʳ, preface; e4ᵛ, blank; A1ʳ, title for the first part (verso blank); A2ʳ-L3ᵛ, text of the first part; L4, blank; χ1ʳ, title for the second part (verso blank); χ2, Dedication to Mary Countess Dowager of Northampton; 2A1ʳ-2L4ᵛ, text of the second part; ¶1ʳ, title for the third part (verso blank); ¶2, Dedication to Frances Countess of Carbery; 3A1ʳ-3M3ʳ, text of the third part; 3M3ᵛ, blank; 3M4, blank; 3N1ʳ-3O4ᵛ, The Table.
Variants: There are six states of the title-page. The variations are the printing of "His Majesty" or "his Majesty" in line seventeen and three different versions of the imprint. The states are set forth in tabular form.

State 1. "His Majesty | .... | Printed by *R. N.* for *Francis Ash*. 1649."

State 2. "his Majesty | .... | Printed by *R. N.* for *Francis Ash*. 1649."

State 3. "His Majesty | .... | LONDON, | Printed by *R. N.* for *Francis Ash*. 1649."

State 4. "his Majesty | .... | LONDON, | Printed by *R. N.* for *Francis Ash*. 1649."

State 5. "His Majesty | .... | [in red] LONDON, | Printed by R. N. for *Francis Ash*, and are to be sold at the three Pigeons in | [in red] S. [in red] *Pauls* Church-yard. 1649."

State 6. "his Majesty | .... | LONDON, | Printed by R. N. for *Francis Ash*, and are to be sold at the three Pigeons in | [in red] S. *Pauls* Church-yard. 1649."

A careful examination reveals that duplicate title-pages were set, one with "his" the other with "His" and that two copies were printed off at the same time on a single quarto sheet and then cut apart to create two copies of the Π gathering. It is likely that the two internal half-sheets bearing the divisional titles to Parts Two and Three (χ and ¶) were printed in a similar fashion on a single sheet.

The printing of the text was very badly done, and a number of little accidents, often due to the form being badly locked up, happened and were corrected during the printing. Page numberings may be found slipping, missing, or even upside down (over a series of copies examined, one of these mishaps could almost be seen taking place). Signature 3L3 appears at least once as 3K3.

On 2D1ʳ (p. 49 of Part II, line 27), the word "uningenuious" appears. In some copies this reads "uningenious." Since in later editions this becomes "uningenuous," we can be fairly certain that the former is the right reading and that the latter reading is a case of incomplete correction in the press. Such a correction, or attempted correction, indicates that some proof-reading, at least, was done with reference to copy: "uningenuous" was a new word, perhaps invented by Taylor himself (the OED gives 1670 as its earliest use). It is already clear, from one errata leaf added to *The Liberty of Prophesying* (1647), that proofs were not being sent down to Taylor in Wales. Thus, the readings of 2D1ʳ indicate that either Taylor was in London at this time, or that this is a case of the printer's proof-reader making careful comparison with Taylor's manuscript. Mr. Gathorne-Hardy has examined these questions in *The Library*, March, 1948.

2B8 is a cancel. It is sometimes bound with the stub wrapped around the 2C gathering and sometimes pasted on the stub of 2B8. Possibly the cancel leaves bound in and showing a stub were inserted before the sheets had been stitched, and those pasted on the stub of the cancelland were inserted after stitching. No copy has been observed in which the leaf is uncancelled.

Notes: On October 26, 1648, Francis Ash entered *The Great Exemplar* in the Stationers' Register, and on November 24, 1651, this entry was made: "Assigned over unto him [Royston] by vertue of a noate under the hands and seals of Alexander Ash, executors of Fran. Ash, and by order of Cort bearing date this 21st of November 1651, these two copies, Viz Gt. Exemplar and Holy Living." Just how Ash became involved in the publication of works by Taylor (he entered and acted as publisher for the first edition of *Holy Living* [No. 11 A] and his name appears in the imprints of the second edition of *Holy Living* [No. 11 B] and the first edition of *Holy Dying* [No. 15 A]) is not at all clear. He had a shop in Worcester; there is no record of his having any establishment in London; and he had never undertaken the publication of books before (in 1648 he had been a book-seller for twenty-one years). He was a man of Romish inclination, for he is violently attacked by Michael Sparke, himself a London stationer, in *A Second Beacon Fired by Scintilla* (1652).

The engraved ornament on the title-page was used on the divisional title of Part I in the second edition, and on the title-page of the spurious *Discourse of Auxiliary Beauty*, 1656 (No. T 1).

In *Christ's Yoke an easy Yoke*, 1675 (No. 46 A), were printed two sermons, clearly from manuscript. One, incomplete in 1675, was used for Discourse XV in Part III of *The Great Exemplar*; the other was used to compile Additional Section 5 in Part I. As Gosse acutely pointed out, this little publication shows that, in many parts of *The Great Exemplar*, we have some of the early sermons which helped to make Taylor's reputation (Gosse, pp. 59-60).

Copies: BM, Bod, CUL, DC, GK, H(3), P(2); CU, CW, Har, HH, KS, NL, PU, US.

9 B. Second Issue. 1650.

Royston issued the 1649 *Great Exemplar* as a substantial part of *Treatises*, 1650 (No. 10 A).

9 C. Second Edition. 1653. Wing T343.

Title: THE | [all in red] GREAT EXEMPLAR | OF | Sanctity and Holy Life | [all in red] according to the Christian Institution: | Described in the History of the | LIFE and DEATH of the ever blessed | [all in red] JESUS CHRIST | THE | [all in red] SAVIOUR of the WORLD | [rule] | WITH | [all in red] CONSIDERATIONS and DISCOURSES | upon the severall parts of the Story; | [all in red] And PRAYERS fitted to the severall Mysteries. | [rule] | *In three Parts*; *with many Additionals.* | [rule] | [all in red] By [ital.] IER: TAYLOR, D. D. Chaplain in Ordinary | to his late MAJESTY. | [rule] | [in red] *LONDON.* | Printed by *James Flesher,* for *Richard Royston,* at the signe of the | [all in red] Angel in *Ivie-lane.* MDCLIII.

Coll: Fol., mostly in sixes: *⁶ A-B⁶ C⁴, c⁴, D-3D⁶ 3E-3F⁴, 320 leaves; plates 12 (Johnson: Faithorne #5 and engraved half-title before *2, before E1, F2, N4, P3, X5, 2N2, 2T3, 2Y1, 2Z4, 3D1). Paged D1ʳ-3E2ᵛ: pp. 1-568.

Contents: *1, blank; *2ʳ, title-page (verso blank); *3ʳ-*5ᵛ, dedication to Christopher Lord Hatton; *6ʳ-c2ᵛ, preface; c3ʳ-c4ʳ, contents; c4ᵛ, blank; D1ʳ, divisional title for Part I (verso blank); D2ʳ-X2ʳ, text of Part I; X2ᵛ, blank; X3ʳ, divisional title for Part II (verso blank); X4, dedication to the Countess of Northampton; X5ᵛ-2M5ᵛ, text of Part II; 2M6ʳ, divisional title for Part III (verso blank); 2N1ʳ-3E2ᵛ, text of Part III and errata [errata on 3E2ᵛ]; 3E3ʳ-2F3ᵛ, the table; 2F4ʳ, advertisement (verso blank).

Variants: The plates in this edition are subject to some variation, but this matter will be dealt with in the notes on the plates in the following section since they do not affect the text.

Some copies have two different 2N1 leaves. Frances Countess of Carbery, to whom the third part was dedicated (the dedication is found on 2N1 recto and verso), died in childbirth on October 9, 1650. In July, 1651, Lord Carbery married Lady Alice Egerton (as a girl she had taken the part of the Lady in the original production of *Comus*). Taylor wrote a dedication to her, which became a normal part of the book in the third edition of 1657 (9 D.), where it followed the dedication to her predecessor; however, a few copies were printed on a separate leaf, and inserted into the 1653 edition; this leaf is signed "Nn," the signature to be found on the earlier dedication to Frances. Gosse said that the later dedication was substituted for the earlier in the 1657 edition (p. 127). This is not so, and his error may have arisen from his having seen an abnormal copy of the second edition. Seven copies have been observed with the cancel dedication; in two Alice is substituted for the Countess of Northampton (X4); in two Alice is immediately inserted after Frances (one of these latter copies, in the British Museum has the figure "2" added in manuscript to the cancel leaf).

All copies containing the cancel dedication, except the EC and H copies, have plates in early states (cf. notes on the plates below). The signature on the cancel leaf indicates that it was probably meant to be substituted for the old dedication to Frances. We appear to be witnessing a struggle between sentiment and worldly wisdom; it must have seemed advisable for Taylor to honor the new wife of his patron; and yet how could he give up, or even obscure, the memory of his adored and revered, dead patroness? He was evidently in a difficult position; the new Lady Carbery might have resented mention of her dead precursor, while Lord Carbery might equally have resented the removal of the "dear saint," as both he and Taylor had spoken of her. When the third edition appeared in 1657, Taylor, sick of Wales, was somewhat estranged from the Carberys.

Copies with the leaf of dedication to Alice Countess of Carbery are: BC, BM, EC, H, HM, MC, PCC.

Notes: PLATES. There is a portrait of Taylor, engraved by P. Lombart. It was engraved, with variations, from the painting at All Souls' College, Oxford, which is the original of all formal portraits used in early editions of Taylor. Lombart's plate was to be used for more than half a century in all but a few of the works by Taylor which were published in folio. From examples used during Taylor's lifetime, four recognizable states can be noted; a description of them is provided elsewhere in this work. In this edition of *The Great Exemplar,* it should be found in State I.

The other plates are engraved by Faithorne; they consist of an engraved half-title page which, like Lombart's portrait, are often inserted between *1 and *2. The remainder are illustrations of the text; they all have directions to the binder on them. A list of the ten plates are: (1) The Annunciation, (2) St. Matthew, (3) St. Mark, (4) St. Luke, (5) The Marriage at Cana, (6) St. John, (7) The Agony in the Garden, (8) The Betrayal, (9) The Last Supper, and (10) The Ascension. A plate of the Crucifixion, normally among those added to the third edition of 1657, may occasionally be found in an early state in the second edition; it is then bound in facing 3C3^r. It will be described under the third edition.

Six plates, namely the Four Evangelists (2,3,4,6), the Agony in the Garden (7), and the Last Supper (9), may be found in earlier states. Perhaps the most interesting of these is St. Matthew (2) which, in its earliest state, is known only from a copy in the British Museum. The engravings of the evangelists each have a quatrain in English at the foot, and these have usually been attributed to Taylor. Grosart, in his edition of Taylor's poems, rather ostentatiously called attention to his inclusion of these unmeritorious verses. Now, in that exceptional plate of St. Matthew there is engraved across the panel at the foot of it, on each side of the quatrain, "And are to be sold by | William Peake at Holburne's Conduit." The year and Faithorne's name have been added in manuscript. In a normal copy of the plate, faint traces of this inscription can be seen where it was burnished out. In the plate of St. John (6), the shading in the panel is burnished away on each side of the quatrain into two blank spaces; this, although no remains of an inscription are apparent, may show where the printseller's name was engraved; the year and Faithorne's name have been engraved over these spaces. The plates of the other two evangelists (3 and 4) show no evidence of such treatment; nevertheless it seems obvious that Royston, to make up his book, had bought four plates already prepared for the market. It is immensely improbable that Taylor had written the quatrains for an obscure printseller, and they should be removed from the canon of his work. The BM copy has, as well, plates 3 and 6 without directions to the binder, a unique state; this was perhaps the condition of the plates as acquired by Royston.

Five of the six plates to be found in earlier states have different directions to the binder; these, being wrong, are usually corrected in manuscript. These are the plates with their faulty directions: (3) "St. Mark, Place this fig Sect P: 11.", (4) "St. Luke, Place this in Sect: 14 P 213.", (6) "St. John, Place this in P: 345.", (7) "The Agony in the Garden, Place this in Sect: 14. P. 426.", and (9) "The Last Supper, Place this before ye 13 Sect-. P: 387."

In the case of the remaining variable plate, St. Matthew (2), a strip was cut away from the right hand side. In the earlier state there is about a quarter of an inch between the saint's left elbow and the edge of the plate; the shadow of an inkpot below is complete. In the later state, part of the drapery on the arm touches the edge, and the shadow of the inkpot has been cut through. Copies with plates in an early state are: BM (2, 3, 6); MC (3, 4, 6, 7, 9); PCC (2, 3, 4, 6, 7, 9); BC (3, 4, 2, 6, 7); HM (4, 6, 7, 9); H (2, 3, 4, 6, 7, 9); WSC (3, 4, 6, 7, 9); I (2, 3, 4, 6, 7, 9).

The advertisement on 3F4^r is a "Catalogue" of books published by Royston and lists the following works by Taylor: ". . . 1. A course of Sermons . . . in *fol.* 2. Episcopacy asserted, in 4°. 3. The Liberty of Prophesying, in 4°. 4. An Apologie for authorized and Set-forms of Liturgie; in 4°. 5. A Discourse of Baptism . . . in 4°. 6. The Rule and Exercises of holy living, in 12°. 7. The Rule and Exercises of holy dying, in 12°. 8. A short Catechism for institution of young persons in the Christian Religion, in 12°. . . . The Psalter of *David*, with Titles and Collects according to the matter of each Psalm, by the Right honourable *Chr: Hatton*, in 12°. . . ."

On April 11, 1653, Taylor wrote to Gilbert Sheldon, afterwards Archbishop of Canterbury, saying, "I have given Royston order together with this to present you with . . . the Life of Christ in a fairer character and with some enlargements and advantages." Certain small changes were made in the text between editions, and it was perhaps these that Taylor was thinking of when he spoke of "advantages." As to "enlargements," apart from the occasional appearance of the new dedication, these consisted of two discourses, *Of Baptism,* and *Of Baptizing Infants,* which had already been published as *A Discourse of Baptisme* in 1652 (No. 17 A). In a fragmentary letter to Sir William Dugdale, dated April 1, 1651, Taylor speaks of ". . . writing a tract in defence of baptisme," and he goes on, "I would desire those . . . true Sons of the Church to answer the arguments its [opponen]ts make use of, out of my books." In this damaged passage he must be alluding at least to his first plan of the two discourses on baptism, which were incorporated in this edition of *The Great Exemplar.* Later in the same letter he implies that he means "to adde to the life of Christ which is to be [. . .] summer." This would seem to indicate that he planned some other addition which was never made. Since this is mentioned in the same letter as the tract on baptism, he can hardly be referring to that work again. We can also deduce from this valuable although mutilated letter that he originally expected to reprint *The Great Exemplar* during the summer of 1651.

A very curious echo from the portrait and engraved half-title of this, or the following edition, is to be found in an obscure mystical poem, *Mundorum Explicatio,* printed by T. R. for Lodowick Lloyd, in 1661. This is a Behmenist poem; the first part foreshadows Milton, with a narrative of the fall, while the second and third parts, anticipating Bunyan, tell of a pilgrim's journey through life to heaven. It has been attributed to Samuel Pordage, or to his father Dr. John Pordage, or even jointly to both of them. The father, during part of the Commonwealth, was incumbent of Bradfield in Berkshire, the next parish to Mr. Gathorne-Hardy's own; in his rectory, Dr. Pordage carried on a strange cult, which eventually led to his ejectment from "scandal, ignorance, and insufficiency proved against him." One charge was that the devil appearing to him by night "made on the Brick-Wall, over his Chimney, the likeness of a Coach drawn by Tygers, so deeply impressed, that they were fain to use a Pick-Ax to cut it out of the Bricks." For Samuel Pordage, or his father John, or some unknown author, while writing the preface to his poem, there came to mind the image of Taylor's portrait, and the title of his book. On one line the phrase "Christ the great Exemplar" is found and below on the same page, from the legend on the portrait, "non magna loquimur sed vivimur [sic 'vivimus'], let us live well rather than talk well."

Copies: BC, BM, Bod, EC, H, HM, MC, MO, PCC, SE; HH, I, KS, KU, WSC, W, Y.

9 D. Third Edition. 1657. Wing T344.

Title: THE | [all in red] GREAT EXEMPLAR | OF | Sanctity and Holy Life | [all in red] according to the Christian Institution: | Described in the History of the | LIFE and DEATH of the ever Blessed | [all in red] JESUS CHRIST | THE | SAVIOUR of the WORLD. | [rule] | WITH | [all in red] CONSIDERATIONS and DISCOURSES | upon the several parts of the story; | [all in red] And PRAYERS fitted to the several MYSTERIES. | [rule] | *The Third Edition.* In three Parts. | [rule] | [all in red] *By* JER: TAYLOR, *D. D.* Chaplain in Ordinary | to his late MAJESTIE. | [rule] | [in red] *LONDON,* | Printed by *R. Norton,* for *Richard Royston,* at the signe of the | [all in red] Angel in *Ivie-lane.* MDCLVII.

Coll: Fol., mostly in sixes: A-3H⁶ 3I⁸, 422 leaves; plates 14 (two before A1; opposite F3ʳ, G4ʳ, K1ʳ; two-leaf plate before N4; opposite O4ʳ, R1ʳ, Z5ʳ, 2Y5ʳ, 3B3ʳ, 3D1ʳ, 3G2ʳ, 3H1ʳ). Paged E3ʳ-3I2ᵛ: pp. 1-600.

NOTE: Missignings: A3 for A2, 3Y2 for Y2.

Contents: A1ʳ, title-page (verso blank); A2ʳ-A5ʳ, Dedication to Christopher Lord Hatton; A5ᵛ, blank; A6, The Contents; B1ʳ-E2ᵛ, The Preface; E3ʳ, title for Part I (verso blank); E4ʳ-Z2ᵛ, text of Part I; Z3ʳ, title for Part II (verso blank); Z4, Dedication to the Countess of Northampton; Z6ʳ-2P4ʳ, text of

Part II; 2P4^v, blank; 2P5^r, title for Part III (verso blank); 2P6, Dedication to Frances Countess of Carbery; 2Q1, Dedication to Alice Countess of Carbery; 2Q2^r-3I2^v, text of Part III; 3I3^r-3I7^v, The Table; 3I8^r, advertisement (verso blank).

Notes: PLATES. There was added to this edition four illustrations, two of them on a single plate. The double plate has "Antwerp" engraved to one side, and it is not unlikely that the plates had been imported. They are as follows, with the directions for insertion: (11) The Massacre of the Innocents, "Sect vi. P. 99."; (12-13) The Scourging and The Crowning with Thorns [these two on a single plate], "Page 547."; (14) The Crucifixion, "page 575." Plate 14 is known to exist in three states. Across the foot of the plate is a narrow band, with a Latin inscription. In State I there is no direction; it appears thus in its two known appearances in the second edition (1653). In State II "p. 575" is engraved to the left of the strip; this state is known only in the H copy of the 1657 edition. In State III the whole strip has been cut away, and a new blank strip burnished across from the left to a plant on the right, one leaf of which overlaps. On this new strip has been engraved "p. 575" and the Latin inscription.

All ten plates used in the 1653 edition were used again in this edition. All of the plates except two have had some alteration, usually consisting of changing the inscription to suit the date and make-up of the new edition. The Ascension (10) has been extensively touched up. This can most easily be seen about one figure on the right-hand side, and in the footprints of Christ. The figure in question, standing against the sky, with an outstretched arm, has in 1653 the sky blank between arm and hill; in 1657 the space between arm and hill has lines engraved across it. In 1653 the left footprint reaches to the top of the hill upon which, against the sky, blades of grass can be seen; in 1657 the top of the hill has been raised about a quarter of an inch above the footprint, and the surface is smooth.

This edition was set up from the second; this is shown by the fact that on the title-page of Part I the compositor has put into type the legend from the ornament of the second edition while this edition bears another ornament in its place.

On Z2 is the Syriac text, with a translation into English, of a prayer supposed to have been uttered by Christ at His baptism; it is followed by a discussion as to the authenticity of the prayer. With this small addition the text of *The Great Exemplar* became complete. A note in the margin says that the original was supplied by Dudley Loftus, Professor of Oriental Languages at Dublin. He came of a notable Anglo-Irish family which had been established in Ireland by his great-grandfather, Adam Loftus, Archbishop of Dublin and Armagh. The archbishop was instrumental in founding the University in Dublin. Dudley had been at Oxford in 1639, when he probably became acquainted with Taylor. In a letter to Evelyn of November 15, 1656, Taylor said,

"I have lately received from a learned person beyond sea certain extracts of the Easterne and Southerne Antiquities, which very much confirm my opinion and doctrine; for the learned man was pleased to expresse great pleasure in the reasonablenesse of it and my discourse concerning it." He was alluding to his trouble over original sin (see *Deus Justificatus*, No. 26), in which this communication from Loftus was made use of. It was with these comforting papers, no doubt, that Taylor received the Syriac prayer. According to Charles Page Eden, the Syriac manuscript was in Dublin when he re-edited Heber's collected edition, and the Oriental text, in his edition, was corrected from the original.

Copies: BM, Bod, BO, E, H, TCD; Cla, HH, KS, LC, W, Y.

9 E. Fourth Edition. 1667. Wing T345.

Title: THE │ [all in red] GREAT EXEMPLAR │ OF │ Sanctity and Holy Life │ [all in red] according to the Christian Institution: │ DESCRIBED │ In the HISTORY of the │ LIFE and DEATH │ of the ever-Blessed │ [all in red] JESUS CHRIST, │ THE SAVIOUR of the WORLD. │ [rule] │ WITH │ [all in red] CONSIDERATIONS and DISCOURSES │ upon the several parts of the Story; │ And PRAYERS fitted to the several MYSTERIES. │ [rule] │ In three Parts │ [rule] │ *The Fourth Edition.* │ [rule] │ [all in red] By JER. TAYLOR, Chaplain in Ordinary to King │ *CHARLES* the First, and late Lord Bishop of │ *DOUN* and *CONNER.* │ [rule] │ [in red] *LONDON,* │ Printed by *J. Flesher,* for *Richard Royston,* at the sign of the │ Angel in S. Bartholomew's Hospital. MDCLXVII.

Coll: Fol., in sixes: A-3D⁶ 3E⁴ 3F-3H², 424 leaves; plates 11 (two before A1; facing N3ʳ, Y1ʳ; two-leaf plate before 2Y3; two-leaf plate before 2Z6; two-leaf plate before 3A2; facing 3A4ʳ, 3B2ʳ, 3C4ʳ; two-leaf plate before 3D3ʳ). Paged A4ʳ-D6ᵛ: pp. i-xl; E1ʳ-E5ʳ: pp. i-ix; F3ʳ-3E3ᵛ: pp. 1-542.

Contents: A1ʳ, title-page (verso blank); A2ʳ-A5ʳ, Dedication to Christopher Lord Hatton; A5ᵛ, blank; A6, The Contents; B1ʳ-E2ᵛ, The Preface; E3ʳ-F1ʳ, "An Exhortation to the Imitation of the Life of Christ"; F1ᵛ, blank; F2ʳ, sub-title (verso blank); F3ʳ-3E3ᵛ, text; 3E4, blank; 3F1ʳ-3H2ᵛ, The Table.

Notes: PLATES. The plates of the four evangelists were not used in this edition. The double plate of the third edition was divided and each of the parts shows a plate-mark all around. The remainder, excluding the portrait and engraved title, have the following inscriptions: (1) "Place this figure before the tytle of ye 1 part." (5) "Place this figure before the title of the 2nd part." (7) "Place this figure before page 487:" [still dated 1653.] (8) "Place this figure before page 490:" [still dated 1653.] (9) "Place this figure before page 496:" [still dated 1653.] (10) "Place this figure page 529." (11) "Sect vi. P 84." (12) "Place this page 495." (13) "Place this page 503." (14) "Place this page 519." At Magdalen College, Oxford, there is a copy with a variant plate 10 reading "Sect vi. P. 81." and corrected in manuscript to "84."

The engraved title is still dated 1657, but has been re-engraved since that date. This is most easily detected in the panel behind the Greek inscription, at the foot of the plate. In 1653 and 1657 this has only vertical and horizontal lines in it; for the 1667 edition heavy diagonals were scored across.

Forty-four smaller illustrations were added to this edition. They are printed in pairs—some on two plates, some coupled on a single plate—at the head of various sections. In the last pair of all, on p. 419 (2S2^r), one represents Christ at prayer. This plate was first used as the frontispiece to *A Collection of Offices,* 1658 (No. 30 A). It was then cut down and re-engraved; in this form it was used in 1660, and for a number of years, as a frontispiece to the sixth and following editions of *Holy Living* (No. 11 F).

The new business address for Royston was brought about by the burning of the old Angel in the Great Fire of 1666. Taylor died in August, 1667, and the preliminaries at least must have been printed after that date since Taylor is called the "late Lord Bishop" on the title-page. Much of the text, however, was probably printed during his lifetime, and it is by no means impossible that the text bears authorial corrections.

Copies: AS, BM, Bod, CUL, JR; Har, I, KS, US, Y.

9 F. Fifth Edition. 1675. Wing T287.

Antiquitates Christianae: or, the History of the Life and Death of the Holy Jesus: as also the Lives, Acts and Martyrdoms of His Apostles . . . London, Printed by R. Norton, for R. Royston, Bookseller to his most Sacred Majesty, at the Angel in Amen-Corner, MDCLXXV. Fol.

For the remainder of the seventeenth century and well into the eighteenth (1742), *The Great Exemplar* was published with William Cave's work, *Antiquitates Christianae, or the Lives, Acts, and Martyrdoms of the Apostles,* which also supplied the title for the composite volume. Cave also provided an "Apparatus" for the whole volume, which consisted of a long essay on "the three great dispensations of the church, Patriarchal, Mosaical and Evangelical." This edition and most subsequent editions can be found with any of the parts bound separately, including the "Apparatus." This edition was advertised in the Term Catalogue for Easter, 1675.

The top and bottom inscribed panels of the engraved title-page have been burnished out and re-engraved, so that now the whole reads: "——Antiquitates Christianae——The Life and Death of the Holy Jesus——As also the Lives, Acts and Martyrdoms of the Apostles." Of the old plates, only four remain, the portrait, the engraved title-page, (1) and (11). These four plates, worn away and clumsily touched up, were to be retained for many years. Some of the forty-four small plates are kept in this edition, including Christ at prayer; and beside it there turns up again, routed out of the stores and faint with wear, another plate already associated with Taylor, namely Vaughan's engraving of King David, which in 1644 had been the title-page of *The Psalter of David*

(No. 3 A1). This edition also has an allegorized folding plate which was also used in *Polemical Discourses,* 1674 (No. 28 B).
Copies: BM, Bod, E, Hai, LI; Har, I, KS, LC, PU, RU.
9 G. Sixth Edition. 1678. Wing T287A.
Antiquitates Christianae. . . . Printed by E. Flesher, and R. Norton, for R. Royston. MDCLXXVIII. Fol.
This edition is advertised, with no publisher's name, in the Term Catalogue for Easter, 1678.
Copies: C; Pb, US.
9 H. Seventh Edition. 1684. Wing T288.
Antiquitates Christianae. . . . Printed by J. Macock and M. Fletcher, for R. Royston. MDCLXXXIV. Fol.
The title to Part I is simply: "Printed for Richard Royston, 1684"; to Part II "Printed by J. Macock . . . 1683"; and to Part III "Printed by M. Flesher, 1684." Cave's part of the volume is also "Printed by M. Flesher, 1684." It would seem that the two printers were not partners but separate firms.
Copies: BM; Har, US.
9 I. Eighth Edition. 1694. No Wing number.
Antiquitates Christianae. . . . Printed by R. N. for Luke Meredith, at the Sign of the Star in St. Paul's Church-Yard, MDCXCIV. Fol.
This edition was advertised in the Term Catalogue for Michaelmas, 1693.
Copies: Bod, CUL, Et; I, KS, NL, Y.
The Lombart Portrait: The portrait of Taylor engraved by Peter Lombart can be found up to 1667 in four states. What follows is a description of the variations by which they can be detected and some further notes on their appearance.
State I. As normally found in *The Great Exemplar,* 1653 (No. 9 C).
State II. A few lines have been added to the whites of the eyes. Just under the front and right side of the chin (left side of the plate), about a quarter of an inch from the middle of the collar, there have been engraved a few vertical lines which are absent in State I. The hand also is slightly different; in State I, on the inner side, next to the thumb, patches of white show, while in State II this part, together with the thumb itself, has been darkened all along with cross-hatching.
State III. The shadow under the ledge on which stands the oval frame of the portrait has been changed. In earlier states longitudinal lines are darkened by diagonals sloping inwards on each side of the middle; in State III other diagonals have been engraved upwards across these, roughly at right angles. The right cheek (left of the plate) is shaded in States I and II by lines running up and down; in State III lines have been engraved horizontally across these, up to the level of the top of the cheek.
State IV. A few lines have been added to the face. The roughly horizontal

lines across the cheek have been extended up to the level of the eye. In State I and II the wrinkles running down from the right nostril (left of the plate) are all longitudinal; in State III there is a hint of cross-hatching at the top of it; in State IV, this is continued all along.

It will be seen that these four can be divided into two groups; only small alterations were made between States I and II, as between States III and IV. State II was probably prepared for *Polemical Discourses,* 1657 (No. 28 A) and *The Great Exemplar,* 1657 (No. 9 D), and State III for *Ductor Dubitantium* of 1660 (No. 32 A). However, all four states can be found in various editions. The following is a rough sampling of appearance:

State I: 1653, 1655, 1657, 1660.
State II: 1655, 1657.
State III: 1660, 1668.
State IV: 1667.

It is possible that copies of the plate might have been printed off, not only for binding, but also for sale, separately. A specimen of State III, in the library of Christ Church, Oxford, is stuck, not bound, into *Ductor Dubitantium* (1660) and on it is written, in what seems to be a contemporary hand, "Pret 1—O." This is the normal state of the portrait for this book, although other states can be found in copies.

If it be true that the portrait was offered for sale as a single print, it would follow that more copies would have been printed than were needed as frontispieces; then, if there had been a large stock of earlier impressions, left-over specimens could easily get mixed with those newly brightened up.

Anybody at all familiar with seventeenth-century English books will know of cases where illustrated volumes, perfect and untouched in appearance, are lacking in requisite plates. It is not impossible that copies of such books may have varied in price according to the number of plates included; or copies in which certain plates are wanting could have been bought from workmen, selling dishonestly or by customary right. It seems probable that, in the cases of books of this period with illustrations printed separately, "perfection" is bibliographically a relative term; but here the only certainty is that there exists one copy of the Lombart portrait with a price written on it.

10 A. *Treatises.* First Edition. 1650. Wing T404.
General Title: TREATISES | OF | 1. The *Liberty* of *Prophesying.* | 2. Episcopacie. 3. The History of the Life & Death | of the ever blessed *Jesus Christ.* | 4. An *Apologie* for Authorized and | Set-forms of *Lyturgie.* | TOGETHER WITH | A Sermon Preached at *Oxon.* on the | Anniversary of the 5. of November. | [rule] | *IN TWO VOLUMES.* | [rule] | By Jer: Taylor

D. D. Chaplaine in Ordinarie | to His late MAJESTIE. | [rule] | [row of 5 roses] | [rule] | *LONDON,* | Printed for R. ROYSTON, at the | Angel in *Ivie-lane.* 1650.

Coll: Quarto: Π², Numbers 6 A, 2 B, 8 A, and 9 A. No accurate collation can be provided because of the lack of examples and the variable character of this collection (cf. No. 7 A).

Contents: Π1, blank; Π2ʳ, general title-page (verso blank). The collection was intended to contain *The Liberty of Prophesying* (1647), *Episcopacy Asserted* (1647), *An Apology for Liturgy* (1649), *Gunpowder Sermon* (1638), and *Great Exemplar* (1649).

Notes: The only known copy of the composite work is at Trinity College, Cambridge, and is, unfortunately, mutilated. This copy has the new title-page but lacks the *Gunpowder Sermon* and *Great Exemplar,* the second volume of the issue. Further, the second edition of *A Discourse of Baptisme,* 1653 (No. 17 B) is bound in at the end of the existing volume.

It cannot be determined, of course, if there was ever a new title-page for the second volume of this edition of *Treatises.* The second volume was no doubt to contain the rather lengthy *Great Exemplar.*

Copies: TCC.

11 A. *Holy Living.* First Edition. 1650. Wing T371 and T371A.

Title: THE RVLE | AND | EXERCISES | OF | HOLY LIVING. | *In which are described* | The MEANS and INSTRUMENTS | of obtaining every Vertue, and the | Remedies against every Vice, and | Considerations serving to the | resisting all temptations. | Together with | Prayers containing the whole duty of | A Christian, and the parts of Devotion | fitted to all Occasions, and furnish'd | for all Necessities | [rule] | [flower enclosed in a box of fleurs-de-lis orns.] | [rule] | LONDON, | Printed for *Richard Royston* at the | Angel in *Ivie-Lane.* | MDCL.

Coll: 12mo: ¶¹² A-R¹² S⁴, 220 leaves; plates 1 (Johnson: Faithorne #11 before ¶3). Paged A1ʳ-S1ᵛ: pp. 1-410.

Contents: ¶1-¶2, blank; ¶3ʳ, title-page (verso blank); ¶4ʳ-¶10ʳ, dedication to the Earl of Carbery; ¶10ᵛ-¶12ᵛ, the table; A1ʳ-S1ᵛ, text; S2ʳ-S3ʳ, appendix; S3ᵛ, blank; S4ʳ, colophon, "[row of orns.] | LONDON, | Printed by *R. Norton.* | MDCL. | [row of orns.]" (verso blank).

Variants: Two other states of the title-page exist. Since it is probable that these two are earlier than the one reproduced above, which we will call State III, they will be designated as States I and II. State I varies by having line six ("In which are described") set in roman instead of italic, the initial letter of line fourteen ("a Christian . . .") set in lower case rather than upper, and an imprint reading: "LONDON, | Printed for Francis Ash, Book- | Seller in

Worcester. | MDCL." Copies having State I are: Bod, H(1), and Har. State II agrees with State III, in the readings for lines six and fourteen, but agrees with State I in the reading of the imprint. Only one copy, H(2), with this state is known.

Some copies with State III title-pages lack S2 and S3, the "Appendix" which contained prayers for the King. Signature S was printed as an octavo half-sheet (the chain-lines are vertical) and apparently in some copies for London circulation the leaves were discreetly supressed. Copies lacking the "Appendix" are: Th, CUL(2), HH.

Copy H(2) is the only known copy with p. 273 misnumbered 173.

The Th copy has a two-leaf plate tipped in between ¶2 and ¶ 3. It depicts Taylor (?) on a pedestal at left on which is written "MERCVRIVS | CHRISTIANVS". At the top right Christ offers a crown and a ray of light falls diagonally to Taylor's feet. On the ray is written, *"Ad te quacunq vocas dulcisime Jesu."* At the bottom right is the devil, in fire, offering bags, and on a path of cross-hatching, edged in weeds and flowers is written, "Who can dwell with the | everlasting burnings. *Isay.* 33. 14." The plate is not signed.

Notes: Holy Living was entered in the Stationers' Register by Francis Ash on March 7, 1649/50. On November 24, 1651, it was transferred to Royston, together with *The Great Exemplar* (9 A). In spite of Ash's primary interest, it is evident that Royston had very early on a large interest in the work. The imprint of State III of the title-page is the prototype of the book as it was to be produced over many years.

Thomason's copy is dated May 22, 1650, and *Holy Living* may therefore be confidently put before the *Funeral Sermon on Lady Carbery,* who died in October, 1650.

Copy H(2), the copy with the unique State II title-page, was presented by Taylor to William Wyat, his collaborator in *A New and Easie Institution of Grammar* (No. 5 A). It has corrections and additions in the text, a prayer on the blank S3ᵛ, and a "Table of the Prayers," on the blank S4ʳ and a flyleaf, all in Taylor's hand. The corrections and the prayers were published, with a description of the copy, in *The Times Literary Supplement,* September 20, 1947, p. 484.

Holy Living was one of Taylor's most popular works and one of the most popular books of devotion of the age. Dorothy Osborne read it. In a letter, tentatively dated by Parry as February 19, 1654, she wrote to Temple, "They say you gave order for this vast paper; how do you think I shall ever fill it, or with what? I am not always in the humour to wrangle and dispute. For example, now I had rather agree to what you say, than tell you that Dr. Taylor (whose devote you must know I am) says there is a great advantage to be gained in resigning up one's will to the command of another. . . . Let me practice this towards you as well as preach it to you, and I'll lay a wager you will approve on't" (*Letters from Dorothy Osborne to Sir William Temple,* ed.

E. A. Parry, London, 1888). She is paraphrasing from *Holy Living* a paragraph which begins, "There is very great peace and immunity from sin in
resigning our will up to the command of others" (Ch. III, Sect. 1, para. 2).

An echo of the title can be detected late in the century, in an anonymous
little book, meanly printed on mean paper—*The True Way to Happiness: or,
The Necessity of Holy Living* . . . . London . . . . 1696 (Wing T3128 A).

Early during the eighteenth century, parts of *Holy Living* underwent a
curious metamorphosis. In 1714, there was published by Tonson, in three
volumes, a compilation called *The Ladies Library,* "Written by a Lady" and
"Published by Mr. Steele." It is most noteworthy for the enchanting dedication
to his wife, with which Steele prefaced the third volume. The "Lady" is, by
persistent tradition, presumed to be Taylor's granddaughter, Lady Wray, the
author of that puzzling letter, now lost, about incidents in her grandfather's
life. The work is a sort of mixed grill, improvingly arranged, of extracts from
seventeenth-century divines, with large chunks from Taylor, and predom-
inantly from *Holy Living.* Royston Meredith, who was evidently Royston's
grandson, and co-heir with his sister Elizabeth Meredith, complained that he
was being robbed of his literary property (other works originally published by
Royston, beside those by Taylor, were rifled to fill *The Ladies Library*); he
wrote to Steele, and accused him of theft from "two poor orphans who have
very little else to subsist on." The orphans were presumably himself and his
sister. Later he threatened proceedings on account of his rights in Taylor's
works. Steele retorted with his intention to do "all the good offices I can to the
reverend author's grandchild [Lady Wray?] now in town." Meredith believed
this to be, on Steele's part, merely "a blind excuse for his notorious plagiarisms."
He published the correspondence on November 11, 1714, in *Mr. Steele detected: Or, the Poor and Oppressed Orphan's Letters to the Great and Arbi-
trary Mr. Steele.*

Copies: Bod, CUL(1,2), CHW, H(1,2,3), Th; CW, Har, HH.

11 B. Second Edition. 1651. Wing T372.

Title: THE RVLE | AND | EXERCISES | OF | HOLY LIVING. | *In
which are described* | The MEANS and INSTRUMENTS | of obtaining every Ver-
tue, and the | Remedies against every Vice, and | Considerations serving to the
| resisting all temptations. | Together with | Prayers containing the whole
duty of | A Christian, and the parts of Devotion | fitted to all Occasions, and
furnish'd | for all Necessities. | *The Seeond Edition.* | [rule] | [orn.] | [rule] |
LONDON, | Printed for *Richard Royston* at the | Angel in *Ivie-Lane.* |
MDCLI.

Stet: "The Seeond Edition."

Coll: 12mo: $\P^{12}$ (-$\P$1) A-S^{12}, 228 leaves; plates 1 (Johnson: Faithorne #11 before $\P$2). Paged A1^r-S10^v: pp. 1-428.

Contents: $\P$2^r, title-page (verso blank); $\P$3^r-$\P$9^r, dedication to the Earl of

Carbery; ¶9ᵛ-¶12ᵛ, the table; A1ʳ-S10ᵛ, text; S11, blank; S12ʳ, advertisement (verso blank).

Variants: Some sheets of ¶ were printed before the words *"The Seeond Edition"* were added to the title-page. Copies with this variant are H(1), P(1 and 2), US, and Y. It is possible that these sheets were in the nature of a late proof. In copy H(1) some words have slipped on ¶12ʳ; in other copies they are straight, but in putting them back a space has got into the middle of one word. Also in this form the word *signes* appears as *sgnes* in copy H(1).

Some copies were also printed with a variant imprint, preserved in copy H(2). The title-page is the same except for the imprint which reads: "LONDON, Printed | for *Francis Ashe* Book-seller | in Worcester. | MD CLI."

In one copy not examined and no longer traceable, the book-seller who catalogued it fortunately printed a line block in illustration. This copy has a slip of paper pasted over the Royston imprint which reads: "LONDON, | Printed for *Francis Ashe* Book- | Seller in Worcester. | MDCL." Not only is the setting different by line and by the spelling of Ash's name from the Ash imprint in the first edition and second edition, but the type is much larger and of a different face from both these editions as well. This variant title-page, unfortunately not available for examination, does further suggest that the title-page which lacks *"The Seeond Edition"* is a proof, and that the page with Ash pasted on is a sort of dummy made before Ash's imprint was put into the chase.

In some copies one line is missing at the top of E12ᵛ (p. 120); in other copies the error has been corrected with a cancel. Some copies have page 317 misnumbered 371.

Notes: The engraved title-page is tipped in on the stub of ¶1.

The prayers and passages from the "Appendix" of the first edition have been incorporated in the text. The first such prayer had been originally called "For the King &c.", but has been altered to "For the Ruler &c." in this edition. *King* in the titles of all the other prayers has been altered to *Ruler* but the former word has not been suppressed in the text of the prayers.

Copies: BM, CUL, H(2), P(2); UC, US, Y.

11 C. Third Edition. 1651. Wing T372.

Title: [A line for line resetting of the title-page of No. 11 B with the following exceptions. This is described as the "Second" not "Seeond" edition, and the ornament is a thistle in this edition and a rose in No. 11 B. The imprint is the Royston imprint of 11 B.]

Coll and *Contents:* [As in No. 11 B.]

Variants: The CCC copy lacks the ornament on the title-page. This copy also has the *f* in "of" on line 13 of the title-page missing. This suggests that the absence of both may be due to an accident.

Notes: This edition was probably created to supply the demand for this pop-

ular work, and was no doubt called the "second" edition because of its prox-
imity in time to the actual second edition and as a stimulus to sales. It can be
distinguished from the second by some small differences, in addition to the
two changes in the title-page.

The advertisements on S12^r are printed between two lines of acorns. In the
second edition there are eighteen above and nineteen below; in the third edition, the ornaments being smaller, there are twenty-one both above and below.
In all copies of the third edition known, page 317 is misnumbered 371 and one
line is missing from the top of page 120. Clearly the third edition was set from
a copy of the second edition which embodied both these variants (cf. No. 11 B,
"Variants" above).

The engraved title-page has been re-engraved in all copies of the third edition. Most of the lines have been deepened, and many new ones have been
added. This can be most easily seen on each side of the panel bearing the Latin
text. On each side of this are small crescent-shaped spaces. In the earlier state,
found in the second edition, these vertical lunettes are shaded mainly by
vertical lines. In the later state, found in the third edition, deep horizontals
are scored across the whole way down.

Copy H contains a few manuscript corrections. Eight of these were incorporated in the following edition (No. 11 D). These corrections, though
contemporary, are not in Taylor's hand; but the fact of the necessary alterations
having been made indicates that Taylor was taking care of his text.
Copies: CCC, H.

11 D. Fourth Edition. 1654. Wing T373.
Title: THE | *RULE* and *EXERCISES* | OF | Holy Living. | In which are
described | The *Means* and *Instruments* of obtain- | ing every Virtue, and the
Remedies against | every Vice, and *Considerations* serving | to the resisting all
Temptations. | *Together with* | Prayers containing the whole duty of a |
Christian, and the parts of Devotion fitted to | all Occasions, and furnished for
all Necessities. | [rule] | By Jer: Taylor, D. D. | [rule] | The 4th Edition
corrected: | with Additionals. | [double rule] | *LONDON.* | Printed for
Richard Royston at the Angel | in Ivie-lane. 1654.
Coll: 12mo: A-T^{12} U^6, 234 leaves; plates 1 (before B1). Paged B1^r-U4^r: pp. 1-
439.
Contents: A1, blank; A2^r, engraved half-title (verso blank); A3^r, title-page
(verso blank); A4^r-A9^v, dedication to the Earl of Carbery; A10^r-A12^v, the
table; B1^r-U4^r, text; U4^v-U6^r, advertisement of books published by Royston;
U6^v, blank.
Notes: Except for the date, which has been changed to 1654, the engraved title
appears to be the same as in the previous edition (11 C), but is, in this in-
stance, apparently printed on a leaf conjugate with A11 and thus part of the
sheet A.

The plate inserted before B1 is a folding plate. To the left is the full-length figure of Taylor, standing on a pedestal lettered "Mercurius Christianus." He points with his left hand to a figure of Christ in the sky, holding a banner and a crown; below, surrounded by smoke and flames, is a horned and fanged demon, with a money bag in one hand and a taper in the other, and standing in a dragon's mouth. This design of Christ was added to Hollar's engraving for *The Golden Grove* when it was reprinted in *Polemical Discourses* (No. 28 A). This plate, which first appears in this edition, was obviously designed to match the plate found in all early editions of *Holy Dying*. This plate has been added to copy Th of the first edition of *Holy Living* (No. 11 A) to remedy an imagined defect.

On O9ᵛ (p. 306) of this edition, a new paragraph was added between paragraphs ten and eleven of Chapter 4, Section 7. The added paragraph was given no number. The word *King* was restored in the passages from the "Appendix" in this edition.

Copies: CUL.

11 E. Fifth Edition. 1656. Wing T374.

Title: THE | *RULE* and *EXERCISES* | OF | Holy Living. | *In which are described* | The *Means* and *Instruments* of obtain- |ing every Virtue, and the *Remedies* against | every Vice, and *Considerations* serving | to the resisting all Temptations. | *Together with* | Prayers containing the whole duty of a | Christian, and the parts of Devotion fitted to | all Occasions, and furnished for all Necessities. | [rule] | By Jer: Taylor, D. D. | [rule] | The 5th Edition corrected: | With Additionals | [double rule] | *LONDON.* | Printed for *Richard Royston* at the Angel | in Ivie-lane. 1656.

Coll: 12mo: A-T¹² U⁶, 234 leaves; plates 1 (before B1). Paged B1ʳ-U4ʳ: pp. 1-349.

Contents: A1, blank; A2ʳ, engraved title-page (verso blank); A3ʳ, title-page (verso blank); A4ʳ-A9ᵛ, dedication to the Earl of Carbery; A10ʳ-A12ᵛ, the table; B1ʳ-U4ʳ, text; U4ᵛ-U6ʳ, advertisement of books published by Royston; U6ᵛ, blank.

Notes: That this edition is a page for page reprinting of the fourth edition of 1654 can be seen not only in the similarity of title-pages and collation, but in the advertisement (U4ᵛ-U6ʳ in both editions). The 1656 advertisement duplicates the 1654 advertisement, even though Royston had published *The Golden Grove* (1655, No. 22 A), *Unum Necessarium* (1655, No. 23 A), *A Further Explication* (1656, No. 24 A), and *Deus Justificatus* (No. 26 A) in the two years between the fourth and fifth editions of *Holy Living*. Evidently in the copy of the fourth edition used to set the fifth the advertisement had not been corrected and was allowed to pass in its outdated condition.

The engraved title-page has been renovated and is dated 1657. The folding plate has been very much re-engraved. This can most easily be described from the figure of Taylor, which has been adapted to resemble more closely in the face the Lombart portrait. In the fourth edition, a long lock of hair, coming out from under the skull-cap, turns in towards the right cheek (left on the plate); the mouth is between two and three sixteenths of an inch across; there is a narrow collar which does not meet under the chin. In the fifth edition, we have the familiar priestly locks, short and turning away from the cheek; the mouth is reduced to less than two sixteenths of an inch; the collar is broad, falling almost to the shoulders, and meeting under the chin.

The KCC copy has many corrections in Taylor's hand. These were printed, with those in copy H(2) which was a presentation copy of the first edition (No. 11 A), in *The Times Literary Supplement*, September 20, 1947, p. 484. The KCC copy of this edition has been rebound in the nineteenth century, and all blank leaves and fly-leaves have been removed; it is possible that it too was a presentation copy. Four of the corrections were incorporated in the sixth edition.

Despite the claim of "Additionals" on the title-page there are none, and the new paragraph added in the previous edition is still unnumbered.

Copies: BM, CUL, H, KCC, NCE; PU.

11 F. Sixth Edition. 1660. No Wing number.

Title: [A line for line resetting of 11 E above, including the statement of edition.]

Coll: [As in 11 E above.]

Contents: A1, blank; A2^r, blank; A2^v, frontispiece; A3^r, title-page (verso blank); A4^r-A9^v, dedication to the Earl of Carbery; A10^r-A12^v, the table; B1^r-U4^r, text; U4^v-U5^v, advertisement; U6^r, "[band of orns.] | [rule] | THE | RULE and EXERCISE | OF | Holy Dying | [rule] | [band of orns.]" (verso blank).

Notes: This edition differs from the fifth edition in three respects. First is the difference in the advertisement which had appeared regularly at the end of *Holy Living* since the fourth edition. This edition has three, not four, pages of advertisement. The fourth page is devoted entirely to the elaborate printing of the title of *Holy Dying*. This page may be in the nature of an advertisement, although *Holy Dying* had already been advertised on the preceeding page (U5^v); or it may be evidence of an abandoned plan to print the two works together.

The second difference is the substitution of a frontispiece for the engraved title-page. The frontispiece plate had been used originally for the frontispiece to *A Collection of Offices*, 1658 (No. 30 A). For this edition of *Holy Living* the plate was cut down and re-engraved. The oval frame to the picture has been made smaller, so that the right hand of Christ overlaps it (in 1658 the hand had been inside the frame). Two Latin sentences have been added:— along the top edge of the plate is "Non magna loquimur sed vivimus"; around the inner band of the frame, at the top, is "Qui sequitus me in tenebris non ambulat." The latter text was one already engraved or printed on the title-pages of works by Taylor.

Finally, the third difference between the fifth and sixth editions is that the folding plate has been re-engraved again. This can be most easily detected on the right, receding, side of the pedestal. In 1656, this is shaded with vertical and horizontal lines; in 1660 diagonals have been added, running down from left to right.

Copies: CO, H.

11 G. Seventh Edition. 1663. Wing T375.

Title: [all within double rules] THE | *Rule* and *Exercises* | OF | Holy Living. | *In which are described* | The MEANS and INSTRUMENTS of obtai- | ning every Vertue, and the Remedies against every | Vice, and *Considerations* serving to the resisting | all Temptations. | *Together with,* | PRAYERS | *Containing* | The Whole duty of a *Christian,* | and the parts of *Devotion* fitted to all Occa- | sions, | and furnished for all Necessities. | [rule] | By JER. TAYLOR, D. D. | [rule] | The Seventh Edition. | [rule] | *LONDON,* | Printed by *James Flesher* for *Richard Royston.* | Bookseller to His most Sacred MAJESTIE. | [centered rule] | MDCLXIII.

Coll: 8vo: A-Y^8, 176 leaves. Plates 1 (before B1). Paged B1^r-Y8^r: pp. 1-335.

Contents: A1^r, half-title "THE | *Rule* and *Exercises* | OF | Holy Living"; A1^v, frontispiece; A2^r, title-page (verso blank); A3^r-A6^v, dedication to the Earl of Carbery; A7^r-A8^v, contents; B1^r-Y8^r, text; Y8^v, blank.

Variants: Copy H has an extra folding plate, paired with the normal one, between A8 and B1. This extra plate had already been used in *Unum Neces-sarium,* 1655 (No. 23 A). About half of the plate is missing, but from what remains it can be seen that it has been cut down and re-engraved. In the right corner is inscribed "Holy Living pa: 260." Since the design symbolizes re-pentance, and page 260 treats of anger, the number must be wrong. It is clear no copy of the seventh edition of *Holy Living* need be incomplete for lacking this plate.

Notes: The frontispiece and the folding plate are the same as in the sixth edition, but worn.

Copies: BM, CCO, EmC, H; Y.

11 H. Eighth Edition. 1668. Wing T376.

Title: [all within double rules] THE | *Rule* and *Exercises* | OF | Holy Living. | *In which are described* | The MEANS and INSTRUMENTS of obtai- | ning every Vertue, and the *Remedies* against every | Vice, and *Considerations* serving to the resisting | all Temptations. | *Together with* | PRAYERS | Containing | The whole duty of a *Christian,* | and the parts of *Devotion* fitted to all Occa- | sions, | and furnished for all Necessities. | [rule] | By *JER. TAYLOR,* D. D. | [rule] | The Eighth Edition. | [rule] | *LONDON,* | Printed by *Roger Norton* for *Richard Royston,* | Bookseller to His most Sacred Majesty. | MDCLXVIII.

Coll: [As in 11 G above.]

Contents: [As in 11 G above.]

Notes: This is a reprint of the seventh edition, with the same plates. The alterations in the folding plate can most easily be seen in the sky between the clouds and the hills in the background. In the seventh edition (1663) this consists of horizontal lines, and separate diagonals; in this edition the plate has been darkened here by criss-cross diagonals.

This edition was advertised in the Michaelmas Term Catalogue for 1668. *Copies:* E, EC; Y.

11 I. Second Issue of 11 H. [Ninth Edition.] 1670. Wing T377.
The Rule and Exercises of Holy Living . . . . Printed by Roger Norton for Richard Royston . . . MDCLXX. 8vo.

For the remainder of the century *Holy Living* appeared in a format similar to that found in the seventh edition (1663, 11 G), with a folding plate, roughly of the original design, and sometimes from a new engraving, and the frontispiece. The latter illustration gradually wears away and is last used in 1680 (11 L). *Copies:* BM, CUL: KS.

11 J. Third Issue of 11 H. [Tenth Edition.] 1674. Wing T378.
The Rule and Exercises of Holy Living . . . . Printed by Roger Norton for Richard Royston . . . MDCLXXIV. 8vo.
Copies: E.

11 K. Eleventh Edition. 1676. Wing T379.
The Rule and Exercises of Holy Living . . . . Printed by Roger Norton for Richard Royston . . . MDCLXXVI. 8vo.

On A1^r (the frontispiece is on A1^v) is printed: "THE | *Rule* and *Exercises* | of | Holy Living | and Dying." This appears to be the first time that the two works were explicitly treated as a single one (which they are not). *Copies:* Bod, MO; Y.

11 L. Twelfth Edition. 1680. Wing T380.
The Rule and Exercises of Holy Living . . . . Printed by Miles Flesher for Richard Royston . . . MDCLXXX. 8vo.

We can fix the date of publication for this edition within a few days. In the seventh report of the Historical Manuscripts Commission, a sentence is quoted from a letter written on September 18, 1679, from John Verney to Sir R. Verney: "Taylor's Living and Dying is now reprinting and may be out in 20 days" (p. 475). This edition was advertised in the Michaelmas Term Catalogue for 1679.

This is the last time the frontispiece is used in *Holy Living*. A new engraved title-page is used in this edition. It is Johnson: Anon. 154 and is described as follows: "Two angels bearing candles and a kneeling child before an altar under a canopy; above two cherubs hold sheet on which the title is engraved." Johnson lists this plate under *Holy Living*, but the title on the sheet held by the cherub is "The Rule and Exercises of Holy Living and Dying." *Copies:* H; Y.

11 M. Second Issue of 11 L. [Thirteenth Edition.] 1682. Wing T381.

The Rule and Exercises of Holy Living . . . . Printed by Miles Flesher for Richard Royston . . . MDCLXXXII. 8vo.

This, and all editions down to the twenty-fifth (1739), have the engraved title-page first used in the twelfth edition.

Copies: BM, TCC, TCD; KS, NL, Y.

11 N. Third Issue of 11 L. [Fourteenth Edition.] 1686. Wing T382.

The Rule and Exercises of Holy Living . . . . Printed by Miles Flesher for Richard Royston . . . MDCLXXXVI. 8vo.

Copies: Bod, Hai, LI.

11 O. Fifteenth Edition. 1690. Wing T383.

The Rule and Exercises of Holy Living . . . . Printed by J. H. for Luke Meredith at the Angel in Amen Corner. MDCXC. 8vo.

The printer, to judge from later imprints, must have been John Heptinstall. Luke Meredith had inherited Royston's copies upon his death in 1686. This edition was advertised in the Trinity Term Catalogue for 1690.

Copies: BM, Bod, TCD; Har, PU.

11 P. Sixteenth Edition. 1693. Wing T383A.

The Rule and Exercises of Holy Living . . . . Printed by J. L. for Luke Meredith at the Star in St. Paul's Church-yard. MDCXCIII. 8vo.

Since John Heptinstall is the printer of *Holy Living* through several more editions, it is conjectural that the "J. L." of the title-page is a misprint for "J. H." However, it seems strange that a printer would make this kind of mistake with his own initials.

This edition was advertised in the Michaelmas Term Catalogue for 1693.

Copies: I.

11 Q. Seventeenth Edition. 1695. Wing T384.

The Rule and Exercises of Holy Living . . . . Printed by J. L. for L. Meredith . . . 1695. 8vo.

This edition was advertised in the Term Catalogue for Michaelmas, 1697.

Copies: Har, Y.

12 A. *A Funeral Sermon . . . for the Lady Frances Carbery.* First Edition. 1650. Wing T335.

Title: [all within double rules] A | Funerall Sermon, | *Preached* | At the Obsequies of the Right Honble | and most vertuous Lady, | THE LADY | FRANCES, | Countesse of *CARBERY:* | Who deceased *October* the 9th. 1650. | at her House GOLDEN GROVE | in *CARMARTHEN-SHIRE.* | [rule] | By JER. TAYLOR, D. D. | [rule] | [woodcut device] | [rule] | LONDON, | Printed by *J. F.* for *R. Royston* at the Angel in Ivie-lane. | [centered rule] | M.DC.L.

Coll: Quarto: A-E⁴, 20 leaves. Paged A3ʳ-E4ᵛ: pp. 1-36.

Contents: A1ʳ, title-page (verso blank); A2, epistle to the Earl of Carbery; A3ʳ-E4ᵛ, text.

Notes: Taylor was addicted to abbreviations when writing, and some features of the text of this edition (e.g. "H. and mysterious Trinity" for "Holy and …") indicate that it was perhaps printed from his original manuscript.

In the preface to the sermon, Taylor refers to Lady Carbery as "that Deare and most excellent Soule" and the "Dear departed Saint." It would seem that this may have echoed in her widower's mind. Lord Carbery wrote a formal *Advice to his Son*; this was first printed complete in *The Huntington Library Bulletin* for April, 1937. In it he alludes to his dead wife as "that Deare saint." He mentions his son's "tutor," who was almost certainly Taylor; the conclusion of the *Advice* is dated September 30, 1651, and during its composition, Taylor was officiating as chaplain at Golden Grove. With his schoolmastering experi-ence, he would very probably have been employed in teaching the boy.

Copies: BM, Bod, CUL, H, NLW; NL, Y.

12 B. Second Printing. 1651.

See *Twenty-Eight Sermons,* 1651 (No. 14 A).

Notes: In this printing, a number of small alterations were made in such details as punctuation and the use of capitals. The epistle was reprinted with the sermon.

12 C. Third Printing. 1654.

See *Twenty-Eight Sermons,* 1654 (No. 14 B).

Notes: In this printing there was added, between the epistle and the sermon, a single page bearing on the recto a long epitaph on Lady Carbery, in Latin, and arranged in the shape of a column. There is no reason for believing that this epitaph was not written by Taylor.

12 D. Fourth Printing. 1667.

See *Ten Sermons,* 1667 (No. 44 A).

12 E. Fifth Printing. 1673.

See *Eleven Sermons,* 1673 (No. 44 B).

12 F. Sixth Printing. 1678.

See *Eleven Sermons,* 1678 (No. 44 C).

13 A. *Clerus Domini.* First Edition. 1651. Wing T296.

Title: [all within double rules] *CLERUS DOMINI*: | OR, | A DISCOURSE | OF THE | DIVINE INSTITUTION, | Necessity, Sacrednesse, and Separa-tion | OF THE | OFFICE MINISTERIAL. | *TOGETHER WITH* | THE NATURE AND MANNER OF | its Power and Operation. | [rule] | BY *JER. TAYLOR* D. D. | [rule] | [orn.: arms of Oxford University] | *LON-DON,* | Printed by *James Flesher,* for *R. Royston* at the Angel in | *Ivie-Lane.* 1651.

Coll: Fol.: A-E⁶, 30 leaves. Paged A2ʳ-E5ʳ: pp. 1-55.

Contents: A1ʳ, title-page (verso blank); A2ʳ-E5ʳ, text; E5ᵛ, "The Printer to the Reader"; E6, blank.

Notes: The propriety of describing this as a separate publication may be questioned. It often forms an integral part of *Twenty-Eight Sermons,* 1651 (No. 14 A). The note on E5ᵛ, "The Printer to the Reader," alludes to misprints in "these Sermons, and the Discourse annexed." Lowndes mentions an octavo edition of 1651 but this is certainly a ghost. However, Gosse speaks of a "folio pamphlet .... one of the rarest and most obscure of Taylor's writings, though copies of it are sometimes found bound up with the *Eniautos"* (p. 95). Further-more, it was sold as a separate pamphlet in sufficient numbers that several copies of it are recorded by Wing, and in this bibliography, for its four appear-ances in print in the seventeenth century.

Copy H is uncut, stitched in dark gray wrappers, and very close to being in original condition. An anonymous nineteenth-century manuscript note on the title-page says, "This book appears to have belonged to, and to have been carefully read by Bp. Wm Warner vide marg: passim." It has not been possible to verify this. John Warner, Bishop of Rochester, was a friend with whom Taylor had an unhappy brush in public over the question of original sin (see *A Further Explication,* 1656 [No. 24 A] and *An Answer to a Letter,* 1656 [No. 25 A]). It is not at all improbable that Taylor might have arranged for a separate copy to be sent to Warner for his comments, though in that case, we might have expected some inscribed evidence that this example was a gift.

Copies: Bod, H; Har, HH, S, Y.

13 B. Second Edition. 1655. Wing T297.

Title: [all within double rules] *CLERUS DOMINI*: | OR, | A DISCOURSE | OF THE | DIVINE INSTITUTION, | Necessity, Sacrednesse, and Separa-tion | OF THE | OFFICE MINISTERIAL. | *TOGETHER WITH* | THE NATURE AND MANNER OF | its Power and Operation. | *WRITTEN* | By the speciall command of our late Kɪɴɢ. | [rule] | BY *JER. TAYLOR* D. D. | [rule] | [device] | *LONDON,* | Printed for *R. Royston* at the Angel in | *Ivie-Lane.* 1655.

Coll: Fol.: A-E⁶, 30 leaves. Paged A2ʳ-E5ʳ: pp. 1-55.

Contents: A1ʳ, title-page (verso blank); A2ʳ-E5ʳ, text; E5ᵛ, "The Printer to the Reader"; E6, blank.

Notes: The King's special command, mentioned in the title, was no doubt given at Oxford; *Clerus Domini* clearly forms a third in the group, with *Prayer Ex Tempore* and *On The Reverence Due to the Altar,* of dull, small, early works on the doctrine and discipline of the Church. It forms a pendant to *Episcopacy Asserted,* and it is surprising that it was printed with the sermons, instead of eventually being relegated to *Polemical Discourses.*

Copies: BM, H; Har, I, US, Y.

13 C. Third Edition. 1668. Wing T298.

Clerus Domini . . . . Printed by E. Tyler for Richard Royston . . . 1668. Fol.
Copies: BM; Cla, RU.
13 D. Fourth Edition. 1672. Wing T299.
Clerus Domini . . . . For R. Royston. MDCLXXII. Fol.
   This edition is often bound in as part of *Eleven Sermons,* 1673 (No. 44 B).
Copies: CUL; I, US.

14 A. *Twenty-eight Sermons.* First Edition. 1651. Wing T405.
Title: XXVIII | SERMONS | PREACHED AT | GOLDEN GROVE; |
Being for the Summer half-year, | *BEGINNING ON WHIT-SUNDAY,* |
And ending on the xxv. Sunday after | *TRINITY.* | *TOGETHER WITH*
| A Discourse of the Divine Institution, Necessity, Sacredness, | and Separation
of the Office Ministeriall. | [rule] | BY *JER. TAYLOR,* D. D. | [device: cf.
No. 9 A] | *LONDON,* | Printed by *R. N.* for *Richard Royston* at the Angel |
in *Ivie-Lane.* 1651.
Coll: Fol.: ¶⁴ *⁴ A-2H⁶ 2I⁴, ²A-²E⁶, 228 leaves. Paged A1ʳ-2I3ᵛ: pp. 1-378;
²A2ʳ-²E5ʳ: pp. 1-55.
Contents: ¶1ʳ, title-page (verso blank); ¶2ʳ-*3ᵛ, dedication to the Earl of
Carbery; *4, "Titles of the Sermons"; A1ʳ-2I3ᵛ, text of sermons; 2I4, blank;
²A1ʳ-²E6ᵛ, *Clerus Domini* [see 13 A above].
Variants: Two copies, H and P, have a list of 116 errata. In copy H the errata
list is bound up with *Twenty-Eight Sermons* in a copy of *Eniautos,* 1653 (No.
20 A). It appears after the final index to that composite volume; this suggests
that the leaf may have been printed some time after the book had been published. The other copy, P, is alone in a rebacked contemporary binding with
the errata bound in at the end.
Notes: Twenty-Eight Sermons was entered in the Stationers' Register on
April 8, 1651.
   About three quarters of the errata list is in proper order; then the errors
recorded skip backwards and forwards about the book; finally it ends with a
list of errors in Greek (*Clerus Domini* has a separate list). Some of the corrections are themselves misprinted. All but a few of the English errors are
amended in the second edition. Of the twenty-four misprints in Greek, only
four are corrected in the second edition; these four are together in the list,
although the pages involved are not all in regular order.
   A few of the corrections might be stylistic, but most are to remedy misprints.
It must be certain that they were supplied by the author. The picture is irresistible of Taylor discovering many errors in his book, and hurriedly sending
in a list of necessary corrections; then he looks through again; finds more
errors, and sends in another list; then another, and so on. In fact, our hypothesis
is that the errata list has been made up out of several such lists, some very short,

with which Taylor badgered his publisher (something like this had happened before, to judge by the various errata leaves for *The Liberty of Prophesying*, No. 6 A).

The title-page clearly indicates that *Clerus Domini* was to be part of this volume as well as to enjoy its own separate existence. The device on the title-page was used in *The Great Exemplar*, 1649 (No. 9 A); it is worn, and does not appear to have been touched up in any way.

The twenty-eight sermons are made up of twenty-seven sermons for Sundays and *A Funeral Sermon for Lady Carbery*.

Copies: Bod, CO, H, P, TCC, TCD; HH, KS, PU, Y.

14 B. Second Edition. 1654. Wing T406.

Title: [within double rules, single rule at foot] XXVIII | SERMONS | PREACHED AT | GOLDEN GROVE; | Being for the Summer half-year, | *BEGINNING ON WHIT-SUNDAY,* | And ending on the xxv. Sunday after | *TRINITY.* | *TOGETHER WITH* | A Discourse of the Divine Institution, Necessity, Sacredness, | and Separation of the Office Ministeriall. | [rule] | By *JER. TAYLOR, D. D.* | [rule] | [orn.: a tree with two figures underneath, and a banner across it inscribed "Sic omni tempore verno."] | *LONDON,* | Printed by *R. N.* for *Richard Royston* at the Angel | in *Ivie-Lane*. 1654.

Coll: Fol.: ¶⁴ *⁴ A-2H⁶ 2I⁴ 2K², ²A-²E⁶, 228 leaves. Paged A1ʳ-2K2ᵛ: pp. 1-382 [2G5 unpaged]; ²A2ʳ-²E5ʳ: pp. 1-55.

Contents: ¶1ʳ, title-page (verso blank); ¶2ʳ-*3ᵛ, dedication to the Earl of Carbery; *4, "Titles of the Sermons"; A1ʳ-2G3ᵛ, text of the Sunday sermons; 2G4, dedication of Countess of Carbery's *Funeral Sermon* to Lord Carbery; 2G5ʳ, Latin epitaph on Frances, Countess of Carbery (verso blank); 2G6ʳ-2I4ᵛ, text of *Funeral Sermon*; 2K1ʳ-2K2ᵛ, table; ²A1ʳ-²E6ᵛ, *Clerus Domini* [see No. 13 B above].

Notes: This is the first "complete" edition of this volume.

Except for the addition of the Latin epitaph this is a very close reprinting of the preceding edition. There are occasional small differences in the arrangement of the text; otherwise, with a few exceptions, even the ornaments and the ornamental capitals are the same. With unnecessary care, the publisher's apology for misprints is reproduced on the final page (²E6ᵛ).

This edition, and subsequent editions, are almost always found in joint volumes with the other folio collections of sermons.

Page 382 is mispaged 182.

Copies: BM, Bod; Har, I, KS, US, Y.

14 C. Third Printing. 1668. Wing T407 and T412.

See *Eniautos*, 1668 (No. 20 C).

Notes: This work is an integral part of 1668 *Eniautos*, for its table of contents is conjugate with the title-page of *Twenty-Five Sermons*.

The change in title was occasioned by the transfer of the *Funeral Sermon* to *Ten Sermons* (No. 44 A), so that in this printing this work is styled *Twenty-Seven Sermons*. The *Funeral Sermon* was not put back until the end of the seventeenth century.

Clerus Domini still forms part of the volume.

14 D. Fourth Printing. 1673. Wing T413.

See *Eniautos*, 1673 (No. 20 D).

14 E. Fifth Printing. 1678.

See *Eniautos*, 1678 (No. 20 E).

15 A. *Holy Dying*. First Edition. 1651. Wing T361, T361A, T361B.

Title: THE RVLE | AND | EXERCISES | OF | HOLY DYING. | *In which are described* | The MEANS and INSTRUMENTS | of preparing our selves, and others | respectively, for a blessed Death: | and the remedies against the evils | and temptations proper to the state | of Sicknesse. | *Together with* | Prayers and Acts of Vertue to be used by | sick and dying persons, or by others | standing in their Attendance. | *To which are added.* | Rules for the visitation of the Sick, and offices pro- | per to that Ministery. | [three lines of Greek] | LONDON, | Printed for *R. Royston,* and are to be sold | at the Angel in Ivy-Lane. | MDCLI.

Coll: 12mo: A^{12}, a^8, B-P^{12} Q^4, 192 leaves; plates 2 (before A2 and B1). Paged B1^r-Q2^r: pp. 1-339.

Contents: A1, blank; A2^r, title-page (verso blank); A3^r-a5^v, dedication to the Earl of Carbery; a6^r-a8^v, "The Table"; B1^r-Q2^r, text; Q2^v, blank; Q3, advertisement; Q4, blank.

Variants: There are four variants in the imprint. Four provincial booksellers, from Bristol, Salisbury, Worcester, and Norwich appear in the imprints of some copies. In these examples the first two lines of the imprint read:

LONDON, | Printed for *R. R.* and are to be sold by

The remainder of the imprints read as follows:

i. *William Ballard* in *Corn-street* | *Bristoll*. 1651.

Copies: H(2), US.

ii. *Johu Courtuey* [sic] *Bookseller* in | *Salisbury*. 1651.

Copies: H(3), Har.

iii. *Francis Ash* Bookseller in | *Worcester*. 1651.

Copies: BM, Th.

iv. *Edward Marton* Bookseller in | *Norwich*. 1651.

Copies: HH.

Of these booksellers, Ballard was to have an interest in *A Short Catechism,* 1652 (No. 16 A), and Edward Marton of Norwich may have some connection with Edward Marten of Warwick, whose name appears in another copy of the same book. Ash had already published the first edition of *The Great*

Exemplar, 1649 (No. 9 A), and had, in the beginning, an interest in *Holy Living* (No. 11 A and B).

Page 169 is sometimes unnumbered. The figure "I" is sometimes missing from "Sect. I." at the beginning of the text (B1ʳ).

Notes: Since the advertisement in *Holy Dying* lists *Twenty-Eight Sermons,* and *Holy Dying* was entered in the Stationers' Register on June 23, 1651, it was clearly the second of the two to appear. Thomason's copy is dated 3 September, 1651. On April 1, 1651, Taylor wrote to Sir William Dugdale. The letter is fragmentary but one passage reads, "I have some things now . . . . preparing, The Rule of Holy Dying; have . . . . [n]ow transcribing it." With Thomason's dating, this shows that printing and publication must have taken place within less than five months.

Traces of the engraved title-page stub often show between A11 and A12. This page is by Lombart (Johnson: Lombart #1), and represents a memorial such as stands against the wall of a church. Above is a winged skull, and below it a coat of arms surmounted by an earl's coronet (presumably Lord Carbery's arms). In the middle is an oval panel inscribed: "The Rule | and | Exercises | of | Holy Dying | by Jer. Taylor | D. D." It is signed "PL sculp A londre."

The folding plate, also by Lombart, represents a classic chamber in which are a bearded husband, his young wife, and their little boy, together with a clergyman; the latter wears a high-crowned hat, and is pointing at a looking-glass in which the lady sees herself reflected as a skeleton. The husband is holding up one hand in horror, while the boy points in happy amazement. On the table supporting the looking-glass is engraved "Facies nativitatis suae James I 23"; a scroll at the foot of the plate reads "Vigilate et orate quia nescitis horam." The plate is signed "P. L. fc A londre." There is a tradition that this group represents Taylor and the Carberys. Engravings from this design were to be used with *Holy Dying* until well into the eighteenth century. Copies H(1) and R(London imprints) are in identical bindings which continue this design. They are in contemporary black morocco, simply tooled; in the middle of each cover is the design of a winged skull surmounted by an hour-glass.

The four leaves signed Q are probably part of the same twelve-leaf sheet from which gathering a was taken. The recto of the advertisement is signed, correctly, Q3. This would not have been necessary in a separate printing of only four leaves; but if the leaves in question were part of a 12mo sheet it might have been important to have the leaf noticeably signed, as a help to correct folding and cutting. This supposition is almost certainly borne out by the fact that, in the second edition, these two parts were printed from the standing type of the first edition. A few small corrections were made for the reprinting.

The verso of the advertisement leaf is eccentrically numbered 283.

Colophon: After the advertisement on Q3^v.

Printed for Richard Royston at | the Angel in Ivie-lane.

Holy Dying, as Taylor says in his preface, was written for Lady Carbery, but, she dying, it was dedicated most movingly to her husband.

Copies: BM, Bod, H(3), R, Th, WO; Cla, CW, Har, HH, NL, US, Y.

15 B. Second Edition. 1652. Wing 362.

Title: THE RVLE | AND | EXERCISES | OF | HOLY DYING. | *In which are described* | The MEANS and INSTRUMENTS of | preparing our selves, and others re- | spectively, for a blessed Death: and | the remedies against the evils and | temptations proper to the state of | Sicknesse. | *Together with* | Prayers and Acts of Vertue to be used by sick | and dying persons, or by others standing | in their attendance. | *To which are added.* | Rules for the visitation of the Sick, and offices proper | for that Ministry. | The second EDITION. | [three lines of Greek] | LONDON, | Printed for *R. Royston,* and are to be sold | at the Angel in *Ivy-lane.* | MDCLII.

Coll: 12mo: ¶^{12} A^8 B-P^{12} Q^4, 192 leaves; plates 2 (before ¶2 and B1). Paged B1^r-Q2^r: pp. 1-339.

Contents: ¶1, blank; ¶2^r, title-page (verso blank); ¶3^r-A5^v, dedication to the Earl of Carbery; A6^r-A8^v, "The Table"; B1^r-Q2^r, text; Q2^v, blank; Q3, advertisement; Q4, blank.

Notes: This edition is a very exact reprinting, clearly set up from a printed copy of the first edition, page for page and often line for line, or even word for word, so that, apart from minor ornaments, the two editions are difficult to distinguish internally. As was noted in the preceding entry, gatherings A and Q of this edition were printed from the standing type of gatherings a and Q of the first edition.

The plates are worn, and are not re-engraved. This is the last appearance of the folding plate.

The dedication, which had been signed "Taylor" in the first edition, is signed "Jer. Taylor" in this edition.

Copies: Bod, CUL, H, HM, P, TCC; I, Tex.

15 C. Third Edition. 1655. Wing T363.

Title: THE | *RULE and EXERCISES* | OF | Holy Dying. | *In which are described* | The MEANS and INSTRUMENTS of | preparing our selves, and others respectively | for a blessed Death: and the Remedies against | the evils and temptations proper to the state of | sickness. | *Together with* | Prayers and Acts of Vertue to be used by sick | and dying persons, or by others | standing in their attendance. | *To which are added,* | Rules for the visitation of the Sick, and offices | proper for that Ministery. | The third EDITION. | [rule] | [three lines of Greek] | [rule] | Printed by *James Flesher* for *R. Royston,* and | are to be sold at the Angel | in *Ivy-lane.* 1655.

Coll: 12mo: A-P^{12}, Q^6, 186 leaves. Paged B1^r-Q5^v: pp. 1-346.

Contents: A1^r, engraved title-page (verso blank); A2^r, title-page (verso blank); A3ʳ-A9ᵛ, dedication to the Earl of Carbery; A10ʳ-A12ᵛ, "The Contents"; B1ʳ-Q5ᵛ, text; Q6, advertisements.

Notes: In this edition the engraved title-page appears on A1ʳ. It is further worn, and has no new work on it.

Copies: BM.

15 D. Fourth Edition. 1658. Wing T364.

Title: THE | RULE and EXERCISES | OF | Holy Dying. | *In which are described* | The MEANS and INSTRUMENTS of | preparing our selves, and others respectively for | a blessed Death: and the Remedies against the | evils and temptations proper to the state of sick- | ness. | *Together with* | Prayers and Acts of Vertue to be used by sick | and dying persons, or by others standing | in their attendance. | *To which are added,* | Rules for the visitation of the Sick, and offices | proper for that Ministery. | The Fourth EDITION. | [rule] | [three lines of Greek] | [rule] | *LONDON.* | Printed by JAMES FLESHER for *R. Royston,* | and are to be sold at the Angel in Ivy-lane. 1658.

Coll: 12mo: A-P¹², 180 leaves; plates 1 (before B1). Paged B1ʳ-P12ᵛ: pp. 1-336.

Contents: A1ʳ, engraved title-page (verso blank); A2ʳ, title-page (verso blank); A3ʳ-A10ᵛ, dedication to the Earl of Carbery; A11ʳ-A12ᵛ, "The Contents"; B1ʳ-P12ᵛ, text.

Notes: Lombart's engraved title-page has been extensively touched up. In the first state of the engraving, the plain stone of the tomb-like design is, except for the sculptured parts, shaded almost entirely with horizontal lines; in the new state these parts have been darkened everywhere with vertical lines.

A new folding plate was put in this edition. It is slightly larger than the old one, though the design remains much the same. The most obvious novelty is that the clergyman is wearing a skullcap, and the face is obviously after the Lombart portait. The scroll at the foot now has the text in English, "Watch and pray, because you know not the hour." The Latin text remains on the table. Copy H has the engraving in an early state with no lettering.

In contemporary binding this edition is almost invariably paired with the fifth edition of *Holy Living* (No. 11 E). The KCC copy of this edition, which accompanies, in a nineteenth-century binding, the copy of *Holy Living* (No. 11 E) bearing Taylor's corrections, has three small manuscript alterations so small that the writing cannot possibly be identified. However, consideration of the association of the two copies raises interesting speculations. This volume was mentioned in the item on the KCC copy of *Holy Living* in *The Times Literary Supplement,* September 20, 1947, p. 484.

Copies: CW, H, KCC; PU.

15 E. Fifth Edition. 1663. Wing T364A.

Title: [all within double rules] THE | *Rule* and *Exercises* | OF | Holy Dying. | In which are described | The MEANS and INSTRUMENTS of prepa- | ring our selves and others respectively for a blessed | Death; and the Remedies against the Evils and | Temptations proper to the state of Sickness: | *Together with* |

Praiers and Acts of Vertue to be used by Sick and | Dying persons, or by others standing in their | attendance. | *To which are added* | Rules for the Visitation of the Sick, and offices | proper for that Ministery. | [rule] | [three lines of Greek] | [rule] | *LONDON,* | Printed by *James Flesher* for *Richard Royston,* | Bookseller to His most Sacred MAJESTIE. 1663.

Coll: 8vo: A-R^8 S^4, 140 leaves; plates 2 (before A2 and B1). Paged B1^r-S2^r: pp. 1-259.

Contents: A1^r, engraved title-page (verso-blank); A2^r, title-page (verso blank); A3^r-A8^v, dedication to the Earl of Carbery; B1^r-S2^r, text; S2^v, blank; S3^r-S4^r, "The Contents"; S4^v, blank.

Notes: The plates are unaltered since the previous edition.

This is the first of a series of title-pages of *Holy Dying* which do not have edition numbers. The numbering we have used for these editions merely continues the sequence from the fourth edition onward. The next numbered edition is the twelfth, but there are only six "editions" after the fourth, consequently, there is no eleventh edition recorded.

Copies: BM, Bod, CO, CCO, EmC; Y.

15 F. Second Issue of 15 E. [Sixth Edition.] 1666. No Wing number.

[The title-page has been reprinted without essential change except for the alteration of the date to 1666. The *collation* and *contents* are as in 15 E above].

Notes: For the remainder of the century *Holy Dying* was issued at intervals of from two to four years. In about half of the cases the "edition" is an issue of printed sheets with a new title-page. The octavo format and the organization of the contents of the book, which had become standard by the fifth edition, was the fixed form in which it appeared whether in issue or reprint edition.

Copies: H.

15 G. Seventh Edition. 1668. Wing T365.

The Rule and Exercises of Holy Dying . . . . Printed by Roger Norton for Richard Royston . . . . MDCLXVIII. 8vo.

This edition was advertised in the Term Catalogue for Michaelmas, 1668.

Copies: E; F, NL, Y.

15 H. Second Issue of 15 G [Eighth Edition]. 1670. Wing T366.

The Rule and Exercises of Holy Dying . . . . Printed by Roger Norton for Richard Royston . . . . MDCLXX. 8vo.

Copies: BM, CUL; I.

15 I. Third Issue of 15 G [Ninth Edition]. 1674. No Wing number.

The Rule and Exercises of Holy Dying . . . . Printed by Roger Norton for Richard Royston . . . . MDCLXXIV. 8vo.

Copies: E.

15 J. Tenth Edition. 1676. Wing T367.

The Rule and Exercises of Holy Dying . . . . Printed by Roger Norton for Richard Royston . . . . MDCLXXVI. 8vo.

In this edition a curious change has come over the folding plate, which reminds one of the haunted mezzotint in M. R. James's ghost story, "The Mezzotint." The plate is a new one, and the door in the background, hitherto closed, has been opened, showing trees in the distance; trees and daylight can be seen through the window to the right, which had previously been dark and blank; the furniture of the apartment has become more ornate.

Copies: H; Y.

15 K. Twelfth Edition. 1680. Wing T368.

The Rule and Exercises of Holy Dying .... The Twelfth Edition .... Printed by Miles Flesher for Richard Royston .... MDCLXXX. 8vo.

As we have noted earlier, there is no eleventh "edition." This, and all the following "editions," are numbered. Usually they are found with a copy of *Holy Living,* of the same edition number and publication date. In earlier pairs, when both editions are numbered, *Holy Dying,* as would be expected, is one number behind *Holy Living.* One may suspect, therefore, that the numbering of the present edition was done to correspond with the contemporary edition of *Holy Living.*

This edition was advertised in the Term Catalogue for Michaelmas, 1679.

Copies: BM; Wi.

15 L. Second Issue of 15 K [Thirteenth Edition]. 1682. Wing T369.

The Rule and Exercises of Holy Dying .... The Thirteenth Edition .... Printed by Miles Flesher for Richard Royston .... MDCLXXXII. 8vo.

Copies: KS, Y.

15 M. Third Issue of 15 K [Fourteenth Edition]. 1686. No Wing number.

The Rule and Exercises of Holy Dying .... The Fourteenth Edition .... Printed by M. Flesher for Richard Royston .... MDCLXXXVI. 8vo.

Copies: Bod, Hai, LI.

15 N. Fifteenth Edition. 1690. Wing T369A.

The Rule and Exercises of Holy Dying .... The Fifteenth Edition .... Printed by J. H. for Luke Meredith at the Angel in Amen Corner. MDCXC. 8vo.

This edition was advertised in the Term Catalogue for Trinity, 1690.

For information about the printer of this edition and the change from Royston to Meredith as publisher, see the *Notes* to No. 11 O.

Copies: Har.

15 O. Sixteenth Edition. 1693. No Wing number.

The Rule and Exercises of Holy Dying .... the Sixteenth Edition..... Printed by J. L. [sic] for Luke Meredith at the Star in St. Paul's Church-yard. MDCXCIII. 8vo.

This edition was advertised in the Michaelmas Term Catalogue for 1693.

For a note on the printer of this edition, see No. 11 P.

Copies: H; I.

15 P. Seventeenth Edition. 1695. Wing T370.

The Rule and Exercises of Holy Dying . . . . The Seventeenth Edition . . . . Printed by J. L. [sic] for Luke Meredith . . . . MDCXCV. 8vo.

This edition was advertised in the Michaelmas Term Catalogue for 1697. *Copies:* Y.

16 A. *A Short Catechism.* First Edition. 1652. Wing T397.

Title: [all within double rules] A SHORT | CATECHISM | FOR | The institution of Young Persons | IN THE | Christian Religion. | To which is added, | AN EXPLICATION | OF THE | Apostolical CREED, | [rule] | Easie and useful for these Times. | [rule] | Composed for the use of the | Schools in *South-Wales.* | [rule] | [three lines of Greek] | [three lines of translation] | [rule] | *London,* Printed by *J. Flesher* for *R. Royston,* at | the Angel in *Ivy-Lane,* 1652.

Coll: 12mo: A-B^{12} C^6, 30 leaves. Paged A1^r-C5^r: pp. [1]-[4], 5-57.

Contents: A1, blank; A2^r, title-page (verso blank); A3^r-C5^r, text; C5^v-C6^r, advertisements; C6^v, colophon.

Variants: The colophon on C6^v can be found in three states; the first two lines are always the same:

> *LONDON:* | Printed for *Richard Royston,* and are to be

The varying states are as follows:

> (i) sold by *Edward Marten,* Bookseller in | *Warwick.* | 1652.

Copies: E.

> (ii) sold by *Richard Unitt* Bookseller in | Liechfield. | 1652.

Copies: TCC.

> (iii) sold by *William Ballard* Bookseller in | *Corn-street* in *Bristol.* | 1652.

Copies: Th.

Information about the interest of Ballard and Marten in the first edition of *Holy Dying* can be found in the *Notes* to No. 15 A.

Curiously, copy Th was bought by Thomason on April 15, 1652, and bears the Bristol colophon. Thomason has added "by Jeremy Taylor" to the copy.

Notes: A Short Catechism was entered in the Stationers' Register on March 18, 1651/2.

The main part of this book was reprinted, in 1655, as the first part *(Credenda)* of *The Golden Grove* (No. 22 A). Of four prayers at the end, two for morning and one for evening were reprinted in *The Golden Grove* in the last section *(Postulanda).* At the same time small rearrangements were made in two short translated fragments from Tertullian and Saint Augustine. In *A Short Catechism* these appear at the end of the Catechism (which does not take up all of the book); in *The Golden Grove,* they are transferred to the end of the whole reprinted section, now called *Credenda;* there they join other such quotations, which already occupied that place in *A Short Catechism.*

Since the fourth prayer in *A Short Catechism* has never been reprinted, the text is given here:

> *A Christian Prayer for Adversaires of True Religion*
>
> Merciful God, who hast made all men, and hatest nothing that thou has made, nor wouldest the death of a sinner, but rather that he should be converted and live, have mercy upon all Jewes, Turks, Infidels and Heretiks, and take from them all ignorance, hardness of heart, and contempt of thy word, and so fetch them home (blessed Lord) to thy flocke, that they may be saved among the remnants of the true Israelites, and be made one fold under one shepherd, Jesus Christ our Lord, who liveth and reigneth with thee and the holy Ghost, now and ever. Amen.

Copies: E, TCC, Th.

17 A. *A Discourse of Baptism.* First Edition. 1652. Wing T315.

Title: A | DISCOVRSE | OF | Baptisme, | ITS INSTITUTION, | and Efficacy upon all Believers. | [rule] | *Together with* | A CONSIDERATION | of the Practice of the Church | IN | BAPTIZING INFANTS | of Beleeving Parents: | And the Practise justified | [rule] | By Jer: Taylor D. D. | [rule] | [one line of Greek] | *Suffer little children to come unto me, and forbid them not,* &c. | [rule] | LONDON, | Printed by *J. Flesher* for *R. Royston,* at the *Angel* in *Ivy-Lane.* | [centered rule] | *MDCLII.*

Coll: Quarto: A² B-H⁴ I², 32 leaves. Paged B1ʳ-I2ᵛ: pp. 1-60.

Contents: A1ʳ, title-page (verso blank); A2, "To the Reader"; B1ʳ-I2ᵛ, text.

Notes: This work was entered in the Stationers' Register on July 1, 1652. Thomason's copy is dated November 27, 1652.

In that fragmentary letter to Dugdale, already quoted under *Holy Dying* (No. 15 A) Taylor wrote: ". . . esse, to adde to the life of Christ which is to be . . . summer." He is probably referring to the present little work, for no other substantial additions were made to *The Great Exemplar,* 1653 (No. 9 C). The present work was added at the end of Part One in that edition. The only textual change of any significance, in this transfer, involves a quoted Greek inscription; in *A Discourse* this is printed in lower case, while in *The Great Exemplar* it is printed more appropriately in capitals.

Copies: Bod, CUL, Th; I, NL, US, Y.

17 B. Second Edition. 1653. Wing T316.

Title: [An exact reprinting of the 1652 title-page, only the date being changed to 1653.]

Coll: Quarto: A-H⁴, 32 leaves. Paged A3ʳ-H4ᵛ: pp. 1-60.

Contents: A1ʳ, title-page (verso blank); A2, "To the Reader"; A3ʳ-H4ᵛ, text. *Notes:* The imposition was altered clearly to avoid the awkward use of the two half-sheet gatherings, A and I, of the earlier edition.

The preface has never been reprinted since the appearance of this edition. *Copies:* BM, Bod, CUL, MO, TCC; C, I, Tex.

18 A. *Two Discourses.* First Edition. 1653. Wing T414.
General Title: TWO | DISCOURSES | 1. of { | BAPTISME, | Its Institution, and Efficacy upon | all Believers. | 2. Of { | PRAYER *Ex tempore,* | OR | By pretence of the Spirit. | [rule] | By Jᴇʀ. Tᴀʏʟᴏʀ D. D. | [rule] | 1 Cᴏʀ. 14. 32. | [three lines of Greek and three lines of translation] | [double rule] | LONDON, | Printed by *J. Flesher* for *R. Royston,* at the *Angel* in *Ivy-Lane.* | [centered rule] | MDCLIII.
Coll: Quarto: II², *Discourse of Baptisme,* 1652 or 1653 (Nos. 17 A or B) and *Prayer Ex Tempore,* 1647 (No. 4 C), 50 leaves.
Contents: II1, blank; II2ʳ, general title-page (verso blank); *Discourse of Baptisme; Prayer Ex Tempore.*
Variants: Copy Th lacks *Discourse of Baptisme;* copies AO and NL have the first edition of the discourse (1652); other copies have the second edition (1653).
Notes: The title-page of *Prayer Ex Tempore* is often missing, the work commencing on A2ʳ, the first page of text.

Thomason dated his copy December 3, 1652. It is possible that this is a slip for 1653, but, as can be seen from other instances, several of Royston's publications were given the date of the following year.
Copies: AO, CD, CO, J, Th; NL, US.

19 A. *Twenty-Five Sermons.* First Edition. 1653. Wing T408.
Title: [all within double rules] XXV |SERMONS | PREACHED AT | GOLDEN-GROVE: | Being for the Winter half-year, | BEGINNING ON | *ADVENT-SUNDAY,* | UNTILL | *WHIT-SUNDAY.* | [rule] | By *JEREMY TAYLOR,* D.D. | [rule] | *Vae mihi si non Euangelizauero.* | [rule] | [woodcut: an open book] | [rule] | *LONDON,* | Printed by *E. Cotes,* for *Richard Royston* at the Angel | in *Ivie-Lane.* M. DC. LIII.
Coll. Fol.: A-2E⁶ 2F², 170 leaves. Paged B1ʳ-2F1ᵛ: pp. 1-100, 109-334 [*=326*].
Contents: A1ʳ, title-page (verso blank); A2ʳ-A5ʳ, dedication to the Earl of Carbery; A5ᵛ, blank; A6, "Titles of the Sermons"; B1ʳ-2F1ᵛ, text; 2F2ʳ, errata (verso blank).
Notes: Twenty-Five Sermons was entered on May 9, 1653.

This work is almost always found with *Twenty-Eight Sermons* (No. 14 A-B), the first or second edition, and either with or without the general title to *Eniautos*. The inference is that this book was designed to make the composite volume of sermons for the whole year.

The errata are listed out of order, and two refer to pages 100 and 102, where they cannot be found. One erratum had already been corrected in the press.

Two copies are known in contemporary bindings; copies GK and CO.

On April 11, 1653, Taylor wrote to Sheldon, in a letter already quoted under No. 9 C, saying that he had ordered Royston to send him "my second volume of sermons, for the winter half year." This presentation copy, if it exists, is unrecorded. It must presumably have been the separate volume by itself, and not the composite *Eniautos*.

One group of sermons in this book, *The Marriage Ring,* was very popular in the nineteenth century. It was reprinted separately twelve times between 1854 and 1939, and editions of it by Baroness Burdett-Coutts appeared in 1883, 1884, 1892, and 1907.

Copies: BM, BO, Bod, CO, GK; Har, I, S, Y.

19 B. Second Edition. 1655. Wing T409.

Title: [all within double rules] XXV | SERMONS | PREACHED AT | GOLDEN-GROVE: | Being for the Winter half-year, | BEGINNING ON | *ADVENT-SUNDAY,* | UNTILL | *WHIT-SUNDAY.* | [rule] | The Second Edition Corrected. | By *JEREMY TAYLOR,* D. D. | [rule] | *Vae mihi si non Evangelizavero.* | [rule] | [orn.] | [rule] | *LONDON,* | Printed by R. *Norton,* for *Richard Royston* at the Angel | in *Ivie-Lane.* MDCLV.

Coll: Fol.: A-2E⁶ 2F², 170 leaves. Paged B1ʳ-2F1ᵛ: pp. 1-100, 109-334 [=*326*].

Contents: A1ʳ, title-page (verso blank); A2ʳ-A5ʳ, dedication to the Earl of Carbery; A5ᵛ, blank; A6, "Titles of the Sermons . . . ."; B1ʳ-2F1ᵛ, text; 2F2, blank.

Notes: As indicated above, this is so faithful a reprinting of the first edition that the pagination error following page 100 is repeated in this edition.

In this edition all the errata but one have been corrected.

When copies either of this or the previous edition are found as part of the second edition of *Eniautos,* 1655 (No. 20 B), a leaf of contents referring to *Twenty-Eight Sermons* will usually be found after the normal table of contents. This second table is part of a double leaf, the other half bearing the general title; the whole leaf is folded around sheet A.

Copies: Bod, EC, H, P, PCC; Har, PU, UC, US, Y.

19 C. Third Printing. 1668. Wing T410.

See *Eniautos,* 1668 (No. 20 C).

Notes: As printed, this is an essential part of *Eniautos,* 1668, for the table of contents to *Twenty-Eight Sermons* is conjugate with the title-page of *Twenty-Five Sermons.*

The one erratum uncorrected in the second edition remains uncorrected in this printing.

19 D. Fourth Printing. 1673. Wing T411.

See *Eniautos,* 1673 (No. 20 D).

19 E. Fifth Printing. 1678.

See *Eniautos,* 1678 (No. 20 E).

20 A. *Eniautos.* First Edition. 1653. Wing T329.

General Title: [all within double rules] ΕΝΙΑΥΤΟΣ | [rule] | *A* | COVRSE | OF | SERMONS | FOR | All the Sundaies | Of the Year; | Fitted to the great Necessities, and for the supplying | the Wants of *Preaching* in many parts | of this NATION. | [rule] | *Together with* | A Discourse of the Divine Institution, Necessity, Sacredness, | and Separation of the Office *Ministeriall.* | [rule] | By JER. TAYLOR D. D. | [rule] | [two lines of Greek] | —*Commune periclum* | *Omnibus, Una salus.*— | [double rule] | *LONDON.* | Printed for *Richard Royston* at the Angel in Ivie-lane, 1653.

Coll.: Fol., mostly in sixes: Π², *Twenty-Five Sermons,* 1653 (No. 19 A), *Twenty-Eight Sermons,* 1651 (No. 14 A), ³F², 402 leaves.

Contents: Π1, blank; Π2ʳ, general title-page (verso blank); *Twenty-Five Sermons* (1653); *Twenty-Eight Sermons* [including *Clerus Domini*] (1651); ³F1ʳ-³F2ᵛ, "A Table to both the Volumes of Sermons."

Variants: Copy H has the errata leaf to *Twenty-Eight Sermons,* which is bound in after the added Table (³F1-2); this helps confirm the supposition that the list of errata was printed sometime after the publication of the book.

Notes: The double leaf at the end, signed F and F2 (³F1-2), follows the blank leaf at the end of *Clerus Domini.* This blank is ³E6 and the extra leaves were signed, presumably, as a guide to the binder.

It is not very rare to find the two books of sermons bound together in their intended order (without the general title-page and extra leaves); such volumes were probably sold in that form by Royston, and make a parallel with the *Treatises* of 1650 (No. 10 A), the volumes of which, as has been pointed out, except for one curious example, turn up without general title-pages.

Copies: Bod, H, IT, P, RS; Har.

20 B. Second Edition. 1655. Wing T330.

General Title: [all within double rules] [in red] ΕΝΙΑΥΤΟΣ | [rule] | *A* | COVRSE | OF | [in red] SERMONS | FOR | [all in red] All the Sundays | Of the Year. | Fitted to the great Necessities, and for the supplying | the Wants of Preaching in many parts | of this NATION. | *Together with* | A Discourse of the Divine Institution, Necessity, Sacredness, | and Separation of the Office *Ministeriall.* | [rule] | [all in red] By JER. TAYLOR D. D. | [rule] | *The Second*

Edition Corrected. | [rule] | [two lines of Greek] | —*Commune periclum* | *Omnibus, Una salus.*— | [rule] | [in red] *LONDON* : | Printed for *Richard Royston* at the Angel in Invie-Lane, 1655.

Coll: Fol., mostly in sixes: (Π²(Π1+A6), *Twenty-Five Sermons,* 1653 (No. 19 A), *Twenty-Eight Sermons,* 1654 (No. 14 B), ²2K², *Clerus Domini,* 1655 (No. 13 B), 402 leaves.

Contents: Π1ʳ, general title-page (verso blank); Π2ʳ, [after A6ᵛ] contents of *Twenty-Eight Sermons* (verso blank); *Twenty-Five Sermons* (1653); *Twenty-Eight Sermons* (1654); ²2K1-2, "A Brief Table to both the Volumes of Sermons"; *Clerus Domini* (1655).

Variants: Three copies, EC, H, and PCC, have the second, not the first edition of *Twenty-Five Sermons.* Each has the portrait in the first state. Three is too small a number on which to base a conjecture, but it seems possible that all copies in the ordinary form were sold without the portrait, and that it was included in all copies of this variant form. If this was indeed the case, they should perhaps be regarded bibliographically as separate issues.

Notes: The location of Royston's shop in Ivy-lane is misspelled "Invie" on the title-page.

Copies: BM, Bod, EC, H, PCC, SE; Har, I, US, WSC, Y.

20 C. Third Edition. 1668. Wing T331.

General Title: [all within double rules] [in red] ΕΝΙΑΥΤΟΣ. | [rule] | A | COURSE | OF | [in red] SERMONS | FOR | [all in red] All the Sundays | Of the year. | Fitted to the great Necessities, and for the supplying | the Wants of Preaching in many parts of this NATION. | With a Supplement of Ten Sermons Preached since His | MAJESTIES Restauration. | Whereunto is Adjoyned, | A Discourse of the Divine Institution, Necessity, Sacredness, | and Separation of the Office *Ministerial.* | [rule] | By [all in red] *JER. TAYLOR,* | Chaplain in Ordinary to King *Charles* the First, and late | Lord Bishop of *Down* and *Connor.* | [rule] | The Third Edition. | [rule] | [two lines of Greek] | —*Commune periclum* | *Omnibus, Vna salus.*— | [rule] | [in red] *LONDON,* | Printed by *E. Tyler* for *R. Royston* Book-seller to the Kings | most Excellent MAJESTY, MDCLXVIII.

Sect. Title (A2ʳ): [all within double rules] XXV | SERMONS | Preached at | GOLDEN-GROVE | Being for the Winter half-year, | BEGINNING ON | *ADVENT-SUNDAY* | UNTIL | *WHIT-SVNDAY.* | [rule] | The Third Edition Corrected. | [rule] | By *JER. TAYLOR,* | Chaplain in Ordinary to King *Charles* the First, and | late Lord Bishop of *Down* and *Connor.* | [rule] | *Vae mihi si non Evangelizavero.* | [rule] | [orn.] | [rule] | *LONDON,* | Printed by *E. Tyler* for *Richard Royston* Book-seller to the | Kings most Excellent MAJESTY, 1668.

Sect. Title (*1ʳ): [all within double rules] XXVII | SERMONS | PREACHED AT | GOLDEN GROVE; | Being for the Summer half-year, |

BEGINNING ON *WHIT-SVNDAY* | And ending on the xxv. Sunday after | TRINITY. | [rule] | By *JER. TAYLOR,* | Chaplain in Ordinary to King *Charles* the first, and | late Lord Bishop of *Down* and *Connor.* | [rule] | [orn.] | [rule] | *LONDON,* | Printed by *E. Tyler* for *Richard Royston* Book-seller to the | Kings most Excellent MAJESTY, 1668.

Sect. Title (^{3}A1^r) : [all within double rules] *CLERUS DOMINI:* | OR, | A DISCOURSE | OF THE | DIVINE INSTITUTION, | Necessity, Sacredness, and Separation | OF THE | OFFICE MINISTERIAL. | TOGETHER WITH | THE NATURE AND MANNER OF | its Power and Operation. | WRITTEN | By the special Command of King *Charles* the First. | [rule] | By *JER. TAYLOR,* | Chaplain in Ordinary to King *Charles* the First, and | late Lord Bishop of *Down* and *Connor.* | [rule] | [orn.] | [rule] | *LONDON,* | Printed by *E. Tyler* for *Richard Royston* Book-seller to the | Kings most Excellent MAJESTY, 1668.

Sect. Title (^{4}A1^r) : [all within double rules] ΔΕΚΑ᾿Σ ᾿ΕΜΒΟΛΙΜΑΊΟΣ, | A | SUPPLEMENT | TO THE | ᾿ΕΝΙΑΥΤΟΣ, | Or Course of Sermons for the whole Year: | BEING | TEN SERMONS | Explaining the Nature of Faith, and Obedience, | in relation to God, and the Ecclesiastical and | Secular Powers respectively. | [rule] | All that have been Preached and Published | (since the Restauration) | By the Right Reverend Father in God | *JEREMY* Lord Bishop of *Down* and *Connor.* | WITH | His Advice to the Clergy of his Diocess. | [rule] | *LONDON,* | Printed for *R. Royston* Book-seller to the Kings most Ex- | cellent Majesty. 1667.

Sect. Title (^{5}A1^r) : [all within double rules] A | FUNERAL | SERMON, | Preached at the OBSEQUIES | Of the | Right Reverend Father in God | JEREMY | Lord Bishop of Down: | Who deceased at | LYSBURNE | *August* 13th. 1667. | [rule] | By Dr. *GEORGE RVST* Dean of *CONNOR* | [rule] | *LONDON,* | Printed by *E. Tyler* for *Richard Royston* Book-seller to the | King's most excellent Majesty, MDCLXVIII.

Coll: Fol., mostly in sixes: A^8 B-Y^6, *^{6}, ^{2}A-^{2}Y^6 ^{2}Z^4, ^{3}A-^{3}D^6, ^{4}A^4 ^{4}B-^{4}T^6 ^{4}U^2, ^{5}A-^{5}B^6, 313 leaves; plates 1 (before A1).

Contents: A1^r, general title-page (verso blank); A2^r, title-page for *Twenty-Five Sermons* (verso blank); A3^r-A5^r, dedication; A5^v, blank; A6, list of titles of the *Twenty-Five Sermons* (No. 19 C); A7, list of titles of the *Twenty-Seven Sermons* (No. 14 C); A8, list of titles of the *Ten Sermons* (No. 44 A) and three prayers from *A Collection of Offices* (No. 30); B1^r-Y5^v, text of *Twenty-Five Sermons;* Y6, blank; *1^r, title-page for *Twenty-Seven Sermons* (verso blank); *2^r-*6^r, dedication; *6^v, titles of sermons in "the Second Part"; ^{2}A2^r-^{2}Z3^v, text of *Twenty-Seven Sermons;* ^{2}Z4, blank; ^{3}A1^r, title-page for *Clerus Domini;* (No. 13 C) (verso blank); ^{3}A2^r-^{3}D6^v, text of *Clerus Domini;* ^{4}A1^r, title-page for *Ten Sermons* (No. 44 A) (verso blank); ^{4}A2^r-^{4}U2^v, text of *Ten Sermons;* ^{5}A1^r, title-page for Rust's *Funeral Sermon* (verso blank); ^{5}A2^r-^{5}B6^r, text of Rust's *Funeral Sermon;* ^{5}B6^v, advertisement.

Variants: Copy H, in a contemporary binding, lacks *Clerus Domini* and Rust's *Funeral Sermon.*

Notes: Twenty-Seven Sermons is separable as it stands, except that in the table it is described as the second part. *Twenty-Five Sermons,* on the other hand, is ·involved with the preliminaries of the entire book. Yet each part was set up and printed as a separate entity. This is shown by the final blank leaf of *Twenty-Five Sermons* (Y6); had the book been printed as a unit, the title of *Twenty-Seven Sermons* would have been put on this. Further, if the conjugate leaves A1 and A8 were removed and the second list of titles (A7) was cancelled, *Twenty-Five Sermons* could also have been issued as a separate volume. That this was a possibility is enhanced by the fact that no mention of *Twenty-Five Sermons* being the first part is made in its list of titles. We have seen no instances of separate issue; however, copies are likely to have the works arranged in an order other than the one stated here, which we believe to be the intended one.

The catchword on A7^r is "The," which is wrong and was probably absent-mindedly copied from the correct catchword on the preceding leaf.

Copies: BM, Bod, H, TCC, TCD; Cla, Har, HH, RU.

20 D. Fourth Edition. 1673. Wing T332.

Eniautos . . . . The Fourth Edition . . . . Printed by T. Macock for R. Royston . . . . 1673. Fol.

This is a reprint of the third edition. It was advertised in the Term Catalogue for Easter, 1673.

Variants at the end of *Eleven Sermons* are described under *Ten Sermons* (No. 44 B). Copy NCE is peculiar in having the 1667 *Ten Sermons* at the end, instead of the 1673 *Eleven Sermons.* The title-page of *Clerus Domini* is dated 1672 (No. 13 D).

Copies: BM, CO, CUL, MO, NCE, TCD; Har, I, Tex, US.

20 E. Fifth Edition. 1678. Wing T333.

Eniautos . . . . The Fifth Edition . . . . Printed by J. Macock for R. Royston . . . . 1678. Fol.

The imprint on *Eleven Sermons* title-page has "Printed by R. Norton for R. Royston."

This edition was advertised in the Easter Term Catalogue for 1678.

Copies: BM, Bod, D, MeO, TCC; Cla, Har, I, KS, PU, Y.

21 A. *The Real Presence.* First Edition. 1654. Wing T358.

Title: THE | [all in red] REAL PRESENCE | AND | [in red] Spirituall | OF | [in red] CHRIST | IN THE | [all in red] Blessed Sacrament | PROVED | Against the Doctrine of | *TRANSUBSTANTIATION.* | [rule] | [all in red] By *Jer. Taylor,* D. D. | [rule] | *Oportuit enim certé ut non solùm anima per*

Spiritum | *Sanctum in beatam vitam ascenderet, verùmetiam ut rude,* | *atque* | *terrestre hoc corpus cognato sibi gustua, tactu, & cibo* | *ad immortalitatem* | *reduceretur.* S. Cyril. in Joh. 1. 4. c. 14. | *Literam sequi, & signa pro rebus* | *accipere servilis in-* | *firmitatis est.* S. August. 1. 3. de doct. Christ. | [rule] | LONDON, | [all in red] Printed by *James Flesher,* for *Richard Royston* at the | Angel in Ivie-lane. 1654.

Coll: 8vo: A-Z⁸, 184 leaves. Paged B1ʳ-Z6ʳ: pp. 1-347.

Contents: A1ʳ, title-page (verso blank); A2ʳ-A7ʳ, epistle to Dr. Warner, Bishop of Rochester; A7ᵛ-A8ᵛ, contents; B1ʳ-Z6ʳ, text; Z6ᵛ-Z8ʳ, advertisements; Z8ᵛ, blank.

Notes: The Real Presence was entered in the Stationers' Register on November 9, 1653, and Thomason dated his copy on November 23 of the same year.

On April 11, 1653, in that letter to Sheldon in which is mentioned to him the gift of *The Great Exemplar* (No. 9 C) and the second volume of sermons (No. 19 A), Taylor says, "Sr, I have now sent to the Presse, but first to my L. Bp. of Salisbury to be perused, a discourse of the Real Presence, occasioned by my conference with a Jesuit in these parts. It hath pass'd all the Welch censure I could well obtaine for it, and I have put as much care and industry upon the Qu. as I could; it's greatest infelicity is, it cannot find your leisure and opportunity to peruse."

The Real Presence is not so dull as his early controversial works; there is an aphoristic gusto and a wit, even a rude wit, in the writing; and it may be that he has stated more penetratingly than anywhere else the unstatable Anglican doctrine about the real presence.

Copies: BO, Bod, DC, H, PCC, R, Th; Har, I, PU, US, Y.

21 B. Second Printing. 1657.

See *Polemical Discourses,* 1657 (No. 28 A).

21 C. Third Printing. 1674.

See *Polemical Discourses,* 1674 (No. 28 B).

Among the errata at the end of the volume, a number refer to *The Real Presence.* Of these, six restore errors, taken over from the second printing, to the correct reading of the first; one corrects an error which appears in both the previous printings. One, more interesting than the others, slightly alters a reading. In the first edition there is a passage which speaks of Christ's "conversation" in Palestine; in the second and third printings this appears as "conversion"; in the errata of the third printing it was altered to "conversing." This suggests that when, in the 1674 reprints, errors taken over from the second printing were restored to the correct reading of the first, the amendments were not made from the original printed version; and such a change as this was not very likely to have been made by a publisher's reader, however sensitive. It looks like an author's emendation.

22 A. *Golden Grove.* First Edition. 1655. Wing T336.
Title: THE | *GOLDEN GROVE,* | OR, | A MANUALL | OF | Daily
Prayers and *Letanies,* | Fitted to the dayes of the Week. | Containing a short
Summary of | *What is to be* { | Believed, Practised, Desired. | [rule] | *ALSO* |
FESTIVAL HYMNS, | According to the manner of | *The Ancient Church.*
| [rule] | Composed for the Use of the Devout, especially | of Younger Per-
sons; By the Author of | *The Great Exemplar.* | [rule] | *London,* Printed by
J. F. for *R. Royston,* at the | Angel in *Ivie-lane.* 1655.
Coll: 12mo: Π² (—Π2), A⁸ B-H¹² I⁴, 98 leaves; plates 1 (before A1). Paged
B1ʳ-I2ʳ: pp. 1-161 [=*170*].
Contents: Π1ʳ, half-title (verso blank); A1ʳ, title-page (verso blank); A2ʳ-A8ᵛ,
"To The Reader" and errata; B1ʳ-I2ʳ, text; I2ᵛ, blank; I3ʳ-I4ᵛ, advertisements.
Variants: Copy H has another state of the title-page. In the line beginning
"Composed" the *y* of the last word in the line, "especially," is missing; the
address in the imprint reads "Ivi-lane."
Notes: The Golden Grove was entered in the Stationers' Register on January
25, 1654/5. This was probably after publication, as Thomason's copy is dated
December 13, 1654.

It is not entirely accurate to refer to the first leaf (Π1) as the half-title, for it
bears not the title of the work but the alternative title always given to the work.
Π1ʳ reads:

THE | GUIDE | OF | Infant-Devotion.

The prose text is divided into three sections, *Credenda* (B1ʳ-C10ᵛ: pp.
1-44), *Agenda* (C11ʳ-E6ʳ: pp. 45-83), and *Postulanda* (E7ʳ-G12ʳ: pp. 85-143).
Included in this reckoning are separate sectional titles (B1ʳ, C11ʳ, and E7ʳ)
with blank versos. The last page of the *Agenda* (E6ᵛ: p. [84]) and of the
Postulanda (G12ᵛ: p. [144]) are blank. There follows the *Festival Hymns* with
a similar sectional title (H1ʳ, verso blank). Pagination should begin again at
page 147, but for the rest of the book runs on erroneously from 137.

The folding plate is by Hollar. To the left an angel holds in his right hand a
cross with a crown on it; with his left hand he is leading a boy; the boy holds in
his left hand a coiled snake with a dove perched on it. Behind is a river valley
in mountainous country. This is quite clearly intended to represent the Towey
Valley at Golden Grove; I have stood on the road at almost the exact spot from
which the original must have been taken. To the right, in the engraving, is the
old house of Golden Grove, now vanished; the valley beyond is curved away
more than in nature, and a castle, now in ruins, has been moved from its proper
site to the virgin summit of Grongar Hill. The buildings are probably romanti-
cised, but the departures from geographical exactitude are no more than would
be found in the work of any landscape painter. It would be interesting to learn

if Hollar ever worked in South Wales. If the original was by another hand, it must have been one of the first "pure" landscapes ever drawn by an English artist. In the first edition, the plate appears without any lettering, except for Hollar's signature.

Golden Grove was the seat of the Earl of Carbery, Taylor's patron. The poetical place-name had already been given to a book: *The Golden-grove moralized in three books: a worke very necessary for all such, as would know how to governe themselves, their houses, or their countrey. Made by* W. Vaughan, *Master of Artes,* and student in the civill law. *Printed at London by Simon Stafford, dwelling on Adling Hill.* 1600 (STC 24610). The author was William Vaughan, one of the first colonisers of Newfoundland. The book is dedicated to his brother, Sir John Vaughan of Golden Grove, first Earl of Carbery, and father of Taylor's patron. To anybody living in the place, the title would have been irresistible, but it is certain that Taylor must have known and read the earlier work, for echoes of it appear in his own writings: "They knew mans lyfe to be but a bubble on the face of the earth. They considered with themselves our miserable estate; for as soone as wee are borne, wee seem to flourish for a small moment, but straightway we die, and there is little memorial left behind." This little passage, like the seed of a magical tree, expanded into one of Taylor's most noble paragraphs.

The Golden Grove was equal in popularity with Taylor's other works during this century. It is also interesting because it eventually contained all of his original poems, as opposed to his translations and paraphrases. There are twenty-three in this edition. They are rather tepid and appear to have been influenced by Henry Vaughan. The two had probably met, since both were acquainted with Katharine Philips, the "Matchless Orinda." Vaughan's *Mount of Olives,* published in 1652 (Wing V122), shows affinity with Taylor's verse. The two penitential hymns, "Great Good, and just" and "Lord, I have sinn'd," were later set to music, one by Purcell and the other by Pelham Humphryes (see *Harmonia Sacra,* 1688 [No. C 8]).

Some twenty years later an odd fate befell eleven of the hymns. Samuel Speed, an obscure publisher, was imprisoned for debt in Ludgate and beguiled his tedium with literary work. One result was *Prison-pietie: or, Meditations Divine and Moral. Digested into Poetical Heads* (Wing S4902). Since Speed's initials are part of the imprint ("London: Printed by J. C. for S. S. and sold by the booksellers of London and Westminster.") it may be presumed that he hoped to purchase his release by the profits. Speed's own poems in this book—some are beautiful imitations of Vaughan—are full of echoes; the eleven Taylor poems have many alterations in Speed's book, usually but not always, for the worse. If these eleven poems had been found in the same form in a manuscript, it would have been confidently assumed that this was an earlier version from the author's own hand. The poems in question are: the first three hymns for Christmas day, the first and second hymns for Advent, the first penitential hymn, "A hymn upon St. John's Day," "A Meditation of Death," "Of the Day of Judgement," "Of Heaven," and "Of Hell."

The *Festival Hymns,* with a few other verses by Taylor, and the spurious quatrains from the folio *Great Exemplar* (No. 9 C), were collected together for the first time by Grosart in *The Poems and Verse Translations of Jeremy Taylor* (1870).

Writing to Taylor in February of 1654/5, and commiserating with him on his imprisonment, Evelyn said, "I had read the preface long since to your Golden Grove, remember, and infinitely justifie all that you have there asserted . . . . it is a blessing if men escape so in these dayes, when not the safties only, but the souls of men are betrayed: whilst such as you and such excellent assistances as they afford us, are rendered criminal and suffer." The preface contains a poetic and bitter attack on the government.

Copies: H, P, Th; HH.

22 B. Second Edition. 1655. No Wing number.

Title: [Exact reprinting of the title-page of the first edition.]

Coll: 12mo: A-H¹², 96 leaves; plates 1 (before A1). Paged A10ʳ-H10ʳ: pp. 1-169.

Contents: A1ʳ, half-title (verso blank); A2ʳ, title-page (verso blank); A3ʳ-A9ᵛ, "To the Reader"; A10ʳ-H10ʳ, text; H10ᵛ, blank; H11ʳ-H12ᵛ, advertisements.

Notes: Thomason bought a copy of this edition and dated it March 12. The date on the title-page of this copy has been altered by hand to 1654.

This book, which initially might appear to be only an issue of No. 22 A, has been reset throughout, the errata have been corrected, and the pagination adjusted. One book, *The Matching of the Magistrates Authority,* William Lyford, 1654 (Wing L3549), has been added to the last page of the advertisements.

The folding plate has been altered to its second state. Lettering has been added in these places: close to the angel's wings "Dux viae," above the crowned cross "Coronata tides" [sic], above the serpent and dove "prudens simplicitas." In all known copies "tides" is corrected to "fides" in manuscript.

The Thomason copies of the first and second editions are bound in a single volume.

Copies: Bod, H, P, QC, Th.

22 C.   Third Printing. 1657.

See *Polemical Discourses,* 1657 (No. 28 A).

Notes: B1ʳ is a sort of half-title, part of which reads "The Guide to Infant-Devotion." Lower down is the Hollar plate; additions have been made to it. The words "The golden grove" have been engraved above the representation of that mansion. In the top right corner has been added much the same figure of Christ as appears on the folding plate of the fourth edition of *Holy Living,* 1654 (No. 11 D). The text "Non magna loquimur, sed vivimus" is added in type on the same page.

In this printing Taylor is named as the author for the first time, the preface being signed "Jer: Taylor."

The separate internal titles are, in this printing, reduced to head titles.

22 D. Fourth Edition. 1659. Wing T337.

Title: THE | *GOLDEN GROVE,* | OR, | A MANUALL, | OF, | Daily *Prayers* and *Letanies,* | Fitted to the dayes of the Week; Containing a short summary of, | *what is to be* { | Believed, Practised, Desired. | [rule] | *ALSO* | FESTIVAL HYMNS, | According to the manner of | *The Ancient Church.* | [rule] | *The fourth Edition.* | [rule] | Composed for the Use of the devout, especially | of Younger Persons, | *By Jer. Taylor D. D.* | [rule] | *London,* Printed by *J. F.* for *R. Royston* at the | Angel in *Ivie-lane.* 1659.

Coll: 12mo: A-H^{12}, 96 leaves; plates 2 (engraved title [Johnson: Marshall #20] and folding plate before A2). Paged A10^r-H11^r: pp. 1-171.

Contents: A1, blank; A2^r, title-page; A3^r-A9^v, "To the Reader"; A10^r-H11^r, text; H11^v, blank; H12, blank.

Variants: At least one copy, not now locatable, has been seen with advertisements on H11^v.

Notes: In this edition Hollar's plate makes its last appearance. It has already lasted too long, and here it is crudely touched up.

The engraved title is pasted onto the blank A1^r. Johnson says of this plate, "copy is found in Jeremy Taylor's *Guide to Infant Devotion.* [1674?]." The date is obviously too late, as the present is its first appearance. The plate seems to have been touched up and is not, in 1659, worthy of Marshall. The plate is of Prudence; across the top is inscribed "Non magna loquimur sed vivimus"; over a curtain at the base is "THE | GUIDE | of | Infant-Devotion."

Thomason also bought this edition and his copy is dated June, 1659.

Down to page 150 (G12^v) this is a page for page reprint of the second edition; the same is true from page 153 (H2^r) to the end. The change is caused by the addition, in this edition, of a fourth "Hymn for Christmas Day" which takes up pages 151-52 (H1). At this time Taylor had been in Ireland for many months, and the new poem was probably sent to Royston by itself with instructions as to its proper place.

Copies: DC, H, NLW, Th.

22 E. Fifth Edition. 1664. Wing T290.

Title: [all within double rules] *A* | Choice Manual, | CONTAINING | What is to be *Believed, Practised,* | and *Desired* or *Praied for*; the | *Praiers* being fitted to the | several daies of the Week. | [rule] | ALSO | Festival Hymns, | According to | *The manner of the ancient Church.* | [rule] | Composed for the Use of the Devout, | especially of younger Persons, | By *Jeremy Taylor* D. D. | [rule] | *LONDON,* | Printed by *J. F.* for *R. Royston,* | Bookseller to his most Sacred | MAJESTY.

Note: The title-page bears no date.

WORKS BY JEREMY TAYLOR TO 1700

Coll: 12mo: A^{10} B-F^{12} G^6 H^2 I-K^{12}, 102 leaves. Paged B1^r-H2^r: pp. 1-135; I4^r-K12^v: pp. 1-42.

Contents: A1^r, general title-page; A1^v, portrait; A2^r, engraved title (verso blank); A3^r, title-page of *Golden Grove* (verso blank); A4^r-A10^v, "To the Reader"; B1^r-H2^r, text; H2^v, blank; I1^r, title of *A Guide to the Penitent* (verso blank); I2^r-I3^v, "To the Christian Reader"; I4^r-K12^v, text.

Notes: It seems probable that the fold H was originally part of the sheet containing gathering A. If this was the case, it implies that *The Golden Grove* was set up as a separate work and that the preliminaries were done last, as was customary as partners with the final two leaves of text.

A Guide to the Penitent, whose addition brought about the change of title for the collection, was written by Brian Duppa, Bishop of Salisbury, and it was to be for many years the stable companion of *The Golden Grove.* It was first published in 1660 (Wing D2659) and also in a separate quarto edition of 1664 (Wing D2660). In this edition it has the imprint: "Printed by *J. Flesher,* for *R. Royston* | Bookseller to his most Sacred *Majesty.* | MDCLXIV." It is from this imprint that the whole volume has been dated.

Duppa was one of the two bishops to whom Taylor addressed the preface of *Unum Necessarium,* 1655 (No. 23 A), an action which, because of Taylor's opinions about original sin, gravely distressed the elderly bishop. For all that, to judge from this work, he had profited by Taylor's example as a stylist.

In the engraved title a strip has been cut from the top of the plate, removing the Latin text; the sheet at the bottom has been extended to the very edge of the plate, in order to take in the additional words: "together with | a Guide for the Penitent." The plate was used in this form until it wore away.

This is the first appearance of a portrait with *The Golden Grove.* It is founded on the Lombart portrait, or else on the original painting from which that was engraved. It was first used in the second edition of *Friendship,* 1657 (No. 29 C) and next, a little worn, in the third edition of that work, 1662. This is its third appearance, and it has been touched up. The different states can be easily detected. In *Friendship* "Non magna loquimur &c." is engraved across the bottom; in the 1664 and some subsequent editions of *The Golden Grove* there is added "Nihil opinionis Gratia omnia Conscientiae faciam."

This is the first of what might be called the popular editions of the book which, as will be seen, has now got three titles; this was the model edition until the plates wore out. The names of the four parts are not, as previously, given in the headlines; the separate titles are reduced to head titles.

Copies: CUL, Ex, H; US.

22 F. First Issue of 22 E [Sixth Edition]. 1667. Wing T291.

A Choice Manual . . . . Printed by J. Flesher for R. Royston, Bookseller to his most Sacred Majesty, at the Angel in S. Bartolemew's Hospital. 1667. 12mo.

Copies: CO; CW, Y.

22 G. Seventh Edition. 1669. No Wing number.

A Choice Manual . . . . Printed by J. Flesher for R. Royston . . . . 1669. 12mo.

This edition differs from all others in having *A Guide for the Penitent* printed before *Festival Hymns.*

Copy H is in a "Mearne" binding. Mearne was a bookseller, and it may be assumed that he bought a number of sets of sheets, and put them all into what was meant to be the same expensive binding.

Copies: H.

22 H. Eighth Edition. 1674. Wing T291A.

A Choice Manual . . . . Printed by E. Flesher for R. Royston . . . . 1674. 12mo.

This edition was advertised in the Trinity Term Catalogue for 1674.

Copies: Cla.

22 I. Ninth Edition ["Eleventh"]. 1677. Wing T292.

A Choice Manual . . . . Printed by J. Groves for R. Royston . . . . 1677. 12mo.

To our knowledge, this is the ninth appearance of this work under either the title *Golden Grove* or *Choice Manual,* and we have therefore given it such a number although the rudimentary half-title says: "THE | Golden Grove | [rule] | *The Eleventh Edition.* | [rule]" Since the remainder of this work's history has other numbering slips, we will give both the actual and printed edition numbers where conflicts are involved.

The *Festival Hymns* follow the *Guide to the Penitent,* but without a separate title-page.

The BM copy is inscribed "My booke ye gift of Bishop Fleetwood."

Copies: BM.

22 J. Tenth Edition. ["Twelfth"]. 1680. Wing T338.

The Golden Grove . . . . Printed for R. Royston . . . . 1680. 12mo.

It is with this edition that the work resumes the title it had originally had but which had not been used since the fourth edition of 1659 (No. 22 D).

It is presumably this edition which is advertised in the Michaelmas Term Catalogue for 1679.

Copies: AO; Cla, Y.

22 K. First Issue of 22 J ["Thirteenth Edition"]. 1681. Wing T338A.

The Golden Grove . . . . Printed by J. M. for R. Royston . . . . 1681. 12mo.

Copies: PU.

22 L. Second Issue of 22 J ["Fourteenth Edition"]. 1683. No Wing number.

The Golden Grove . . . . Printed by J. M. for R. Royston . . . . 1683. 12mo.

Copies: BM.

22 M. Eleventh Edition ["Fifteenth"]. 1685. Wing T339.

The Golden Grove . . . . Printed by J. M. for R. Royston . . . . 1685. 12mo.

This is the first edition to appear after the original plates had worn out. A new frontispiece was added representing a clergyman standing beside a coffin; out of his mouth appear the words "This is the period of all human glory." The plate is headed "Diverse Considerations" and is obviously more appropriate for *Holy Dying* than *Golden Grove*.

Copies: BM, CUL; NL, UC.

22 N. (?) Twelfth Edition. 1689/90. No Wing number.

No copy of this "edition," or "editions," is known to exist, and the only references to its existence are contained in the Term Catalogues for Easter 1689 and Trinity 1690, in which an edition "Printed for L. Meredith at the Angel in Amen-Corner" is advertised.

22 O. Thirteenth Edition ["Eighteenth"]. 1692. Wing T340.

The Golden Grove . . . . Printed by J. H. for L. Meredith at the Star in St Paul's Church-yard. 1692. 12mo.

This edition was advertised in the Term Catalogue for Michaelmas of 1692.

Copies: CU, US.

22 P. First Issue of 22 O ["Eighteenth Edition"]. 1695 .Wing T341.

The Golden Grove . . . . Printed by J. L. for Luke Meredith . . . . 1695. 12mo.

The printed edition number duplicates that of No. 22 O. In the Michaelmas Term Catalogue for 1694 this "edition" is called the eighteenth.

Copies: V.

22 Q. Second Issue of 22 O. ["Twentieth Edition"]. 1700. Wing T341A.

The Golden Grove . . . . Printed by J. L. for Luke Meredith . . . . 1700. 12mo.

It is presumably this issue which is advertised in the 1699 Hilary Term Catalogue as the "nineteenth" edition.

Copies: Y.

23 A. *Unum Necessarium.* First Edition. 1655. Wing T415.

Title: [rule] | *Vnum Necessarium.* | [rule] | OR, | The Doctrine and Practice | OF | REPENTANCE. | *DESCRIBING* | The Necessities and Measures of a | Strict, a Holy, and a Christian Life. | AND | *Rescued from Popular Errors.* | [rule] | By *JER. TAYLOR* D. D. | [rule] | *Poenitentiae compensatione redimendam proponit impunitatem* | *Deus.* | Tertullian. de Poenit. | *Praevoniamus faciem ejus in confessione.* | [rule] | *LONDON,* | Printed by *James Flesher* for *R. Royston,* at the Angel | in *Ivy-lane.* 1655.

Coll: 8vo: A-2Z⁸ 3A⁴, 372 leaves; plates 1 (before D1). Paged D1ʳ-3A1ᵛ: pp. 1-690.

Contents: A1ʳ, half-title(verso blank); A2ʳ, title-page (verso blank); A3ʳ-A6ᵛ, dedication to Carbery; A7ʳ-C4ᵛ, preface to Brian Lord Bishop of Sarum and John Lord Bishop of Rochester and to the clergy of England; C5ʳ-C8ᵛ, contents; D1ʳ-3A1ᵛ, text [errata on 3A1ᵛ]; 3A2ʳ-3A4ᵛ, "The Table."

Variants: The page number of page 384 can be found printed upside down.

Most copies have *A Further Explication,* 1656 (No. 24 A) inserted after

Chapter VI. All copies examined which lacked it were in contemporary bindings. They are copies CO, GK, H, KS, NLW, and PCC. All of these copies, except CO, also lack the folding plate. The lack of *A Further Explication* and the folding plate in these copies may indicate that they are early copies and that both extra features were afterthoughts. Copy NCL has *A Further Explication* bound in at the end of the work, but lacks the folding plate.

Notes: Unum Necessarium was entered on May 3, 1655. Brian Duppa (see below) mentions March as a time before the book was in press, and Thomason's copy is dated July, 1655.

The cut on the half-title [Johnson: Hertochs #6] was used on the title-page of *Polemical Discourses,* 1657 (No. 28 A), in the second volume of *Ductor Dubitantium,* 1660 (No. 32 A), and in the "fourth edition" of the present work. The entire half-title reads:

> Unum Necessarium | or | The Doctrine and Practise | of | Repentance | Rescued from popular Errors | [oval cut: representation of Christ as the Good Shepherd, signed "P. Lombart, fecit londini"] | Ecce agnus Dei qui tollit peccata Mundi | London | Printed for R. Royston 1655.

The folding plate was used in the seventh edition of *Holy Living,* 1663 (No. 11 G), on the internal title of the present work in *Polemical Discourses,* 1674 (No. 28 B), on the title-page of the fourth edition of *Ductor Dubitantium* (No. 32 D), and in the "fourth edition" of the present work. The plate represents St. Peter and Mary Magdalen, in postures of repentance, and holding up between them a bleeding heart, crowned with thorns. It is signed "P. lombart, fecit londini" and in the lower left corner is engraved "place this before page 1." For its second appearance, a strip was cut off the right-hand side; a text from the bottom was burnished out, and the names of saints added, with a shorter text, and a direction to the binder. In the third appearance, this direction is burnished out, and the background landscape is re-engraved. For its fourth appearance, it is further cut down on each side, and a hand appears writing on the heart; this addition is copied from part of a device on the title-page of *Ductor Dubitantium,* 1660.

Unum Necessarium was regarded by Taylor more as a devotional than a theological work, and it contains many passages of his finest quality. Chapter VI is entitled "Of Concupiscence, and Original sin, and whether or no, or how far we are bound to repent of it." With what, to a modern mind, seems charitable common sense Taylor concludes that for this kind of sin no repentance is necessary. This opinion and his relevant deductions gravely and inordinately scandalized his contemporaries. An enormous storm broke upon him, and it was probably as a result of this that he was not, at his request, translated by Sheldon to an English bishopric, from the intolerable vexations of presbyterian Ulster in 1661.

Brian Duppa, the Bishop of Salisbury, wrote to a friend on October 25, 1655, saying that Taylor had arranged for sheets to be sent to him before publication—"some pieces without either beginning or ending, which I being greedy to read, presently lighted upon the sixth chapter, where I met with the *coloquintida* that spoiled all the broth." He goes on to say that he expostulated with Taylor, who had thus given "his poor desolate mother the church . . . a greater wound by this unwary blow of his (for I cannot but absolutely clear him from having any malicious intent in it) than by all the unreasonable acts of persecution which her malicious enemies have done against her." He adds, with what Gosse calls a scream of indignation, "he was pleased to make use of my name in the very forehead of it."

Duppa spoke of receiving the sheets "some two or three months past," which would, at the furthest, date the dispatch of those sheets at about the time when Thomason bought his complete copy. Obviously relying on this, Gosse talks confidently, as though from ascertained fact, of the printing being deliberately held up by Royston. In this Gosse was confusing *Unum* with *A Further Explication* (Gosse, pp. 121-23). It is not at all improbable that Duppa, in his dreadful agitation, may have got confused about the lapse of time.

The gentle Sanderson was so greatly shocked that wistful ideas of persecution seeped into his saintly mind. Walton printed a letter written to him by Barlow, Sanderson's successor in the see of Lincoln (it is printed on O4^r, closely following the *Life,* in the 1678 edition, Wing W667) :—"Having (in a Letter) named two or three books writ (*ex professo*) against the being of original sin; and that Adam (by his fall) transmitted some calamity only, but no Crime to his posterity; The good old man was exceedingly troubled, and bewailed the misery of these licentious times, and seem'd to wonder (save that the times were such) that any should write, or be permitted to publish any errors so contradictory to truth. . . . I name not the Books, nor their Authors. . . ." Walton, imitating the charity of his episcopal correspondent does not mention the name of Jeremy Taylor.

Sheldon wrote to Taylor, expressing his disapprobation. In his answer, the latter mentions that he had received a letter on the subject from Duppa, and another from John Warner, Bishop of Rochester. Taylor amazed and distressed his friends by resolutely defending his position. In writing at great length to Sheldon, he says, with pathetic resignation, "I am wearied out by answering so often, but I wish you had a sight of those letters I wrote to the bp. of Salisbury"; a wish we may well echo, for the letters have been lost.

At that time, of received opinions, Evelyn's almost alone was favorable. He wrote to Taylor, probably in May of 1655, saying: "I have not yet been so happy as to see those papers which Mr Royston tells me are printing, but I greatly rejoice that you have so happily fortified the batterie, and I doubt not but you will maintain the siege; for you must not be discouraged for the passions of a few. Reason is reason to me where ever I find it, much more when it conduces to a design so salutary and necessary. At least, I wonder that those who are not convinced by yr. arguments, can possibly resist yr. charity, and yr. modesty: but as you have greatly subdued my education in that particular, and controversy; so am I confident tyme will render you many proselytes. And if all doe not come so freely in with their suffrages at first, you must with yr. accustomed patience attend the event." Evelyn had not, it appears, read the book, but Taylor had evidently, in private, expounded the scandalous doctrine to him.

In 1659 there appeared *An Epilogue to the Tragedy of the Church of England* by Herbert Thorndike (Wing T1050). It was printed for Martin Allestry, and Dicas, who published Taylor's *Funeral Sermon on Sir George Dalston* (No. 31 A) and *The Worthy Communicant* (No. 33 A). In Chapter XX, "The Covenant of Grace," the author discusses, under the question of original sin, "that novelty in the doctrine of the Church of England." He alludes to Taylor, not by name, but as "that excellent doctor."

Taylor omitted *Unum* from *Polemical Discourses,* 1657, but in the preface to that collection he says that he has excluded it, with other devotional works, in order not to prevent the publication of cheaper editions. His hopes in this respect were not realized, although, as will be seen in the next appearance of this work, there are slight grounds for believing that he had looked over the text with a view to reprinting.

Copies: Bod, CO, E, GK, H, MO, NLW, PCC, Th, VA; FU, HH, KS, NL, NW, US, Y.

23 B. Second Printing. 1674.

See *Polemical Discourses,* 1674 (No. 28 B).

Notes: This is the first edition of the complete text as it was finally planned by Taylor. *A Further Explication* is printed, together with its introductory epistle, as Chapter VII, the subsequent chapters being renumbered accordingly. In some parts the paragraphs are differently numbered, and on a more convenient system than in the first edition; faulty paragraph numbers are rectified. All the errata in the original list are corrected, except for two superfluous ones, which refer to readings already accurate. The collected volume of 1674 has its own list of errata. So far as *Unum Necessarium* is concerned, these usually refer to mechanical misprints; however, three errors thus corrected here, including one in Greek, were taken over from the first edition, where they had not been noticed. It is not improbable that these three fresh errata had been recorded by Taylor himself, and that the whole text was collated with a copy corrected by him.

24 A. *A Further Explication.* First Edition. 1656. No Wing number.

Title: A further | EXPLICATION | OF | The Doctrine | OF | Originall Sin,

| [rule] | By *JER. TAYLOR* D. D. | [double rules] | *LONDON,* | Printed by *James Flesher* for *R. Royston,* at the Angel | in *Ivy-lane,* | 1656.

Coll: 8vo: 2H-2L^8, 32 leaves. Paged irregularly 2H5^r-2L8^v: pp. 449-504.

Contents: 2H1^r, title-page (verso blank); 2H2^r-2H4^v, epistle to John Bishop of Rochester; 2H5^r-2L8^v, text [errata on 2L8^v].

Variants: Copy CO lacks "The End" on 2L8^v.

Notes: Pages after [493] to the end are numbered in square brackets, 493-4, 496, 407, 497-8, 500-1, 501-2, 404; other single numberings are inaccurate.

In the first gathering (2H) both letters of the signing are in lower case. This pamphlet, when found in *Unum Necessarium,* 1655 (No. 23 A), follows 2H8^v (p. 448).

Two errata are recorded at the foot of 2L8^v.

It is clear from its make-up that this was primarily intended to be inserted into *Unum Necessarium,* where it was eventually incorporated as Chapter VII. It was printed, however, a year later than *Unum.* Taylor's two later pamphlets in the original sin controversy were entered in the Stationers' Register, but not this work. Yet, aside from the date of publication, there are several pieces of internal and external evidence that would point to the work being written for separate publication and that some copies of it were sold as separate pamphlets.

On page 400 of *Unum Necessarium,* Taylor writes of one problem "concerning which I have already given account. . . ." and two lines later "if this were to be understood in the sense which I then reproved"; these two phrases are corrected in the errata to "I have in the next chapter" and "I there reprove." It seems that these sentences must have been written in Chapter VI after *A Further Explication,* the eventual Chapter VII, had been composed. If this was the case, Taylor must have been more sharply aware than has been recognized that his case was a somewhat startling one. It is apparent from Duppa's letter, quoted in the previous entry, that the bishop had seen the sheets before publication. Perhaps, because of Duppa's remonstrances, Taylor decided against separate publication, thinking or hoping that by its insertion immediately after the offending chapter, all complaints would be silenced.

As for external evidence, the CUL copy is badly stained with ancient dirt on the title-page and the verso of the last leaf of the work, indicating that it has spent a large part of its history as a separate pamphlet. The TCC copy is in a seventeenth-century binding, together with a pamphlet by William Sherlock, dated 1674. The CO copy is uncut and is bound up with tracts of various dates. Although it is possible that all these copies were extracted from the larger work (*Unum*), their conditions, particularly the CO and TCC copies, make it seem improbable.

There is one further piece of evidence. A certain Henry Jeanes, "Minister of Gods word at Chedzoy in Somersetshire," published in 1660 a correspondence, between himself and Jeremy Taylor, on the question of original sin (No. C 4). In that book he speaks of meeting "at my house" a Mr. T. C. who spoke in praise of Taylor; Jeanes, according to his account, assented, but with snakish reservations: "I . . . . instanced his doctrine of originall sin; now his further explication of this lay then casually in the window (as I take it) which hereupon I took up, and turned unto the passage now under debate." The reference to a passage of Taylor's makes it indisputable that Jeanes was referring to *A Further Explication*. It is impossible that Taylor would have sent his work to such a man as Jeanes, and the conclusion is almost irresistible that this copy was bought in the ordinary way, like any other book.

On November 17, 1655, Taylor wrote to Warner from Wales, mentioning "a little tract, giving a further account of that doctrine," which he was sending up to Royston. He says later on in the same letter: "I have given order to Royston to consigne these papers into your Lor^p's hands, to peruse, censure, acquit, or condemne, as your Lor^p pleases. If the written copy be too troublesome to read, your Lor^p may receive them from the presse, and yet suppresse them before publication, *si minus probentur.*" Although Warner did not take advantage of this permission to suppress the tract, one cannot but suspect that he may have persuaded Taylor to omit, as he did, from *Polemical Discourses* (1657), the three disturbing works which bore his name in their dedications.

A Further Explication never appeared again except as Chapter VII of *Unum*.

Copies: CO, CUL, TCC.

25 A. *An Answer to A Letter.* First Edition. 1656. Wing T286.

Title: An Answer to a Letter | Written by the R. R. | The Ld Bp of *Rochester*. | Concerning | The Chapter of *Original Sin*, | In the | *Unum Necessarium*. | [rule] | By Jer. Taylor D. D. | [rule] | [woodcut orn.] | *London*, Printed by *E. Cotes* for *R. Royston* | at the Angel in *Ivie-lane*, 1656.

Coll: 12mo: A² B-E¹² F¹⁰, 60 leaves. Paged B1ʳ-F8ʳ: pp. 1-111.

Contents: A1ʳ, blank signed A (verso blank); A2ʳ, title-page (verso blank); B1ʳ-D8ᵛ, text of *An Answer to A Letter;* D9ʳ-D12ᵛ, text of the Bishop of Rochester's letter; E1ʳ-F8ʳ, text of *An Answer to A Letter;* F8ᵛ, errata; F9ʳ-F10ʳ, advertisements; F10ᵛ, blank.

Notes: A1ʳ is a blank except for its being signed "A." The fold, A, was printed as part of the terminal gathering, F.

An Answer was entered on March 24, 1655/6, and Thomason dated his copy June 29, 1656.

In the letter to Sheldon of January 19, 1655/6, already quoted under *Unum Necessarium*, Taylor said: "those [letters] which I wrote to my lord bp. of Rochester will be published." The first letter printed here was written from Chepstow Castle where Taylor was then imprisoned. It begins: "Your Lordships Letter Dated July 28, I received not till Septemb. 11. it seems R. Royston detained it in his hands, supposing it could not come safely to me while I remain a prisoner, But I now have that liberty, that I can receive any Letters, and send any; for the Gentlemen under whose custody I am, as they are careful of their charges, so they are civil to my person. It was necessary I should tell this to your Lordship, that I may not be under a suspicion of neglecting to give accounts in those particulars, which with so much prudence and charity you were pleased to represent in your Letter concerning my discourse of Original Sin."

Copies: BO, Bod, GK, J, TCD, Th; Cla, I, US, Y.

25 B. Second Issue. 1656.

An Answer, together with *Deus Justificatus* (No. 26 A), was issued later in the year under the common title *Deus Justificatus, Two Discourses* (No. 27 A).

25 C. Second Printing. 1674.

See *Polemical Discourses,* 1674 (No. 28 B).

Notes: In the first sentence of the first letter in this work (cited in No. 25 A above) a small, but significant addition has been made in this printing of the work. It now ends "while I remain a prisoner in Chepstow-castle." This suggests that the 1674 text may have been printed from the original manuscript. It might have been thought indiscreet in 1656 to name the place of Taylor's imprisonment, or else this version (1674) was printed from a copy corrected by Taylor. Nobody else would have made such an interpolation.

Two errata noted in the 1674 have been taken over from the first edition. They do not correct misprints, but each substitutes the word *treated* for *healed.* These must almost certainly be author's corrections, a contention borne out by similar corrections in most other works reprinted in this posthumous collection. The error noted in the errata of the first edition is corrected here.

26 A. *Deus Justificatus.* First Edition. 1656. Wing T311.

Title: Deus Justificatus, | [rule] | OR, | A Vindication of the | glory of the Divine | Attributes in the | Question of | ORIGINAL SIN. | Against the Presbyterian way of | Understanding it. | [rule] | By JER. TAYLOR, D. D. | [rule] | *Lucretius.* | Nam neque tam facilis res ulla est, quin ea primum, | Difficilis magis ad credendum conftet— | [rule] | *LONDON,* | Printed by R. N. for R. *Royston* at the | Angel in *Ivie-Lane.* 1656.

Coll: 12mo: A-F^{12} G^6, 78 leaves. Paged A3^r-G1^r: pp. 1-143.

Contents: A1^r, title-page (verso blank); A2^r, dedication to Christian, Countess Dowager of Devonshire (verso blank); A3^r-A7^v, preface; A8^r-G1^r, text; G1^v-G2^r, postscript; G2^v-G5^v, the stationer's postscript; G6^r, advertisements; G6^v, errata.

Variants: This work is usually found in the composite volume *Deus Justi-*

ficatus (No. 27 A). Only two copies of the work alone are recorded, copies CO and P. Copy CO, bound in seventeenth-century morocco, must have been bound very soon after printing for the errata page (G6^v) has offset on the flyleaf.

Copy PCC has an additional errata leaf, unique in our experience, recording twenty-five errata. This copy is part of a copy of the composite volume. The unique errata includes all but two of those printed on G6^v, the usual errata list.

Notes: Deus Justificatus was entered on July 4, 1656.

In "The Stationer's Postscript," which is signed "R. Royston," we are told that it is published "without the Reverend Author's consent; the work," he pleads, "would have been too long in appearing, if I had delayed my hand, till I could, at that great distance from me, where he lives, have consulted with the Author, and received returns from him. And have no lesse hope, that the Honourable Person, into whose Cabinet I have too boldly admitted the common eye, will pardon my presumption." It was probably not so much Taylor's distance in space, as his circumstances, which made Royston think it useless to attempt communication. Taylor was in prison, and it has been seen, under the previous work (No. 25 A), that the publisher evidently imagined that Taylor was not allowed to send or receive letters.

Taylor seems to have accepted with equanimity the pious little piracy. On July 19, 1656, he wrote to Evelyn, first mentioning "a little thing of mine . . . . which is now in Royston's hands, of Original Sin; the evils of which doctrine I have now laid especially at ye Presbyterian doore, and discours'd it accordingly, in a missive to ye countesse dowager of Devonshire." He goes on, "I thank you for your Lucretius. I wished it with mee sooner; for, in my letter to ye countesse of Devonshire, I quote some things out of Lucretius w^h for her sake I was forced to English in very bad verse." *Deus Justificatus* does make a small addition to the corpus of Taylor's poetry, for he translates fragments of Greek and Latin verse in it. As the rest of the letter shows, however, Taylor when he wrote the pamphlet had not seen Evelyn's version, and his own fragmentary translations were over and done with. On August 23, 1656, Taylor acknowledges with fulsome praise Evelyn's *Lucretius,* and goes on, "I have commanded Royston to present to you two copies of a little letter of mine to ye C. dowager of Devon." Evelyn's catalogue is now at Christ Church, Oxford; this tract is entered in it, but unfortunately the particular copy has disappeared (the other had been intended for a mutual friend). On November 15, 1656, Taylor wrote to Evelyn again on the subject: "But S^r, the last papers of mine have a fate like your Lucretius: I mean, so many errata's made by the printer." Hence the unique errata leaf? It is evident that Taylor first saw a printed copy of Evelyn's *Lucretius* sometime between the writing of these two letters.

It is difficult to reconcile these allusions of Taylor's to his little work with

Royston's statement that it was issued without Taylor's knowledge. Perhaps the tract was sent to Royston to forward to the Countess of Devon (Royston normally helped Taylor with the delivery of his letters) and Royston hastily printed the tract. This, and the fact that Taylor saw no proofs, would account for the large number of errors in so short a work.

Copies: BM, Bod, CO, CUL, P, PCC, TCD; Cla, US.

26 B. Second Issue. 1656.

Deus Justificatus, together with *An Answer* (No. 25 A) was issued later in the year under the common title *Deus Justificatus, Two Discourses* (No. 27 A).

26 C. Second Printing. 1657.

See *Polemical Discourses,* 1657 (No. 28 A).

Notes: All the errata, except two, in the lists mentioned are corrected in this printing. Two unnoted errors in the Spanish quotation are corrected. In this printing large additions have been made to the text, together with many little alterations. It is probable that Taylor had not originally intended the work to be published in the form that was sent to the Countess of Devonshire. Among the additions is a passage with Taylor's comments, from "the Æthiopic version of the New-Testament translated by . . . Dr. *Dudley Loftus*" (see *Great Exemplar,* 1657 [No. 9 D]).

It is evident that great care was taken here to conceal the name and rank of the recipient. The dedication is omitted; the phrase "your honour" is several times altered to "you." In the sentence "you are . . . mother of an honourable posterity," "fair and hopeful" is substituted for "honourable." In the same paragraph "Latimers," the country home of the Earl of Devonshire, is changed to "London."

The publisher's postscript, being unnecessary for this printing, is omitted.

26 D. Third Printing. 1674.

See *Polemical Discourses,* 1674 (No. 28 B).

Notes: The dedication to the Countess of Devonshire is restored.

Two errata are listed; one slightly alters the sense, and the other corrects a Latin quotation. As with other works reprinted in this posthumous volume, these changes are such as could hardly have been made by anyone other than the author.

27 A. *Deus Justificatus, Two Discourses.* 1656. Wing T311.

General Title: [all within double rules] DEUS JUSTIFICATUS. | [rule] | TWO | DISCOVRSES | OF | *ORIGINAL SIN,* | Contained in two Letters | TO | Persons of Honour, | Wherein the question is rightly | stated, several objections answe- | red, and the truth further cleared | and proved by many arguments | newly added or explain'd. | [rule] | By *Jer. Taylor. D. D.* | [rule] | *LONDON,* | Printed for *Richard Royston* 1656.

Coll: 12mo: Π², *Deus Justificatus,* 1656 (No. 26 A) and *An Answer,* 1656 (No. 25 A), 140 leaves.

Contents: Π1, blank; Π2ʳ, general title-page (verso blank); *Deus Justificatus; An Answer.*

Variants: Copy TCD has the general title-page bound in between the two tracts in the middle of the volume.

Notes: The composite book was entered in the Stationers' Register on September 12, 1656, rather unnecessarily since the component parts had already been entered.

Copies: BM, Bod, CO, CUL, P, PCC, TCD; Cla, US.

28 A. *Polemical Discourses.* First Edition. 1657. Wing T398.

General Title: ΣΥΜΒΟΛΟΝ ΗΘΙΚΟΠΟΛΕΜΙΚΟΝ | OR A | Collection of Polemical | and | Moral Discourses. | [rule] | *By* JER: TAYLOR *D. D.* Chaplain in Ordinary | to his late MAJESTY. | [rule] | *S. Bartholomoeus* | [one line of Greek] | [engraving by Lombart: inscribed *"Ecce Agnus Dei qui tollit peccata Mundi"*] | *London* | *Printed for R. Royston 1657.*

Coll: Fol., in sixes: A⁶, a⁴, B-3T⁶, χ², 396 leaves; plates 1 (before A1). Paged: See *Notes.*

Contents: A1, blank; A2ʳ, general title-page (verso blank); A3ʳ-a1ᵛ, epistle to Chrstopher Lord Hatton; a2ʳ-a4ʳ, contents; a4ᵛ, blank; B1ʳ, engraved half-title for *Golden Grove* (verso blank); B2ʳ, title-page (verso blank); B3ʳ-B5ʳ, "To the Pious and Devout Reader"; B5ᵛ, blank; B6ʳ-G3ʳ, text of *Golden Grove;* G3ᵛ, blank; G4ʳ, title-page for *Apology for Liturgy* (verso blank); G5, dedication; G6ʳ-L4ᵛ, text of *Apology for Liturgy;* L5ʳ, title-page for *Episcopacy Asserted* (verso blank); L6ʳ-M2ᵛ, dedication; M3ʳ-2B6ʳ, text of *Episcopacy Asserted;* 2B6ᵛ, blank; 2C1ʳ, title-page for *Real Presence* (verso blank); 2C2ʳ-2D1ᵛ, dedication; 2D2ʳ-2O4ʳ, text of *Real Presence;* 2O4ᵛ, blank; 2O5ʳ, engraved title for *Liberty of Prophesying* (verso blank); 2O6ʳ, title-page (verso blank); 2P1ʳ-2Q4ᵛ, dedication; 2Q5ʳ-3K1ᵛ, text of *Liberty of Prophesying;* 3K2ʳ, title-page for *Deus Justificatus* (verso blank); 3K3ʳ-3K4ᵛ, preface; 3K5ʳ-3N3ᵛ, text of *Deus Justificatus;* 3N4ʳ-3P3ʳ, text of *Friendship;* 3P3ᵛ, *Postscript;* 3P4ʳ, title-page for *Gunpowder Sermon* (verso blank); 3P5ʳ-3Q1ʳ, dedication; 3Q1ᵛ, blank; 3Q2ʳ-3S4ᵛ, text of *Gunpowder Sermon;* 3S5ʳ-3T6ᵛ, text of *Two Letters;* χ1, advertisements; χ2, blank.

Notes: Polemical Discourses was entered on June 8, 1657.

The engraved portrait, the plate which appears before A1ʳ, is in State II.

This book appears not to have been consistently arranged. Two of the works included—*An Apology* and *The Gunpowder Sermon*—have their titles and preliminaries reckoned in the pagination, while all the other works have their preliminaries unreckoned. The pagination is continuous except for the preliminaries and the inclusion of these for the two works just mentioned, and there are no errors. Paging begins on C1^r and ends on 3T6^v at page number 718. *Liberty of Prophesying* and *Golden Grove* have what might be called sectional titles; each of these has an engraving already associated with the work in question, and they have been described under the entries for these two books. *Friendship* and *Two Letters* have no titles of any kind.

The plan of this volume appears to have been altered during printing. In the contents, *Friendship* is listed in its proper place and then is listed again as the last work in the volume. It is possible that the collection was meant to end with *Deus Justificatus* (significantly there is no catchword on 3N3^v, although catchwords do not appear consistently in such a location), but while the book was still being printed the copy for *Friendship* and *Two Letters* arrived, which had almost certainly not been printed before. With these, possibly at Taylor's suggestion, the *Gunpowder Sermon* was added, thus causing a slight confusion in the contents. Certainly the *Gunpowder Sermon* is more polemical than hortatory and could properly have been included.

The different works were mostly set from printed copy. This is most apparent with *Episcopacy Asserted*. The first two full pages of text (pp. 112-3, M4^v-5^r) have, as a headline "The Sacred Order | and Offices of Episcopacy &c." All other pages have "Episcopacy Asserted" on each page, except for the fourth (M5^v), which has the second part of the longer headline. The longer headline is taken from the first edition, where it only appears in the first gathering of the text (See *Notes* for No. 2 A).

In all observed copies five manuscript corrections have been found. These occur on A4^v-A5^r, the title of *An Apology* [G4^r], 3T2^r, 3T4^v, and 3T6^r. They have obviously been made before sale at the publisher's.

On June 2, 1657, Taylor wrote to an unnamed recipient "I have caused Mr. Royston to deliver for you my collection of discourses, which he hath printed in folio. There are some new things with it and additions to the old; esp. the Liberty of Prophesying, in which I have answered all the arguments for the anabaptists." The certainly new writings which appeared in this volume are the general preliminary epistle to Lord Hatton, and the additions to *The Liberty of Prophesying;* the latter have been described under their proper entry. To these should most probably be added *Friendship* and *Two Letters*.

As will be found under those entries, *An Apology* and *Episcopacy Asserted* were entered in the Stationers' Register only some fourteen months before *Polemical Discourses*. Neither the former in its original form, nor the latter had been first published by Royston, although both had already appeared under his imprint. It was, no doubt, the prospect of the present volume appearing which induced him thus to make certain of his rights.

Copy H is inscribed on the fly-leaf, not in Taylor's hand, "Donum Authoris. 22. March. 1657. E:C:". This is clearly Taylor's patron Edward, Earl of Conway; he was in the habit of signing himself "Edward Conway." Immediately below appears the name A. Rawdon. Arthur Rawdon was the nephew of Lord Conway, being the eldest son of Sir George Rawdon, who had married Lord Conway's sister Dorothy. Lord Conway, having become childless, intended to make Arthur Rawdon his heir and superintended his education. The date is of a little interest; the earliest Conway letter referring to Taylor is one from Lady Conway, written on April 9, 1658. The inscription in this volume (March, 1657/8) puts back by a short period the record of their acquaintance. This is not the copy in the letter quoted above, the beginning of which shows clearly that it was not addressed to a nobleman.

Copies: BM, Bod, CUL, E, H, JR; Cla, Har, HH, LC, NL, Pb, US, Y.

28 B. Second Edition ["Third"]. 1674. Wing T399.

General Title: ΣΥΜΒΟΛΟΝ ΘΕΟΛΟΓΙΚΟΝ: | OR A | [in red] COLLECTION | OF | Polemicall Discourses | Wherein the | [in red] CHURCH of [in red] ENGLAND. | IN ITS WORST | As well as more Flourishing Condition, is defended in many | material Points, against the Attempts of the *PAPISTS* | on one hand, and the *FANATICKS* on the other. | [all in red] TOGETHER WITH | Some Additional Pieces addressed to the Promotion of *Practicall* | *Religion* and *Daily Devotion.* | [rule] | By [two words in red] *JER. TAYLOR,* Chaplain in Ordinary to King | *CHARLES* the First, and the late Lord Bishop of *Down* and *Connor.* | [rule] | [black letter] The Third Edition Enlarged. | [rule] | [in red] *LONDON,* | Printed by *R. Norton* for *R. Royston,* Bookseller to the King's most Excellent | Majesty, at the *Angel* in *Amen-Corner,* M. DC. LXXIV.

Coll: Fol., in sixes: [A]², a-c⁶, B-4H⁶ 4I⁴ 4K-4Y⁶ 4Z⁴, ²A-²F⁶ ²G⁴ ²H-²Q², 620 leaves; plates 2 (two before A1, one irregularly but often before E3 or F1). Paged C1ʳ-4Z4ᵛ: pp. 1-1079; ²A1ʳ-²G4ᵛ: pp. 1-67 [preliminaries unpaged for each work].

Contents: [A]1ʳ, engraved title (verso blank); [A]2ʳ, general title-page (verso blank); a1ʳ-a4ʳ, general dedication; a4ᵛ, blank; a5ʳ-b2ʳ, the contents; b2ᵛ, blank; b3ʳ-c6ʳ, "Author's Preface"; c6ᵛ, blank; B1ʳ, title-page for *Apology for Liturgy* (verso blank); B2, dedication; B3ʳ-E2ᵛ, text of *Apology for Liturgy;* E3ʳ, title-page for *Episcopacy Asserted* (verso blank); E4ʳ-E5ᵛ, dedication; E6ʳ-F1ᵛ, blank; F2ʳ-Q2ᵛ, text of *Episcopacy Asserted;* Q3ʳ, title-page for *Real Presence* (verso blank); Q4ʳ-R2ʳ, dedication; R2ᵛ, blank; R3ʳ-2A6ʳ, text of *Real Presence;* 2A6ᵛ, blank; 2B1ʳ, title-page for *First Part of the Dissuasive from Popery* (verso blank); 2B2ʳ-2B6ʳ, preface; 2B6ᵛ, blank; 2C1ʳ-2H2ʳ, text of *First Part of the Dissuasive from Popery;* 2H2ᵛ, blank; 2H3ʳ, title-page for *Second Part of the Dissuasive from Popery* (verso blank); 2H4ʳ-2K6ᵛ, introduction; 2L1ʳ-3B4ʳ, text of *Second Part of the Dissuasive from Popery;* 3B4ᵛ, blank; 3B5ʳ, title-page for *Unum Necessarium* (verso blank); 3B6ʳ-3C1ʳ, dedication; 3C2ʳ-3C6ᵛ, "Preface to the Clergy of England"; 3D1ʳ-3S1ᵛ, text of *Unum Necessarium;* 3S2ʳ-3S3ʳ, dedication for *A Further Explication;* 3S3ᵛ, blank; 3S4ʳ-4E1ᵛ, text of *A Further Explication;* 4E2ʳ, title-page for *Deus*

Justificatus (verso blank); 4E3^r-4E4^r, dedication; 4E4^v, blank; 4E5^r-4G5^r, text of *Deus Justificatus;* 4G5^v, blank; 4G6^r-4H5^r, text of *Answer to a Letter;* 4H5^v, blank; 4H6^r-4I4^r, text of *The Two Letters;* 4I4^v, blank; 4K1^r, title-page for *Liberty of Prophesying* (verso blank); 4K2^r-4L5^r, dedication; 4L5^v, blank; 4L6^r-4Z4^r, text of *Liberty of Prophesying;* 4Z4^v, blank; 4Z5^r, title-page for *Confirmation* (verso blank); 4Z6^r-^{2}A5^r, dedication; ^{2}A5^v, blank; ^{2}A6^r-^{2}D4^r, text of *Confirmation;* ^{2}D4^v, blank; ^{2}D5^r-^{2}F1^r, text of *Friendship;* ^{2}F1^v, *Postscript;* ^{2}F2^r-^{2}G2^r, text of *Two Letters;* ^{2}G2^v, blank; ^{2}G3^r-^{2}G4^v, text of *Three Letters;* ^{2}H1^r-^{2}Q1^v, table and errata; ^{2}Q2^r, advertisements (verso blank).

Variants: In copy H leaves B1-2, containing the title and dedication of *Apology,* have been detached and put before the "Author's Preface."

Notes: This volume is erroneously described on the general title as the third edition. With the exception of *Friendship* and the five accompanying letters, this was the third printing of all the works taken over from the 1657 edition of *Polemical Discourses,* and hence, no doubt, the statement of edition.

Only the general title-page is dated 1674. All the internal titles are dated 1673; it was advertised in the Term Catalogue for Trinity, 1674.

Lowndes falsely describes this volume as "The Church of England Defended, Lond. 1674, folio." This has been a source of confusion for students of Taylor, but it is certainly to this volume that he refers.

Three engravings are associated with this volume. In most copies there is a late version of the Lombart portrait. Most copies have an engraved title by Hertochs, representing the facade of a church, in front of which lies a figure, representing the church, in black clothes, and weeping. According to Johnson, this was first used in Gauden's *Ecclesia Anglicana,* published by Royston in 1659 (Wing G359). That title is engraved on the face of the church; below is engraved "ΣΥΜΒΟΛΟΝ ΘΕΟΛΟΓΙΚΟΝ." A reduced version is used as the frontispiece for the second edition of *A Dissuasive from Popery,* 1664 (No. 42 C). The third engraving is the folding plate of a tree, representing the Catholic Church; it was to be used next in Cave's part of *Antiquitates Christianae,* 1675 (No. 9 F).

The dedication of *Apology* was originally for *A Collection of Offices,* 1658 (No. 30 A).

This edition is not a direct reprint of the first edition. References under their separate entries to the works included show that this, although published about seven years after Taylor's death, is a book of some textual importance. We probably have here the text as it was finally approved by Taylor. In every work reprinted in this volume there is at least one, and often more than one, correction of an error which had persisted through all previous editions. Some are in learned languages, Hebrew, Greek or Latin; some are corrections of sense. One or two such corrections alone would not be a great deal to go on; but this consistency is impressive and, as we have pointed out under the several entries, strongly suggests the author's hand. It is not a wild surmise that

Taylor recorded these corrections for a reprint of *Polemical Discourses. The Liberty of Prophesying* falls into this group, and thus implies that Taylor never—as some have suggested, and Coleridge most virulently of all—desired to repudiate and suppress this, his noblest if not his most beautiful work.

However, the book as it appears can hardly be exactly as Taylor would have planned it. If he had overseen the addition of *A Further Explication* (No. 24 A) to *Unum Necessarium* (No. 23 A), he would surely have omitted from the smaller work the dedication which its absorption had made super-fluous. The "preface" to *An Apology* is clearly a publisher's afterthought. Most of this "preface" is an essay in praise of *The Book of Common Prayer;* only the three final paragraphs refer especially to *A Collection of Offices,* and they are not reprinted here.

Copies: AS, BM, Bod, CUL, DW, EmC, H, SE, TCD; Col, Har, HH, I, NL, US, Y.

29 A.   *A Discourse of Friendship.* First Printing. 1657.
  See *Polemical Discourses,* 1657 (No. 28 A).
29 B.   First Edition. 1657. Wing T317.
First Title ([A]1^r): [all within single rules] A | Discourse of the Nature, | Offices and Measures of | Friendship, | with | Rules of conducting it. | Written in answer to a Letter from | the most ingenious and vertuous | *M. K. P.* | [rule] | *By* J. T. D. D. | [rule] | [two lines of Greek] | Dion. orat. 1. de regno. | [rule] | *LONDON,* | Printed for *R. Royston* at the Angel | in *Ivie-lane.* 1657. *Second Title* ([A]2^r): [all within single rules] To which are added | Two Letters written to per- | sons newly changed in their | Religion. | The first to a Gentlewoman sedu- | ced to the Roman Church, | The other to a person return-ing to the | Church of *England.* | [rule] | *By* J. T. D. D. | *Volo Solidum Perenne.*
Coll: 12mo: [A]^2 B-H^{12} I^6, 90 leaves. Paged B1^r-I4^v: pp. 1-176.
Contents: [A]1^r, first title-page (verso blank); [A]2^r, second title-page (verso blank); B1^r-F3^r, text of *Friendship;* F3^v-F4^v, postscript; F5^r-H9^v, text of "First Letter"; H10^r-I4^v, text of "Second Letter"; I5-I6, blank.
Notes: Friendship has been put after *Polemical Discourses* for these reasons: it was not entered in the Stationers' Register, although Royston was evidently most wary about securing his rights in Taylor's works; presumably his entry of *Polemical Discourses* assured his interest in *Friendship;* all advertisements noted in books published by Royston about this time list *Polemical Discourses* and then, later in the lists, *Friendship;* the advertisements in the former vol-ume do not list *Friendship;* and, *Friendship* is one of only two works in *Polemical Discourses* which appear not to have been set from printed copy

(the other is *Two Letters*), all other works in the collection have internal titles taken from editions already in print.

It is possible that the 12mo and folio versions were set and printed more or less simultaneously. As has been noted in entry No. 28 A, the last work listed in the contents of *Polemical Discourses,* 1657, is *Two Letters,* which are there grouped, wrongly for that volume, with *Friendship.* Perhaps this comes from the careless following of the same copy as that used for the two title-pages for the separate edition. This contention is further supported by the fact that the two versions were quite evidently set from different manuscripts.

In the first place, the titles are slightly different. The folio version is described as "A Discourse of the Nature and Offices of Friendship," and Orinda is called "Most ingenious and excellent." In the separate edition the work is "A Discourse of the Nature, Offices and Measures of Friendship," while Orinda becomes "most ingenious and vertuous" (M.K.P. stands for Mrs. Katherine Philips). In addition, there are some seventy to eighty small differences between the two texts. They are, for the main part, variations in punctuation, spelling, and the use of capitals. They seem not to be the result of correction, and there are too many in such a short work for them to be attributable to the vagaries of the compositor.

Differences more substantial also support the hypothesis of two manuscripts. One often quoted passage begins in the separate, and all subsequent, editions: "For thus the sun is the Eye of the World"; but the folio reads: ". . . of all the World." Later in the same passage the separate edition reads: "the fluxures of heaven and earth," while the folio reads "flexures." There are a few other substantial variations. On the whole, the separate edition has the better text.

Why the two versions were published so nearly simultaneously is perhaps explained by the postscript of Taylor's letter to Katherine Philips, "the Matchless Orinda": "If you shall think fit that these papers passe further then your own eye and Closet, I desire they may be consign'd into the hands of my worthy friend Dr. Wedderburne." No doubt "Orinda" immediately carried out Taylor's wishes and gave a copy to Wedderburne, who sent it to Royston.

The *Two Letters* do not show the same degree of variation between the *Polemical Discourses* version and the separate edition.

Copies: BM, Bod, J, TCC.

29 C. Second Edition. 1657. Wing T350.

Title: THE | MEASURES | *AND* | OFFICES OF | *FRIENDSHIP*: | *WITH* Rules of Conducting it. | *To which are added,* | Two Letters written to persons | newly changed in their Religion. | [rule] | *The second Edition.* | [rule] | *By* Jer: Taylor *D. D.* | [rule] | Dion. Orat. 1. de Regno. | [two lines of Greek] | [rule] | *LONDON* | Printed by *J. G.* for *R. Royston* at | the Angel in Ivie-lane. 1657.

Coll: 12mo: A-I¹², 108 leaves. Paged A1ʳ-I8ʳ: pp. 1-203.

Contents: A1ʳ, blank; A1ᵛ, engraved portrait; A2ʳ, title-page (verso blank); A3ʳ-G12ᵛ, text of *Friendship;* F1ʳ, title for *Two Letters* (verso blank); F2ʳ-H11ʳ, text of First Letter; H11ᵛ, blank; H12ʳ-I8ʳ, text of Second Letter; I8ᵛ, blank; I9, postscript to *Friendship;* I10ʳ-I12ʳ, advertisements; I12ᵛ, blank.

Notes: The title has been altered, and *Two Letters* are now a more integrated part of the volume. "Orinda" is now moved to the heading of *Friendship,* where she becomes "ingenious and excellent" instead of "ingenious and vertuous." This phrase derives from the folio edition while the text comes from the first separate edition.

The running titles read: "Measures and Offices. . . ."

This is the first appearance of the small portrait of Taylor. It has already been discussed in the entry on *Golden Grove,* 1664 (No. 22 E).

After a passage, to be mentioned under the fourth edition where it is altered, a phrase is added in this edition, the second. After "Mandana . . . or the Countess of Exeter" is added "or any of the most perfect beauties and the real excellencies of the World."

Copies: BM, Bod, GK, H, TCC.

29 D. Third Edition. 1662. Wing T351.

Title: THE | MEASURES | *AND* | OFFICES | OF | *FRIENDSHIP*: *WITH* | Rᴜʟᴇs of Conducting it. | *To which are added,* | Two Letters written to persons | Changed in their Religion. | [rules] | *The Third Edition.* [rule] | *By* Jᴇʀ: Tᴀʏʟᴏʀ *D. D.* Lord | Bishop of *Down* and *Connor.* | [rule] | Dion. Orat. i. de Regno. | [two lines of Greek] | [rule] | *LONDON* | Printed for *R. Royston,* Stationer to | the Kings Majesty, 1662.

Coll: 12mo: A-D¹² E⁶ F-H¹² I⁴, 94 leaves. Paged A1ʳ-I3ᵛ: pp. 1-184.

Contents: A1ʳ, blank; A1ᵛ, portrait; A2ʳ, title-page (verso blank); A3ʳ-E6ᵛ, text of *Friendship;* F1ʳ, title for *Two Letters* (verso blank); F2ʳ-I3ᵛ, text of *Two Letters;* I4, blank.

Notes: The postscript was omitted from this edition.

The running title reads *"A Discourse of the Nature | and Measures of Friendship."*

It would appear that Taylor corrected the proofs or a copy for use in this edition, even though he was in Ireland. We know from the case of *Ductor Dubitantium* (No. 32) that proofs were sent overseas to him and in the case of *Bramhall's Funeral Sermon* (No. 39 A) Taylor sent Royston a large addition. This edition, the third, follows the first separate edition in the readings of "eye of the World" and "fluxures," but follows the folio of 1657 in other readings and in omitting the "or any of the most perfect beauties" phrase. It is not likely that the compositor would have a chance to pick out the readings he preferred from different texts, and it is beyond belief that accident would restore two old readings.

Copies: BM, CUL, H.

29 E. Fourth Edition. 1671. Wing T318.

A Discourse of the Nature, Offices and Measures of Friendship . . . . also Three Letters to a Gentleman that was Tempted to the Communion of the Romish Church . . . Printed for R. Royston, 1671. 12mo.

This edition was advertised in the Hilary Term Catalogue for 1670/1.

It will be seen that the full title has been restored. However, it was an unstable compound. In the running title we get "measures and offices," in the heading "nature and offices." Also the *Three Letters* were first published in this edition. They are dated January to March, 1657/8. If these dates are correct, it is difficult to see why they were not published before.

In the heading, M.K.P. is expanded to Mrs. Katherine Philips for the first time.

The text of this edition contains almost all of the first separate edition readings. There is one final alteration of the text in this edition which can only be Taylor's. In the passage dealing with Mandana, cited earlier, the Countess of Exeter is replaced by the Infanta of Spain.

Copies: BM, GK, H; Har, PU, Y.

29 F. Fifth Printing. 1674.

See *Polemical Discourses,* 1674 (No. 28 B).

29 G. Sixth Edition. 1678. Wing T356.

Title: B. TAYLOR'S | *OPUSCULA* | [rule] | THE | [black letter] Measures of [black letter] Friendship. | WITH | ADDITIONAL TRACTS. | *To which is now Added,* | His *Moral Demonstration,* proving that | the Religion of *Jesus Christ* is from *GOD.* | Never before Printed in the Volume. | [cut: two angels in clouds holding an open book, a hand with a pen above; on the left page is "Ecclus. 14. 13. | *Do good* | *unto thy* | *Friend* | *before thou* | *dye.*" on the right "Greg. Nyssen | (five lines of Greek)."] | LONDON, Printed for Rich. Royston | Bookseller to His most Sacred Majesty, 1678.

Coll: 12mo. A⁴ B-I¹² K⁸, 108 leaves. Paged B1ʳ-K8ʳ: pp. 1-207.

Contents: A1ʳ, blank; A1ᵛ, portrait; A2ʳ, title-page (verso blank); A3, advertisements; A4, contents; B1ʳ-E1ᵛ, text of *Friendship;* E2ʳ, title for *Five Letters More to Persons Changed in their Religion* (verso blank); E3ʳ-H2ʳ, text of *Five Letters;* H2ᵛ, blank; H3ʳ, title for *Moral Demonstration* (verso blank); H4, preface addressed to Royston and signed "A. B."; H5ʳ-K8ʳ, text of *Moral Demonstration;* K8ᵛ, blank.

Notes: This edition was advertised in the Michaelmas Term Catalogue of 1678.

This is a reprinting of the fourth edition, the postscript is restored to the text after *Two Letters,* with the addition of the *Moral Demonstration* (Book I, Chapter IV of *Ductor Dubitantium*). This work was added on the recommendation of a correspondent of Royston's, and the letter is printed as an introduction to the discourse and is signed "A. B." The *Moral Demonstration* enjoyed a vogue and was reprinted ten times in the eighteenth and nineteenth centuries.

In the British Museum Catalogue an edition of *Opuscula* is dated 1675; this is an error for 1678. Wing lists a copy at Union Seminary dated 1658; this also is an error for 1678.

This edition has been given rather more full treatment because of the considerable change in the form of *Friendship* in this appearance.
Copies: BM, Bod, CUL; Har, I, KS, NL, Tex, US, Y.
29 H. Seventh Edition. 1684. Wing T357.
B. Taylor's Opuscula . . . Printed for R. Royston, 1684. 12mo.
Copies: BM, CUL, VA; Cla.
29 I. Eighth Printing of *Two Letters.* 1686. Wing T323.
See *Dissuasive from Popery,* 1686 (No. 42 F).
29 J. Eighth Edition of *A Copy of A Letter.* 1687. Wing T306.
A Copy of a letter written . . . For L. Meredith. 1687. 8vo.

This is a separate reprinting of the first letter from *Friendship.* It was published as a pamphlet, priced 2d. It has an *Imprimatur* dated June 3, 1687, and was evidently issued because of the topical interest at that time in the religion of James II.
Copies: Bod; US.

30 A. *A Collection of Offices.* First Edition. 1658. Wing T300.
Title: A | Collection of offices | OR | FORMS of PRAYER | *Publick* and *Private.* | FITTED | To the needs of all Christian | *ASSEMBLIES* | In cases Ordinary and Extraordinary. | *Taken out of the Scriptures and the ancient Litur-* | *gies of several Churches, especially* | the GREEK. | [rule] | *S. Ignatius* | [two lines in Greek] | [rule] | *LONDON,* | Printed by *J. Flesher* for *R. Royston,* at the sign of | the Angel in Ivy-lane. 1658.
Coll: 8vo: A⁸, a-b⁸ c⁶ d-e⁸, B-X⁸, ²A-²N⁸ ²O², 312 leaves. Unpaginated.
Contents: A1ʳ, half-title; A1ᵛ, frontispiece; A2ʳ, title-page (verso blank); A3ʳ-c6ᵛ, preface; d1ʳ-e8ᵛ, calendar, tables, etc.; B1ʳ-X8ᵛ, text; ²A1ʳ, title for Psalter (verso blank); ²A2ʳ-²O2ᵛ, text of Psalms.
Notes: The half-title reads: FORMS of PRAYER | *Publick* and *Private.* | *Together with* | The PSALTER or PSALMS of *David,* | after the KINGS Translation. | [signed "A" at the foot].

The internal title for the Psalter reads: The PSALTER: or PSALMS of David, | After the KINGS Translation. | With Arguments to every Psalm.

A Collection of Offices was entered in Stationers' Register on June 16, 1657, and Thomason's copy is dated December, and the date on the title-page is altered to 1657. His copy was, however, of the second issue of this edition.

Clearly, therefore, this work was published before *The Funeral Sermon on Sir George Dalston,* 1658 (No. 31 A); Dalston died in September of 1657.

This, but for one small difference, is the title which was entered in the Stationers' Register; "families" was substituted for "assemblies" in line 8. Perhaps even the bold Royston thought the latter too perilously suggestive of the persecuted Anglican conventicles to which Taylor was then ministering.

The title-page of this issue of this edition has a slit cut in it, almost certainly as an indication that it was to be cancelled. A7, being joined to the title-page, is uncancelled also in this state. The only textual change on A7 between the two issues is the changing of the word "Romane" from italic to roman twice (the preface is set in italic).

The frontispiece represents Christ in an attitude of prayer. This was afterwards used as the frontispiece for the sixth, and some subsequent editions, of *Holy Living* (No. 11 F). It was also used in the fourth and fifth editions of *The Great Exemplar* (Nos. 9 E and F).

Copies: H.

30 B. Second Issue of 30 A. 1658. Wing T300.

Title: A | [all in red] Collection of offices | OR | FORMS of PRAYER | IN | [all in red] Cases Ordinary and Extraordinary. | *Taken out of the Scriptures and the ancient Litur-* | *gies of several Churches, especially* | *the* GREEK. | [rule] | *Together with* | [all in red] The Psalter or Psalms of *David,* according to | the Kings Translations; with Argu- | ments to the same. | [rule] | *S. Ignatius.* | [two lines in Greek] | [rule] | *LONDON,* | [all in red] Printed by *J. Flesher* for *R. Royston,* at the sign of | the Angel in *Ivy-lane.* 1658.

Coll: [As in 30 A above, except A2.7 is a cancel.]

Contents: [As in 30 A above.]

Variants: Copy CO is from the Evelyn collection and is inscribed, in Evelyn's hand, "ex dono authoris."

Notes: The earlier title (No. 30 A) describes the prayers as "Publick and Private," and mentions "Christian Assemblies." On the cancel title-page of this issue no "Assemblies" are mentioned and the word "Publick" is omitted. These changes from the form in the Stationers' Register, may be concessions to dangerous times.

The preface, except for the last three paragraphs, was reprinted in *Polemical Discourses,* 1674 (No. 28 B), as an introduction to *Apology* (No. 8). A few prayers from this book were added to the devotions following some later editions of *The Psalter of David* (No. 3).

Had the book ever been widely published in the first issue of this edition, it is almost certain that Evelyn would have received such a copy. As can be seen, it was the later issue which was presented to him by Taylor. Further, that Thomason purchased the second issue is indicative of the smaller number of the earlier form issued.

For some years during the commonwealth, Anglicans had been allowed to take part in the rites and ceremonies of their Church, provided that these were carried out discreetly. In the second part of the 1650s this became increasingly difficult and dangerous. Taylor was at this time hazardously employed in ministering to Anglican conventicles. His latest biographer, Canon C. J. Stranks, has described the situation. He quotes a letter from Hammond to Sheldon (*The Life and Writings of Jeremy Taylor,* 1952, pp. 178-9) : "Your presence will be very useful at Richmond, where some of our ecclesiastical affairs are now afoot, and by what I hear concerning a report made to the Bishop of London by Dr. Jeremy Taylor concerning the clergy's sense to have the Common Prayer taken off and some other form made, I cannot but wish you were there to interpose your judgment and authority." The author goes on "It was probably never intended that the Prayer Book should be wholly withdrawn but only that, in order to tide things over for a time, it should be allowed to fall into the background. . . . It was in order to provide this alternative use that Taylor produced his *Collection of Offices* . . . . In all probability they were the forms which he himself used in public now that the Prayer Book was suppressed." In fact, there was evidently a careful plan for the Church to go underground.

Gosse beautifully speaks of Jeremy Taylor's prayers as being "each like a gush of music." Apart from Cranmer, no Englishman has ever surpassed or even equalled Taylor in liturgical writing. After *The Book of Common Prayer,* this is by far the most beautiful book of the kind in our language.
Copies: Bod, CUL, DC, DW, H, Th; I, KS, US.

30 C. Second Edition. 1690. Wing T301.
A Collection of offices or forms of prayers . . . . Printed for Luke Meredith at the Angel in Amen Corner. 1690. 8vo.

Added to this edition is an explanatory preface, "To the Bookseller on his publishing this Second Edition."

This work was advertised in the Hilary Term Catalogue for 1690 and the Michaelmas Term Catalogue for 1693. It seems that the second entry does not imply either a new edition or an issue, for no later copies are known.
Copies: BM, CCC; HH.

31 A. *Funeral Sermon for Sir George Dalston.* First Edition. 1658. No Wing number.
Title: [all within double rules] A | SERMON | PREACHED | at the Funerall of that worthy Knight | Sr. GEORGE DALSTON | of *DALSTON* in *Cumberland,* | *September* 28. 1657. | [rule] | By *J. T.* D. D. | [rule] | [device] | *LONDON,* | Printed for *John Martin, James Allestrye,* and *Thomas Dicas.* | 1658.
Coll: Quarto: A-E⁴, 20 leaves. Paged A2ʳ-E3ᵛ: pp. 1-36.

Contents: A1ʳ, title-page (verso blank); A2ʳ-E3ᵛ, text; E4, blank.
Notes: This work was entered on June 16, 1658.

This sermon has usually been wrongly catalogued and is, therefore, not often recognized as being Taylor's. It is impossible for the compilers to make an adequate judgment about the number of copies to be found in libraries today.

On April 9, 1659, Taylor wrote to Evelyn from Ireland; in a postscript he said: "If you please at any time to write me, if you sent it to Mr. Allestree, stationer, at the Bell in St. Paul's Church-yard, it will come to me safely." Writing again to Evelyn on June 4, 1659, he said: "Sir, Mr. Martin, bookseller, at the Bell, in S. Paul's Church-yard, is my correspondent in London, and whatsoever he receives he transmits it to me carefully; and so will Mr Royston, though I do not often imploy him now." From this it has been deduced that there was some coldness now between Royston and Taylor; however, with the exceptions of this sermon and *The Worthy Communicant,* Royston was the publisher for all of the later works Taylor was to produce. Royalists were more than ever mistrusted by the government at this time, and it may have been thought insecure to send much correspondence through Royston.
Copies: Bod, ML, TCC.

31 B. Second-seventh Printings. 1674-95.
See *Worthy Communicant,* 1674-95 (Nos. 33 E-K).
Notes: The sermon was reprinted with the *Worthy Communicant* in 1674, and all subsequent editions of that work. It was first associated with the other sermons in Heber's collected edition of 1822.

32 A. *Ductor Dubitantium.* First Edition. 1660. Wing T324.
Title: [Vol. I, A2ʳ]: DUCTOR DUBITANTIUM, | OR | THE RULE | OF | CONSCIENCE | In all her generall measures; | Serving as a great Instrument for the determination of | CASES of CONSCIENCE. | In Four Books. | By JEREMY TAYLOR, D. D. | Prov. 14. 8. | [one line of Greek] | *LONDON,* | Printed by *James Flesher,* for *Richard Royston* at the Angel | in Ivy-lane, 1660.
Note: The title-page is on red ruled paper.
Title: [Vol. II. π1ʳ]: *DUCTOR DUBITANTIUM,* | OR | The Rule of Conscience | In all her generall measures; | Serving as a great Instrument for the determination of | CASES of CONSCIENCE. | The Second Volume, | By JEREMY TAYLOR, D. D. | [rule] | Romans 13. 5. | [one line of Greek] | [engraving, Johnson: Hertochs #6. See 23 A above. Engraved at the foot "*LONDON* printed for R. Roiston at yᵉ *Angell* | in Iuy lane. 1660."]
Note: The title-page is on red ruled paper.
Coll: Fol., in sixes: [Vol. I.] A⁴, a-b⁶ c-d⁴, B-3A⁶ 3B⁴, 304 leaves; plates 1 (before B1). Paged a1ʳ-d4ᵛ: pp. i-xl; B1ʳ-3B4ʳ: pp. 1-559.

[Vol. II.] π¹ A-2Z⁶ (±L6) 3A⁴, 281 leaves. Paged A1ʳ-2X6ʳ: pp. 1-527. *Contents:* [Vol. I.] A1ʳ, blank; A1ᵛ, engraved title; A2ʳ, title-page (verso blank); A3ʳ-A4ᵛ, dedication to Charles II; a1ʳ-b5ʳ, preface; b5ᵛ, blank; b6ʳ-d4ᵛ, contents; B1ʳ-3B4ʳ, text of volume I; 3B4ᵛ, blank.

[Vol. II.] π1ʳ, title-page (verso blank); A1ʳ, title for Book III (verso blank); A2ʳ-2X6ʳ, text of volume II; 2X6ᵛ, blank; 2Y1ʳ-3A3ᵛ, table; 3A4ʳ, errata and advertisement (verso blank).

Variants: Some copies (CCC, H, J) have an extra errata strip pasted on 3A4ʳ of Volume II, as well as the usual errata list found on that leaf.

Some copies do not have L6 (pp. 131-2) of Volume II cancelled. They are: CO, H, J, MeO, PCC.

Notes: The engraved title (Vol. I, A1ᵛ): A hand writing on a heart above a book, called Liber Conscientiae and the following text, "DUCTOR DUBI-TANTIUM | or | The Rule of Conscience | In lumine tuo, Domini, videbimus, lumen."

The Lombart portrait, usually in State III, is normally found facing B1ʳ of Volume I.

Ductor was entered on April 18, 1656.

The cancellation of L6 in Volume II sheds some light on the printing history of *Ductor*. On the leaf is printed part of a chapter about moral duties concerned with the supreme political power—what is now called sovereignty. In the original state of L6ʳ (p. 131), this passage is found: "that's the perfect Monarchy; but yet that is no greater power then is in every kind of Government; for be it where it will, somewhere or other in all Government there must be a Supreme power, and that power is absolute and unlimited. For suppose a King that could be questioned by his Senate, deposed, judg'd, condemn'd as *Diodorus Siculus* tells of the Kings of *Egypt,* yet they that judge the King cannot be judged themselves, if they have the right to judge him; or at least they must stand at a Judicatory that cannot be judg'd, and there is the supremacy plac'd." In the cancelled state this reads "that's the perfect Monarchy: which although it be incomparably the best, and like that by which God governs the world, the first in the whole kind of Government, and therefore the measure of the rest, yet that is no greater power then is in every kind of Government; for be it where it will, somewhere or other in all Government there must be a Supreme power, and that power is absolute and limited."

The return of Charles II altered, for loyalists, the moral relationship between themselves and the government, and it made possible, and even advisable, for Taylor to substitute the passage which was so much more sympathetic to his beliefs. At the foot of the page, and on page 132, alterations are made to much the same effect.

In an undated letter to Sheldon, in answer to one dated November 5, 1654?, Taylor said "I am to thank you for the prudent and friendly advice you were pleased to give me in your other letter relating to my great undertaking in Cases of Conscience. I have only finished the first part yet; the *praecognita* and the generals." In view of the following letter, this was probably written toward the end of 1654. On November 17, 1655, after mentioning their controversy over original sin, he said, "I am very desirous to be permitted quietly to my studies, that I may seasonably publish the first three books of my Cases of Conscience, which I am now preparing to the presse." On October 15, 1656, he wrote to Evelyn; after apologizing for misprints in *Deus Justificatus,* he added "But I hope the printer will make amends in my Rule of Conscience, which I find hitherto he does with more care." Printing had obviously begun between the writing of the last two letters, probably about April, when the book was entered in the Stationers' Register. On March 10, 1658/9, he wrote to Lord Conway from Portmore in Ireland, "I could not send my Rule of Conscience over by Major Rawdon, because he was uncertain of his going; and I am fearful of the sea yet, til Aprill but then I intend to send over a servant on purpose, or else to venture them by Brian Magee." On April 9, 1659, he wrote again to Lord Conway, "My Lord, I am to beg a favour of your Lorp. that when Royston sends to your Lorp. the sheets of my second volume; which I have ordered him to doe, you will be pleased to let some of your servants convey them speedily to me. My Lord I would not have moov'd this trouble to your Lorp. if I could have found another way so safe or so tolerable, save only that your Lorps. trouble ought to be intolerable to me. They will be brought by 8 sheets or 10 at a time, & it may be a fortnight after so many more; that they may not be too grievous or troublesome." This all, as can be seen, probably relates to Book III in Volume II. The preface ends "From my study in *Portmore* in *Kilultagh,* October 5. 1659." The dedication to Charles II must have been written and printed after the Restoration. Taylor was in London at about the time of the King's return, and probably superintended the final arrangement of the book, possibly including the cancellation of offending leaf L6.

The entry in the Stationers' Register shows that the work was first planned in three books; according to the titles, which are given in the entry, these were the first, second and fourth books. The fourth book was evidently planned, and probably written, before he left for Ireland. The third book must have been an afterthought.

The story of the printing becomes fairly clear. The first volume began to be set up in 1656. Fairly soon Taylor must have planned Book IV, and it was decided to make a single volume of books I and II. There followed Taylor's tribulations in Chepstow, and then his busy, secret, dangerous life, ministering to private conventicles of Anglicans (it may have been noticed that nearly three years went by without his producing a new work). In the greater leisure of Ireland, interrupted by one arrest, he completed the book. His main task was probably the writing of the third book, in which occurs the phrase "here in

Ireland." Both Wood, in *Athenae Oxoniensis,* and Rust, in his *Funeral Sermon,* say that he wrote the book at Portmore. It is now evident that probably little more than the third book was written in Ireland.

On June 4, 1659, Taylor wrote in a letter to Evelyn, "I shall be ashamed to make my addresse, or pay thankes in words. . . , till my Rule of Conscience be Publicke, and that is all the way I have to pay my debts; that and my prayers that God would." From this we may assume that at this date the book was not yet ready for publication although the proofs may perhaps have been finished.

As was noted under *Friendship,* 1684 (No. 29 H), *A Moral Demonstration* was extracted from this work and often reprinted. An obscurer extract is *The Jewish Sabbath and The Lord's Day* published or edited by Sir Richard Musgrave, Bart., and printed by J. W. Lindsay in 1834.

Copies: AO, AS, BM, Bod, CCC, CO, CUL, H, J, MeO, PCC, TCD; Har, HH, KS, KU, NIU, NL, PU, US, Y.

32 B.   Second Edition. 1671. Wing T325.

Ductor Dubitantium . . . . The Second Edition . . . . Printed by Roger Norton for Richard Royston . . . . MDCLXXI. Fol.

Above the imprint on the title-page is an engraving of two angels holding up the arms of Cambridge.

The Lombart portrait, before B1, is becoming badly worn.

As in the first edition, books III and IV have internal titles. Each is dated 1670.

This edition was advertised in the Hilary Term Catalogue for 1670/1.

A list of errata is printed at the end of the book (4G2ᵛ). Very few, if any, of these show any evidence of having been originally made by the author. There is hardly an error that could not have been corrected without aid by a publisher's reader of intelligence. From the errata of the first edition, all but three of the forty-eight for the first two books (the original first volume) have been corrected in the second edition. However, of the eighteen for the second two books (originally volume two), only one is corrected in this edition. Further, the cancelled version of the altered pages in the first edition naturally appears in the second edition, but in making the cancel, an error was corrected: "respublica" replaced "republica." Oddly, "republica" appears in the second edition. One cannot help suspecting the officiousness of two successive compositors who each thought he knew better than others how to spell *republic.*

Copies: BM, BO, CUL, EmC; BP, I, KS, KU, PU, US, Y.

32 C.   Third Edition. 1676. Wing T326.

Ductor Dubitantium . . . . Printed by R. Norton for R. Royston . . . . MDCLXXVI. Fol.

This edition was advertised in the Easter Term Catalogue for 1676.

The portrait remains, worn and scratched rather than touched up.

On the title-page appears, badly worn, the plate which formed part of the

folding plate in *Unum Necessarium* (No. 23 A). It has been cut away on each side as far as the skirts of the saints. The design of a writing hand, from the frontispiece of the first edition, appears, reversed, above St. Peter's left arm.
Copies: BM, CUL, DC, SE, TCD; Har, I, PU, WSC, Y.

32 D. Fourth Edition. 1696. Wing T327.
Ductor Dubitantium . . . . Printed by J. L. for Luke Meredith, at the Star in St. Paul's Church-yard. MDCXCVI. Fol.

This edition was advertised in the 1696/7 Hilary Term Catalogue.

This edition has the same plates as the third edition, and they are further worn.

A second printer seems to have taken over at some stage of production. The internal title for Book III makes no mention of any printer and on the title for Book IV appears "Printed by W. H. &c."
Copies: BM, LI, MO; CU, KS.

33 A. *The Worthy Communicant.* First Edition. 1660. Wing T417.
Title: [all within double rules] The Worthy | COMMUNICANT | OR | A Discourse of the Nature, Effects, and | Blessings consequent to the worthy | receiving of the | LORDS SUPPER | And of all the duties required in order to | a worthy preparation: | Together | With the *Cases of Conscience* occuring in | the duty of him that *Ministers* and of him | that *Communicates.* | To which are added | Devotions fitted to every part of the | Ministration. | [rule] | By *Jeremy Taylor* D. D. *and Bishop Elect* of | *Down* and *Connor.* | [rule] | *LONDON,* | Printed by *R. Norton* for *John Martin,* | *James Allestry,* and *Thomas Dicas* at the | *Bell* in *St. Pauls Church-yard,* 1660.
Coll: 8vo: A-2C⁸ 2E-2O⁸, 288 leaves; plates 1 (before A1ʳ). Paged (with variants) B1ʳ-2O8ᵛ: pp. 1-400, 417-576.
Contents: A1ʳ, title-page (verso blank); A2ʳ-A4ᵛ, dedication; A5ʳ-A8ʳ, contents; A8ᵛ, blank; B1ʳ-B7ʳ, introduction; B7ᵛ-2O8ᵛ, text.
Variants: [Variants are discussed under the second issue of this edition, No. 33 B].
Notes: The frontispiece, engraved by Hertochs, represents the interior of a church, where two kneeling angels draw aside curtains to reveal the Sacrament on the altar; above is a panel inscribed "The Worthy Communicant."

The Worthy Communicant was entered on May 27, 1660, and Thomason's copy is dated December 6, 1660. Since Taylor is described as "Bishop Elect," this is evidently later than *Ductor* (No. 32 A), on the title of which his impending rank is not noted.
Copies: Bod, CUL, Th, TCD; Cla, I, NL, US, Y.

33 B. Second Issue. 1661. Wing T417A.
[*Title, Coll,* and *Contents* as in 33 A except "Dovotions" for "Devotions"

(line 15) and *"Lord Bishop"* for *"Bishop Elect"* (line 17), and the alteration of the date.]

Variants: Copies Ab and JC have both the 1660 and 1661 title-pages. In both, the later precedes the earlier and indicates faulty cancellation of the 1660 title.

Page 380 (2B6^v) is sometimes misnumbered 80.

Sheet 2E (pp. 417-32) has in some copies of the inner forme this numbering: pp. 394-95, 398-99, 402-03, 406-07. In some copies the faulty numbering has been corrected. Either state of sheet 2E can be found in either the first edition or the second issue of that edition, and even in one of the copies with both title-pages.

Notes: The apparent absence of a whole sheet in the middle of the volume is probably due to the work having been set up by more than one compositor at the same time, with wrongly prepared instructions. The chapters and sections as they stand correspond to the list in the contents. There is no evidence that any matter has been suppressed. It may perhaps be pointed out that the wrong paging in sheet 2E does not run on from the previous sheet.

This was the last of Taylor's devotional works to be written, and it was also one of the only two publications of Taylor's lifetime which Royston never got his hands on (the other was the *Funeral Sermon on Sir George Dalston* [No. 31] soon to be closely associated with the present work). He sometimes advertised it among books described as "All sold by R. Royston," but added a punctilious qualification, such as, "Printed for J. Martin," or "Sold at the Bell in S. Paul's Churchyard."

In 1642 a divine named Jeremy Dyke had published a book called *A Worthy Communicant: or, a Treatise Shewing the Due Order of Receiving the Sacrament of the Lords Supper* (Wing D2961). It was reprinted in the same year. Taylor had already, in *Holy Dying,* used the phrase incorporated in his title; but it is not impossible that he borrowed from Dyke. In the case of *The Golden Grove,* he had shown himself ready, when it perfectly suited him, to use an earlier title. His own was curiously borrowed by a William Smythies who, in 1683, published *The Unworthy Non-Communicant* (Wing S4379).

Subsequent editions are not numbered, until there suddenly turns up, quite inaccurately described, a so-called sixth edition. All observed editions are octavos, and all have the original plate in various states of alteration; it is sometimes arranged as a frontispiece, as in the first edition, and sometimes as a title-page, with the impression on the recto.

Copies: Ab, JC, MO; Har, I, KU.

33 C. Second Edition. 1667. Wing T418.

The Worthy Communicant . . . . Printed by T. R. for J. Martyn, J. Allestry, and T. Dicas, and are to be sold by Thomas Basset at his shop in St Dunstans Church-yard in Fleetstreet. 1667. 8vo.

Since Taylor is described on the title-page as "Lord Bishop &c." and not "late," it is likely that the printing of this edition at least began before his death in this year.

2D8^r bears an advertisement for books sold by Basset.

Copies: Bod, PCC, TCC; I, PU, UC.

33 D.   Third Edition. 1671. Wing T419.

The Worthy Communicant . . . . Printed by T. R. for J. Martyn, at the Bell in St. Pauls Church-yard. 1671. 8vo.

This edition was advertised in the Easter Term Catalogue for 1671.

In this, and all subsequent seventeenth-century editions, the publisher's or bookseller's name is engraved across the foot of the plate. It is from this edition that the plate is described in Johnson (Anonymous #60) as an engraved title-page. In fact, as noted above, the arrangement of it is capricious.

This is the last time, until the nineteenth century, that *The Worthy Communicant* appears without the *Funeral Sermon on Sir George Dalston* (No. 31) attached.

Copies: BM; Y.

33 E.   Fourth Edition. 1674. Wing T420.

The Worthy Communicant . . . . Printed by T. N. for John Martyn, at the Bell in St. Pauls Churchyard. 1674. 8vo.

This edition was advertised in the Term Catalogue for Easter, 1674.

While preparing this edition, Martyn seems to have remembered his rights in the *Funeral Sermon on George Dalston* (No. 31), and consequently that work was added to the volume in this edition. Two extra lines appear on the title-page: "To which is added a Sermon, never Printed with the Folio Volume of Sermons."

Copies: BM, Bod, TCC; Col, NL.

33 F.   Second Isssue of 33 E. 1677. No Wing number.

[Title as in No. 33 E with date altered to 1677.]

Copies: TCC.

33 G.   Third Issue of 33 E. 1678. No Wing number.

[Title as in No. 33 E with date altered to 1678.]

Copies: J.

33 H.   Fifth Edition. 1683. Wing T421.

The Worthy Communicant . . . . Printed by R. H. for Awnsham Churchill at the Black Swan in Ave-Mary Lane near Amen Corner. 1683. 8vo.

This edition was advertised in the Trinity Term Catalogue for 1683.

Copies: BM, NCE; Bow, Cla, KS.

33 I.   Sixth Edition. 1686. Wing T422.

The Worthy Communicant . . . . Printed for Gilbert Cownly at the Popes-head, at the East end of the lower Walk of the New-Exchange in the Strand. 1686. 8vo.

This edition was advertised in the Easter and Trinity Term Catalogues for 1686.

Copies: CUL.

33 J.   Second Issue of 33 I. 1689. Wing T423.

The Worthy Communicant . . . . Printed for James Partridge at the Post-house between Charing-cross and White-Hall. 1689. 8vo.

This issue was advertised in the Trinity Term Catalogue for 1689.

The only alteration made for publishing this Second Issue was the cancellation of the title-page. The plate, which had been inscribed "Sold by Gilbert Cownly at the Popes Head in the New Exchange" in No. 33 I, has not been altered for this issue and still reads that way.

Copies: BM.

33 K. Third Issue of 33 I. 1695. Wing T424.

The Worthy Communicant . . . . Printed for Francis Wright at the Post-house between Charing-Cross and White-Hall. 1695. 8vo.

Identical to 33 I and 33 J except for the cancelled title-page.

Copies: BM.

34 A. *Consecration Sermon.* First Edition. Dublin, 1661. Wing T391.

Title: [all within a border of type ornaments, seventeen at head and foot, twenty-eight at sides] A SERMON | Preached at the *Consecration* of two | *Archbishops* and ten *Bishops,* | in the | Cathedral Church of S. *Patrick* in Dublin, | *January* 27. 1660. | [rule] | By *Jeremie Taylor* D. D. Ld. Bishop | of *Downe* and *Connor.* | [rule] | *Sal liquifit, ut condiat.* | [rule] | [rule] | *DVBLIN,* | Printed by *W. Bladen* for *John North* | Bookseller in Castlestreet, | *Anno Dom.* 1661.

Coll: Quarto: A-G^4, 28 leaves. Paged B1^r-G4^r: pp. 1-47.

Contents: A1, blank; A2^r, title-page (verso blank); A3^r-A4^v, "To the Christian Reader"; B1^r-G4^r, text; G4^v, blank.

Notes: This sermon was not entered in the Stationers' Register separately but was entered as part of the collection *Seven Sermons* (No. 41 A).

A short errata list is printed at the foot of A4^v.

Dudley Loftus, who supplied the Syriac prayer for the third edition of *The Great Exemplar* (No. 9 D), published an account of the memorable service at which this sermon was preached (his pamphlet is described in another section of this bibliography). The occasion was also mentioned in the prefatory life to Bramhall's *Collected Works,* which were published in folio, by Benjamin Tooke, in Dublin, in 1677 (Wing B4211); in the same life there are several allusions to Taylor and his funeral sermon on Bramhall.

Copies: BM, CCO, CUL, Ex, H, LI, ML, PCD, TCC, TCD; Har, HH, US, Y.

34 B. Second Edition. 1663. Wing T392.

Title: [all within double rules] A | SERMON | Preached at the *Consecration* of | Two *Archbishops* and Ten | *Bishops,* | in the | Cathedral Church of S. *Patrick* in | *DUBLIN.* | *January* 27. 1660. | [rule] | By *Jeremie Taylor* D. D.

L*ORD* | Bishop of *Down* and | *Connor.* | [rule] | *Sal liquifit, ut condiat.* | [rule] | *LONDON,* | Printed for *R. Royston,* Bookseller to the | Kings most Excellent Majesty, 1663.

Coll: Quarto: A-G⁴ H², 30 leaves. Paged B1ʳ-H2ʳ: pp. 1-51.

Contents: A1ʳ, title-page (verso blank); A2ʳ-A4ʳ, "To the Christian Reader"; A4ᵛ, blank; B1ʳ-H2ʳ, text; H2ᵛ, blank.

Notes: Copies of this edition are often bound up as part of *Seven Sermons* of 1663 or 1664 (No. 41 A or No. 41 B).

All but two of the errata on the short list in the first edition are corrected in this edition.

Copies: BM, Ex, H, PCC; Har, US.

34 C-D. Second and Third Issues of 34 B. 1663 and 1664.

The *Consecration Sermon,* second edition, was remaindered as part of the composite volume of *Seven Sermons* in 1663 and 1664 (No. 41 A and No. 41 B).

34 E. Third Printing. 1667.

See *Ten Sermons,* 1667 (No. 44 A).

34 F. Fourth Printing. 1673.

See *Eleven Sermons,* 1673 (No. 44 B).

34 G. Fifth Printing. 1678.

See *Eleven Sermons,* 1678 (No. 44 C).

35 A. *Parliament Sermon.* First Edition. 1661. Wing T393.

Title: [all within double rules] A | SERMON | PREACHED | At the opening of the Parliament | of I*RELAND,* | *May* 8. 1661. | Before the right Honourable | the Lords Justices, and the Lords | Spiritual and Temporal and | the Commons. | [rule] | By J*EREMY* Lord Bishop of | *Down* and *Connor.* | [rule] | *Salus in multitudine consulentium.* | [rule] | *LONDON,* | Printed by *J. F.* for *R. Royston,* Bookseller to his | most Sacred M*AJESTY,* 1661.

Coll: Quarto: A⁴, a⁴, B-G⁴, 32 leaves. Paged B1ʳ-G3ʳ: pp. 1-45.

Contents: A1ʳ, blank; A1ᵛ, request to print; A2ʳ, title-page (verso blank); A3ʳ-a4ᵛ, epistle; B1ʳ-G3ʳ, text; G3ᵛ, blank; G4ʳ, advertisements (verso blank).

Notes: This sermon was later entered collectively in the Stationers' Register as part of *Seven Sermons,* 1663 (No. 41 A).

On the verso of A1 is, first, the recorded thanks from the Speaker, dated May 9, and second, what appears to be the thanks of the Lords Justices, dated May 11. The latter contains also a desire for the work to be printed. With so ceremonial a sermon, it is a little surprising that it was not printed in Dublin.

Copies: BM, CUL, LI, TCC, TCD; Har, HH, NL, US, Y.

35 B-C. Second and Third Issues of 35 A. 1663 and 1664.

The *Parliament Sermon,* first edition, was remaindered as part of the composite volume of *Seven Sermons* in 1663 and 1664 (No. 41 A and No. 41 B).

35 D. Second Printing. 1667.
See *Ten Sermons,* 1667 (No. 44 A).

35 E. Third Printing. 1673.
See *Eleven Sermons,* 1673 (No. 44 B).

35 F. Fourth Printing. 1678.
See *Eleven Sermons,* 1678 (No. 44 C).

36 A. *Rules and Advices to the Clergy.* First Edition. Dublin, 1661. Wing T387.
Title: [all within double rules] RULES | AND | ADVICES | To the | CLERGY | Of the | DIOCESSE | OF | *DOWN* and *CONNOR:* | For their Deportment in their Personal | and Publick Capacities. | *Given by the Bishop at the Visitation,* | *at* LISNEGARVEY. | [rule] | *DUBLIN,* Printed by *John Crook,* Prin- | ter to the King's most Excellent Maje- | sty; and are to be sold by *John North,* | Book-seller in *Castle-Street.* 1661.
Coll: 8vo: A-C⁸, 24 leaves. Paged A2ʳ-C8ᵛ: pp. 1-46.
Contents: A1ʳ, title-page (verso blank); A2ʳ-C8ᵛ, text.
Notes: See the notes to 36 B.
Copies: BM.

36 B. Second Edition. Dublin, 1661. Wing T388.
Title: [all within double rules] RULES | AND | ADVICES | To the | CLERGY | OF THE | DIOCESSE | OF | *DOWN* and *CONNOR*: For their Deportment in their Personal | and Publick Capacities. | [rule] | Given by JER. TAYLOR, Bishop of | that Diocess, at the Visitation at *LISNE-* | *GARVEY.* | [rule] | *DUBLIN,* Printed by *John Crooke,* Printer | to the King's Most Excellent Maje- | sty, 1661.
Coll and *Contents:* [as in 36 A.]
Notes: This work was entered by Andrew Crook on September 18, 1661.

There is no direct evidence for placing one of these editions before the other. However, the present arrangement is supported by some small facts.

The variations in the title-page are significant. No. 36 A is the only certainly authentic Irish publication of Taylor's without his name on the title. It is easy to imagine adding his name in a second edition, but there is no imaginable reason for deliberately dropping it in a reprint.

The text of one edition is not a line for line resetting of the other. In each, the numbered sections begin on the same pages, but in No. 36 A every section heading has a row or more of type ornaments, while in No. 36 B only the first section has such decoration. In No. 36 A, after the first, only two section headings begin a page, but in No. 36 B every section begins a page, no matter where the previous page ended. The lines are slightly longer in No. 36 B.

It is likely that the make-up of one edition was planned to follow that of its predecessor; this is implied by the identical collations and the identical position of the beginnings of sections. These facts suggest that No. 36 B is a more careful reprinting of No. 36 A, done according to the experience of printing the rather clumsy No. 36 A.

A great many small alterations in the text are made between the printing of No. 36 A and No. 36 B. These reveal that the third edition, printed by Royston in 1663 (No. 36 C), was set from No. 36 B. In seventy-two cases where Nos. 36 A and 36 B differ, No. 36 C agrees with No. 36 B; in fourteen cases where Nos. 36 A and 36 B differ, No. 36 C agrees with No. 36 A.

If surmise is permissible, No. 36 A, with its local indication of authorship, was probably hastily printed for provincial sale on the occasion of the visitation, and No. 36 B was prepared for more general distribution from Dublin.

Although it has been generously praised, this little work is undeservedly obscure. It is the most polished of Taylor's aphoristic style; the intention is laudably serious, but the form inevitably lets through many of Taylor's wittiest sentences.

Copies: BM, CUL, CCC (2), NLW, RIA.

36 C. Third Edition ["Second"]. 1663. Wing T389 and T386.

Title: [all within double rules] RULES | and | ADVICES | To the | CLERGY | of the | DIOCESSE | of | *Down* and *Connor:* | For their Deportment in their Personal | and Publick Capacities. | Given By *JER. TAYLOR,* Bishop of | that Dioces, at the Visitation at *LISNE-* | *GARVEY.* | [rule] | The Second Edition | [rule] | *LONDON:* | Printed by *J. G.* for *Richard Royston,* Bookseller to the | Kings most Excellent Majesty, 1663.

Coll: Quarto: A-D⁴, 16 leaves. Paged A2ʳ-D4ᵛ: pp. 1-30.

Contents: A1ʳ, title-page; A1ᵛ, "Titles of the Sections"; A2ʳ-D4ᵛ, text.

Notes: In Nos. 36 A and 36 B the paragraphs were numbered twice over; one series refers to the whole book, and the other to each separate section. In this edition that arrangement was discarded, and a complete series of numberings is printed in the margin. As further evidence that this edition was set from a copy of No. 36 B (for other evidence see the notes to No. 36 B), in No. 36 A these numbers appear within the lines of text, but in No. 36 B they appear in the margins as they do here.

Copies: Bod, MeO; Har, US, Y.

36 D-E. Second and Third Issue of 36 C. 1663 and 1664.

Remainders of 36 C were issued as part of the composite volume *Seven Sermons* in 1663 and 1664 (No. 41 A and No. 41 B).

36 F. Fourth Printing. 1667.

See *Ten Sermons,* 1667 (No. 44 A).

36 G. Fifth Printing. 1673.

See *Eleven Sermons,* 1673 (No. 44 B).

36 H. Sixth Printing. 1678.

See *Eleven Sermons,* 1678 (No. 44 C).

37 A. *Via Intelligentiae.* First Edition. 1662. Wing T416.

Title: [all within double rules] Via Intelligentiae. | A | SERMOM | Preached to the | UNIVERSITY | OF | DUBLIN: | Shewing by what means the Scho- | lars shall become most Learned and | most Usefull. | *Published at their desire.* | By the R. R. Father in God, JEREMY Lord Bi- | shop of *Downe,* &c. and Vicechancellour of | that UNIVERSITY. | [rule] | *Ad majorem Dei gloriam.* | [rule] | *LONDON:* | Printed for *R. Royston* Bookseller to the Kings most | Excellent Majesty, 1662.

Stet: SERMOM

Coll: Quarto: A-I⁴, 36 leaves. Paged B1ʳ-I4ᵛ: pp. 1-64.

Contents: A1, blank; A2ʳ, title-page (verso blank); A3ʳ-A4ʳ, "To the Reader"; A4ᵛ, advertisements; B1ʳ-I4ᵛ, text.

Notes: This sermon was entered collectively with the other works in the composite volume *Seven Sermons* (No. 41 A).

In the preface, Taylor says: "When I first spake my thoughts . . . before the Little, but Excellent, University of *Dublin* . . . they were pleas'd with some earnestness to desire me to publish it to the World." He goes on to say that he was reluctant "Till by a Second communication of these thoughts, though in differing words, I had publish'd it also to my *Clergy* at the *Metropolitical Visitation* of the most Reverend and Learned Lord *Primate* of *Armagh* in my own Diocese." This visitation was probably in August, 1661. What exact text we have of this sermon cannot be known, but it is probably the original university sermon somewhat revised. Taylor was evidently depressed at this time, and dissatisfied with his work. On November 16, 1661, he had written to Evelyn that "Royston hath two Sermons and a little collection of Rules for my clergy, which had been presented to you if I had thought fitt for notice, or to send to my dearest friends."

As in the case of the *Parliament Sermon* (No. 35 A), it is a little strange that this work composed specially for Irish bodies should never have been published in Ireland.

This sermon is built on the principle of Platonists, that wisdom will come of its own accord to the virtuous, or, as Rust put it in the funeral sermon, "that Obedience is the only way to true Knowledge." In November of 1659, Taylor had written to Evelyn: "I promise to myselfe . . . that you are entered into the experimental and secret way of religion"; and he goes on, "My retirement in this solitary place hath been, I hope, of some advantage to me as to this state of religion, in which I am yet but a novice, but by the goodness of God I see fine things before me whither I am contending." This approach to mysticism was almost certainly the result of his close and friendly intercourse with Henry More, and perhaps other of the Cambridge Platonists, in the household of the Conways. Its effects appear in *The Worthy Communicant*, but perhaps most noticeably in *Via Intelligentiae*.

Copies: BM, Bod, CUL, TCC; Har, I, NL, PU, US, Y.

37 B. Second Issue. 1663.

37 A was issued as one of the works in the composite volume of *Seven Sermons,* 1663 (No. 41 A).

37 C. Second Printing. 1667.

See *Ten Sermons,* 1667 (No. 44 A).

37 D. Third Printing. 1673.

See *Eleven Sermons,* 1673 (No. 44 B).

37 E. Fourth Printing. 1678.

See *Eleven Sermons,* 1678 (No. 44 C).

38 A. *The Righteousness Evangelical.* First Edition. Dublin, 1663. Wing T360.

Title: THE | Righteousness Evangelicall | *DESCRIB'D.* | THE | CHRIS-TIANS CONQUEST | Over the Body of Sin. | *FIDES FORMATA,* | OR | FAITH working by LOVE. | [rule] | IN THREE | SERMONS | PREACH'D AT | CHRIST-CHURCH, | *DUBLIN.* | [rule] | BY THE | Right Reverend Father in God | *JEREMIAH,* | Lord Bishop of *Down* and *Connor.* | [rule] | *Dublin,* Printed by *John Crook,* Printer to | the Kings most Excellent Majesty, for *Samuel* | *Dancer* Bookseller in *Castle-street,* 1663.

Coll: 8vo: a^4, A-O^8, 116 leaves. Paged A1^r-O7^r: pp. 1-221.

Contents: a1^r, title-page (verso blank); a2^r-a3^v, dedication to the Duchess of Ormonde; a4^r, title of first sermon (verso blank); A1^r-E4^r, text of first sermon; E4^v, blank; E5^r, title of second sermon (verso blank); E6^r-I7^v, text of second sermon; I8^r, title of third sermon (verso blank); K1^r-O7^r, text of third sermon; O7^v-O8^v, blank.

Notes: The sermons in this book were entered collectively with the composite volume of *Seven Sermons* of 1663 (No. 41 A).

The internal titles give the dates on which each sermon was preached. The first is February 15, 1662/63, the second August 10, 1662, and the third May 4, 1662. In the dedication Taylor says that the Duchess of Ormonde had asked that the first sermon be printed and that he had added the other two to make up a book of adequate size. Because of the dates we have put this before the *Funeral Sermon on Bramhall* (No. 39 A) which was preached some five months after the latest of these. If this ordering is not accurate for the printing, it certainly is for the composition and preaching of the works in question. The dedication is signed "*J. D.*", clearly an error for "J. T."

Copies: Bod, CUL, ML, P, TCD.

38 B.   Second Edition. 1663. Wing T359.

Title: [all within double rules] THE | Righteousness Evangelical | *DE-SCRIB'D.* | THE | CHRISTIANS CONQUEST | Over the Body of Sin. | *FIDES FORMATA,* | OR | Faith working by Love. | [rule] | IN THREE | SERMONS | PREACHED AT | CHRIST-CHURCH, | *DUBLIN.* | [rule] | By the Right Reverend Father in God | *JEREMIAH,* | Lord Bishop of *Down* and *Connor.* | [rule] | *The second Edition.* | [rule] | *London,* Printed for *R. Royston,* Book-seller to the | Kings most Excellent Majesty, 1663.

Coll: Quarto: A² B-S⁴, 70 leaves. Paged B1ʳ-S4ᵛ: pp. 1-136.

Contents: A1ʳ, title-page; A1ᵛ, imprimatur; A2, dedication; B1ʳ-S4ᵛ, text of the three sermons.

Variants: Copy ML has been used, perhaps contemporaneously, to make up an imperfect copy of Royston's edition of the *Funeral Sermon on Bramhall;* probably through an error on the part of the original binder.

In copy H, which is bound as part of *Seven Sermons,* the title-page and dedication of *Righteousness Evangelical* are between the general title-page and contents of the composite volume.

Notes: The imprimatur is dated September 21, 1663.

The separate internal titles to the three sermons, with the dates of preaching, are omitted from this edition.

Copies: H, ML; Har, US.

38 C.   Second Issue of 38 B. 1663.

Copies of 38 B were used to make up the composite volume, *Seven Sermons,* 1663 (No. 41 A).

38 D.   Third Printing. 1667.

See *Ten Sermons,* 1667 (No. 44 A).

38 E.   Fourth Printing. 1673.

See *Eleven Sermons,* 1673 (No. 44 B).

38 F.   Fifth Printing. 1678.

See *Eleven Sermons,* 1678 (No. 44 C).

39 A.   *Funeral Sermon on Bramhall.* First Edition. Dublin, 1663. Wing T394.

Title: A | SERMON | Preached in | CHRIST-CHURCH, | *DUBLIN*: | at the Funeral | of | The most Reverend Father in God, | JOHN, | Late Lord Arch-bishop of *Armagh,* | and | Primate of all *Ireland:* | with | *A succinct Narrative of his whole Life.* | [rule] | By | The Right Reverend Father in God, | JEREMY, | Lord Bishop of *Down* and *Connor.* | [rule] | *Dublin,*

Printed by *John Crooke,* Printer to the | Kings Most Excellent Majesty, and are to be sold by | *Samuel Dancer* in *Castle-Street,* 1663.

Coll: Quarto: Π² A-E⁴ F², 24 leaves. Paged A1ʳ-F2ᵛ: pp. 1-44.

Contents: Π1, blank; Π2ʳ, title-page (verso blank); A1ʳ-F2ᵛ, text.

Variants: In copies TCD (1), CD, H, and CUL (1 and 2), there is a blank space on p. 28 (D2ᵛ). In copies TCD (2) and NI, and in the second edition, the correct Greek word, ἀγαθοεργίκ, is added. In the copies of this edition it appears that the word has been stamped in by hand.

Notes: This sermon was entered collectively with *Seven Sermons,* 1663 (No. 41 A).

In Wing this edition and the two succeeding editions are listed under different titles, Nos. 39 B and C being separated from No. 39 A.

Certain small features of this edition, such as the abbreviation "Our B. S." which is expanded into "our blessed Saviour" in the next edition, indicate that it was set from Taylor's manuscript.

The narrative part of the sermon is an important source for Bramhall's biography. It was carelessly reprinted, without acknowledgement, in *Memoires of the Lives, Actions, Sufferings & Deaths of those* .... *excellent personages* .... *for the Protestant Religion, and* .... *Allegiance to their Sovereigne* .... *by Da[vid] Lloyd* .... *London* .... *MDCLXVIII;* in other words, Lloyd's *Memoires of the Loyalists* (Wing L2642). It is interesting to note that this version must have been printed from the Dublin edition; although the word ἀγαθοεργίκ is included, "our B. S." is reprinted. The last paragraph is omitted, and in its place is a Latin epitaph. This contains a paraphrase of a passage from Pliny quoted in the sermon. It seems not unlikely that this epitaph was written by Taylor; however, there is no direct evidence.

The biographical section was also reprinted, this time with acknowledgement, in *A Remembrancer of Excellent Men* .... *London, Printed for John Martyn* .... 1670 (Wing B806). This is a compilation, or anthology of biographies, put together by Clement Barksdale; it includes a summary of Walton's *Life of Hooker,* and a portrait of Duppa by Jasper Mayne. Taylor's work is very much truncated, and most of the learned quotations are cut out of it.

Copies: CD, CUL (2), H, NI, TCD (2); Har.

39 B. Second Edition. 1663. Wing T395.

Title: A | SERMON | Preached in | CHRIST-CHURCH, | *DUBLIN:* | AT THE | FUNERAL | OF | The most Reverend FATHER in GOD, | JOHN, | Late Lord Archbishop of *ARMAGH,* | AND | PRIMATE of all *IRELAND:* | WITH | *A succinct Narrative of his whole Life.* | [rule] | BY | The Right Reverend Father in GOD, | Dr. *JEREMY TAYLOR,* | Lord Bishop of *Down* and *Connor.* | [rule] | *LONDON,* | Printed for *John Crooke,* at the Sign of the | Ship in St *Paul's* Church-yard. 1663.

Coll: Quarto: A-F⁴, 24 leaves. Paged A3ʳ-F4ᵛ: pp. 1-44.

Contents: A1ʳ, blank; A1ᵛ, imprimatur; A2ʳ, title-page (verso blank); A3ʳ-F4ᵛ, text.

Variants: In most copies the first leaf of text is signed A3. However, in the TCC and I copies this leaf of text is not signed. In the Bod (1) and RIA copies A1 and A2 are in reverse order, possibly a result of rebinding.

Notes: The imprimatur is signed "Geo. Stradlin," and is dated "21. Aug. 1663."

Comparison of this edition with the first edition indicates that this one (No. 39 B) was set from the first edition (No. 39 A). The missing Greek word is always printed in 39 B. It is, however, a very close reprinting, often following page for page, and occasionally line for line.

Copies: BM, Bod (2), CUL, MO, RIA, TCC; Cla, I, WSC, Y.

39 C. Third Edition. 1663. Wing T396.

Title: [all within double rules] A | SERMON | Preached in | *Christ-Church,* *Dublin,* | *July* 16. 1663. | AT THE FUNERAL | Of the most Reverend Father in God, | *JOHN,* | *Late Lord Archbishop of* Armagh, *and* | *Primate of all* Ireland: | WITH | *A succinct Narrative of his whole Life.* | [rule] | The third Edition, enlarged. | [rule] | *By the Right Reverend Father in God,* | JEREMY, | *Lord Bishop of* Down *and* Connor. | [rule] | *LONDON:* | Printed by *J. G.* for *Richard Royston,* Bookseller to the | Kings most Excellent Majesty, 1663.

Coll: Quarto: [A]⁴B-I⁴, 36 leaves. Paged [A]3ʳ-I3ᵛ: pp. 1-66.

Contents: [A]1ʳ, blank; [A]1ᵛ, imprimatur; [A]2ʳ, title-page (verso blank); [A]3ʳ-I3ᵛ, text; I4, blank.

Notes: The date of the service is added to the title of this edition.

The imprimatur is signed "M. Franck," and is dated September 21, 1663.

The printer was probably John Grismond.

This edition gives us the text as Taylor was probably satisfied with it, just as the first edition gives us the text as it was probably preached. More than a page of material was added to this edition.

Copies: BM, Bod, DC, LI, MO; Har, NL (2), US.

39 D. Second Issue of 39 C. 1663.

The sheets of No. 39 C were used in the composite volume. *Seven Sermons,* 1663 (No. 41 A).

39 E. Fourth Printing. 1667.

See *Ten Sermons,* 1667 (No. 44 A).

39 F. Fifth Printing. 1673.

See *Eleven Sermons,* 1673 (No. 44 B).

39 G. Sixth Printing. 1678.

See *Eleven Sermons,* 1678 (No. 44 C).

40 A. *A Discourse of Confirmation.* First Edition. Dublin, 1663. Wing T293.

Title: ΧΡΙΣΙΣ ΤΕΛΕΙΩΤΙΚΗ. | A | DISCOURSE | OF | Confirmation. |

For the use of the Clergy and Instruction | of the People of *Ireland*. | [rule] | By Jeremy *Lord Bishop of* Down. | [rule] | *Publish'd by Order of Convocation*. | [rule] | AND | Dedicated to His Grace *James* Duke, Marquess | and Earl of *Ormonde*, &c. Lord Lieutenant Ge- | neral, and General Governour of His Majesties | Kingdom of *Ireland*, | [rule] | *DVBLIN*, | Printed by *John Crooke*, Printer to the Kings Most Ex- | cellent Majesty, and are to be sold by *Samuel Dancer* | next door to the *Beare* and *Ragged-staffe* in | *Castle-street*, 1663.

Coll: Quarto: A⁴, a², B-M⁴ N², 52 leaves. Paged B1ʳ-N1ᵛ: pp. 1-90.

Contents: A1ʳ, title-page (verso blank); A2ʳ-a2ᵛ, dedication to the Duke of Ormonde; B1ʳ-N1ᵛ, text; N2ʳ, advertisements (verso blank).

Variants: Copy ML is bound up with *A Dissuasive from Popery*, 1664 (No. 42), with a general title-page for both works. This is an unique form in our experience.

Notes: In the advertisements at the end (N2ʳ), *Righteousness Evangelical* (No. 38) and *Funeral Sermon on Bramhall* (No. 39) are both listed; this work must therefore have been published later. *A Dissuasive from Popery* (No. 42) is advertised as forthcoming. There is little evidence as to whether *Confirmation* appeared before *Seven Sermons;* however, Royston entered it in the Stationers' Register on October 28, 1663, some ten weeks before that collection.

Copies: CD (2), CUL, ML, RIA, TCD (3).

40 B. Second Edition. 1664. Wing T294.

Title: ΧΡΙΣΙΣ ΤΕΛΕΙΩΤΙΚΗ. | A | DISCOURSE | OF | Confirmation. | [rule] | BY | JEREMY *Lord Bishop of* Down. | [rule] | Acts 19. 2. | [one line of Greek] | [rule] | *LONDON,* | Printed for *Richard Royston,* Book-seller | to His most Sacred MAJESTY. | [centered rule] | M DC LXIV.

Coll: 8vo: A⁸, a⁴, B-K⁸ L⁴, 88 leaves. Paged B1ʳ-L4ʳ: pp. 1-151.

Contents: A1ʳ, blank; A1ᵛ, portrait; A2ʳ, title-page (verso blank); A3ʳ-a3ʳ, dedication to the Duke of Ormonde; a3ᵛ, blank; a4, contents; B1ʳ-L4ʳ, text; L4ᵛ, blank.

Notes: There are grounds for thinking that the two half-sheets a and L are not, as one might expect, the divided halves of a single sheet. Copy H has watermarks on a1, a2, and every leaf of L has some piece of watermark. Although there is no need for two halves of a divided sheet to appear in the same copy, it is difficult to reconcile the arrangement of the watermarks in sheet a with any normal octavo printing; it is what is to be expected from the divided sheet of a quarto. Whatever this makeshift arrangement might have been, it suggests that this edition was not set from a complete printed copy. It is possible that Royston's printer was working either from a second manuscript, or else from Irish sheets sent over as they were printed off for No. 40 A. This latter method would involve the text being set first, even in what was, in a sense, a reprint.

Copies: Bod, CUL, H, TCD; HH, I, Tex, US, Y.

40 C.   Third Printing. 1674.

See *Polemical Discourses,* 1674 (No. 28 B).

Notes: The text of this printing seems to have been set from the second edition (No. 40 B).

41 A.   *Seven Sermons.* First Edition. 1663. Wing T328.

General Title: [all within double rules] ἘΒΔΟΜᾺΣ ʼΕΜΒΟΛΙΜΑῖΟΣ, | A SUPPLEMENT | TO THE | ΕΝΙΑΤΤΟΣ, | Or Course of Sermons for the whole year: | BEING | SEVEN SERMONS | Explaining the Nature of Faith, and Obedience; | in relation to God and the Ecclesiastical and Secular | Powers respectively. | [rule] | All that have been Preached and Published | (since the Restauration) | *By the Right Reverend Father in God,* | JEREMY, | *Lord Bishop of* DOWN *and* CONNOR. | *To which is adjoyned,* | His Advice to the Clergy of his Diocese. | [rule] | *LONDON:* | Printed for *Richard Royston,* Bookseller to the Kings | most Sacred Majesty, 1663.

Coll: Quarto: Π², Nos. 38 B, 34 A, 35 A, 37 A, 39 C, 36 C; plates 1 (frontispiece before Π1). No accurate collation can be given because of the wide variation in make-up from copy to copy.

Contents: Π1ʳ, general title-page (verso blank); Π2, contents; *Righteousness Evangelical,* 1663 (38 B); *Consecration Sermon,* 1661 (34 A); *Parliament Sermon,* 1661 (35 A); *Via Intelligentiae,* 1662 (37 A); *Bramhall Funeral Sermon,* 1663 (39 C); and normally *Rules and Advices,* 1663 (36 C).

Variants: Copy BM lacks *Rules and Advices* (No. 36 C), and BM and H copies lack the frontispiece.

The BM and PCC copies have the second edition of the *Consecration Sermon,* 1663 (No. 34 B).

Notes: Seven Sermons was entered on February 15, 1663/4.

As was noted under *Righteousness Evangelical* (No. 38), it is possible that the preliminary two leaves of *Seven Sermons* may have been printed on one sheet with the first two leaves of the former work.

Copies normally have as a frontispiece an engraving by Hertochs of the royal arms. This was used with other works, and it often, but not always, appears with the *Second Dissuasive from Popery* (No. 45 A).

Two extra works appear in most copies. These are two writings by Jasper Mayne, *A Sermon Preached at the Consecration of . . . Herbert, Lord Bishop of Hereford . . . Printed for R. Royston . . .* 1662 (Wing M1478), and *Concio ad Academiam Oxoniensem . . . apud R. Royston . . .* 1662 (Wing M1469). This parasitical association is curious, and evidently an ideal copy would contain both these works.

Copies: BM, CO, H, J, PCC; Har, US.

41 B.   ?Second Edition. 1664. No Wing number.

[The title-page and contents leaf are exactly reprinted from the first edition (No. 41 A), the only alteration being the changed date to 1664.]

Notes: The main contents are the same as in the previous edition. This has the London edition of the *Consecration Sermon* (No. 34 B) and the Hertochs frontispiece. It seems probable that by some miscalculation, the general title-page and contents of 1663 had been used up, and since a few sets of the separate works remained, the extra pair of leaves were reprinted. The reprinting is so faithful as to reproduce a catchword inaccuracy at the foot of II2ᵛ from the first edition.

This edition also has two parasitical works, found in both recorded copies. The first is Mayne's *Consecration Sermon,* as in the first edition. The second is more obscure, but more interesting: *A Sermon preached at the Funeral of Mr. Lucas Lucie Merchant, October 23, 1663. By Nathaniel Waker, Rector of S. Catherin-Coleman Church in London . . . Printed for R. Royston . . . 1664* (Wing W280). Waker was an obscure, laborious, not quite untalented, close imitator of Taylor. The sermon is not far from being a paraphrase of the opening parts of *Holy Dying.* In one place even, Waker misquotes, with a marginal acknowledgement, as "the Elegant words of a most acute Prelate," Taylor's famous simile of the rose. The introductory epistle to this sermon is dated December 12, 1663.

Copies: Ex, H.

42 A. *A Dissuasive from Popery.* First Edition. Dublin, 1664. No Wing number.

Title: [all within double rules] A | DISSUASIVE | FROM | POPERY | To the People of | IRELAND. | [rule] | BY | Jeremy *Lord Bishop of* Down. | [rule] | *DUBLIN,* | Printed by *John Crooke,* Printer to the Kings Most | Excellent Majesty, and are to be sold by | *Samuel Dancer,* 1664.

Coll: Quarto: A⁴, a⁴, B-Z⁴, 96 leaves. Paged B1ʳ-Z4ʳ: pp. 1-173 [=175].

Contents: A1ʳ, blank; A1ᵛ, imprimatur; A2ʳ, title-page (verso blank); A3ʳ-a4ʳ, preface; a4ᵛ, blank; B1ʳ-Z4ʳ, text; Z4ᵛ, blank.

Notes: There is a paging error on U1, the recto being incorrectly 143 [=145] and the verso 144 [=146]. The paging then continues in error.

A second state of this edition, and its most common form, is for the title-page to appear without the enclosing double rules. In all other respects the two states are identical.

Copies: CD, ML, TCD.

42 B. Second Issue. 1664. Wing T319 and T320.

Title: [all within double rules] A | Dissuasive | FROM | POPERY | To the People of | IRELAND. | [rule] | By the Right Reverend Father in God | *JEREMY TAYLOR, D. D.* | Lord Bishop of *Down* and *Connor.* | [rule] |

Printed at *Dublin* by *John Crook,* Printer to the | KINGS most Excellent Majesty: | And Reprinted at *London* for *THO.* [capitals and small capitals] *JOHNSON*, at | the *Key* in St. *Pauls* Church-Yard, 1664.

Coll and *Contents:* [As in 42 A, except for the cancel title-page for this issue.] *Notes:* There is a second state of the cancel title-page of this issue, in which the imprint is modified to "Printed at Dublin by John Crook: and reprinted at London for Tho. Johnson."

The imprimatur is signed "Geo. Stradling" and is dated March 15, 1663.

Copies: AS, Bod (2), BM, CM, CUL, TCD; Cla, I, NL, NW, PU.

42 C. Second Edition ["Third"]. 1664. Wing T321.

Title: [all within double rules] A | Dissuasive | FROM | POPERY. | [double rules] | *By* JEREMY *Lord Bishop of* Down. | [double rules] | *The third Edition, revised and corrected* | *by the Author.* | [double rules] | *LONDON*: | Printed by *J. G.* for *Rich. Royston,* Bookseller to | the Kings most Excellent Majesty. | [centered rule] | *MDCLXIV.*

Coll: 8vo: A^8, a^8, B-T^8 V^4, 164 leaves; plates 2 (before A2, folding plate before B1). Paged B1^r-V3^v: pp. 1-294.

Contents: A1, blank; A2^r, title-page (verso blank); A3^r-a8^r, "The Preface to the Reader"; a8^v, contents; B1^r-V3^v, text; V4^r, advertisements (verso blank). *Notes: The Dissuasive from Popery* was entered on February 15, 1663.

The folding plate, before B1, is of five Jesuit fathers. The plate, normally found before A2, is the *Ecclesia Anglicana* plate by Hertochs, already discussed under *Polemical Discourses, 1674* (No. 28 B).

Four small alterations in the text and the correction of a few misprints were made between the first and second editions. Some of the alterations may be authorial. These few examples perhaps rescue the words "revised," etc. from complete mendaciousness. The authoritative sentence may have been put in by Royston to assert his rights against Thomas Johnson's London issue of the Dublin edition (Nos. 42 A and B).

Copies: BM, CUL, H; Har, HH, I, Tex, US, Y.

42 D. Third Edition ["Fourth"]. 1668. Wing T322.

A Dissuasive from Popery. The First Part . . . . The Fourth Edition, Revised and Corrected by the Author . . . . London, Printed by *E. Tyler,* for Rich. Royston . . . . MDCLXVIII. Quarto.

Copy CCC is a large paper copy bound up with a large paper copy of the *Second Dissuasive* (No. 45 A), and Rust's *Funeral Sermon.*

This edition was printed in quarto presumably in order that it might be bound up with the *Second Dissuasive* of the previous year. This is further indicated by the addition of "The First Part" to the title-page. No copies have been observed except bound up with the *Second Dissuasive.*

This edition, too, is described as revised and corrected, and again, two or three little alterations perhaps justify the claim.

Copies: BM, Bod, CCC, CUL, LS; Har, HH, I, KS, US, Y.

42 E. Fourth Printing. 1674.

See *Polemical Discourses,* 1674 (No. 28 B).

The plate of the Jesuit fathers, now much worn, appears on the internal title, which is dated 1673.

The work is again described as revised and corrected. One or two alterations do indeed appear; and the errata list corrects one Greek error which had persisted through all previous editions.

42 F. Fifth Edition. 1686. Wing T323.

A Dissuasive from Popery ... Together with II. Additional Letters to Persons changed in their Religion .... London, Printed for R. Royston ... MDCLXXXVI. 8vo.

This edition was advertised in the Term Catalogue for Easter and Trinity, 1686

At the end of this edition *Two Letters* (first published as a part of *Friendship,* 1657 (No. 29 A-B) are added.

Copies: BO, LS; KS, UC, Y.

43 A. *A Dissuasive from Popery* and *Confirmation.* Dublin, 1664. No Wing number.

General Title: [all within double rules] A | DISSUASIVE | FROM | POPERY | To the People of | IRELAND. | *To which is added,* | A Treatise of CONFIRMATION. | [rule] | BY | JEREMY *Lord Bishop of* Down. | [rule] | *DUBLIN,* | Printed by *John Crooke,* Printer to the Kings Most | Excellent Majesty, and are to be sold by | *Samuel Dancer,* 1664.

Coll: Quarto: Π¹, Nos. 42 A and 40 A. A composite volume.

Contents: Π1ʳ, general title-page (verso blank); *Dissuasive from Popery,* 1664 (42 A); *Confirmation,* 1663 (40 A).

Notes: Only one copy of this composite volume is preserved, and it seems questionable just how many copies were issued.

Copies: ML.

44 A. *Ten Sermons.* First Edition. 1667. Wing T308 and T310.

Title: [all within double rules] ΔΕΚΑΣ ΕΜΒΟΛΙΜΑΙΟΣ, | A | SUPPLEMENT | TO THE | ΕΝΙΑΤΤΟΣ, | Or Course of Sermons for the whole Year: | BEING | TEN SERMONS | Explaining the Nature of Faith, and Obedience, | in relation to God, and the Ecclesiastical and | Secular Powers respectively. | [rule] | All that have been Preached and Published | (since the Restauration) | By the Right Reverend Father in God | *JEREMY* Lord Bishop of *Down* and *Connor.* | WITH | His Advice to the Clergy of his Diocess |

[rule] | *LONDON,* | Printed for *R. Royston* Book-seller to the Kings Most Ex- | cellent Majesty. 1667.

Coll: Fol.: A⁴ B-T⁶ U², 114 leaves. Paged B1ʳ-U2ʳ: pp. 1-219.

Contents: A1ʳ, title-page (verso blank); A2ʳ, title for *Righteousness Evangelical* (verso blank); A3, dedication; A4ʳ, contents; A4ᵛ, imprimatur; B1ʳ-E5ʳ, text of *Righteousness Evangelical;* E5ᵛ, blank; E6ʳ, title for *Consecration Sermon* (verso blank); F1ʳ-F2ʳ, preface; F2ᵛ, blank; F3ʳ-G5ʳ, text of *Consecration Sermon;* G5ᵛ, orders to print; G6ʳ, title for *Parliament Sermon* (verso blank); H1ʳ-H3ᵛ, introduction; H4ʳ-I5ʳ, text of *Parliament Sermon;* I5ᵛ, blank; I6ʳ, title for *Via Intelligentiae* (verso blank); K1, introduction; K2ʳ-M1ʳ, text of *Via Intelligentiae;* M1ᵛ, blank; M2ʳ, title for *Bramhall Funeral Sermon* (verso blank); M3ʳ-O2ʳ, text of *Bramhall Funeral Sermon;* O2ᵛ, blank; O3ʳ, title for *Carbery Funeral Sermon* (verso blank); O4, dedication; O5ʳ, epitaph (verso blank); O6ʳ-Q2ᵛ, text of *Carbery Funeral Sermon;* Q3ʳ, title for *The Whole Duty of the Clergy;* Q3ᵛ, imprimatur; Q4ʳ-T1ᵛ, text of *The Whole Duty of the Clergy;* T2ʳ, title for *Rules and Advices;* T2ᵛ, contents; T3ʳ-U2ʳ, text of *Rules and Advices;* U2ᵛ, blank.

Notes: Ten Sermons was not entered in the Stationers' Register.

This is a reprint, in a single volume, of the sermons contained in *Seven Sermons* (No. 41), with the addition of the *Carbery Funeral Sermon* (No. 12) and two sermons never before published. These latter two sermons were never to appear outside this collection but were given the separate title, *The Whole Duty of the Clergy.* The internal title-page (Q3ʳ) is as follows:

[all within double rules] THE | Whole Duty | OF THE | CLERGY | IN | LIFE, BELIEF, | AND | DOCTRINE: |Described, and pressed effectually upon their Con- | sciences in Two Sermons on *Tit.* 2. 7. 8. | Preached in so many several | VISITATIONS. | [rule] | By the Right Reverend Father in God | *JEREMY* Lord Bishop of *Down* and *Connor.* | [double rule] | *LONDON,* | Printed for *R. Royston* Bookseller to the Kings Most Ex- | cellent Majesty. 1666.

It will be seen that a separate imprimatur was obtained for these two sermons. This rather suggests that it was originally intended to make a separate publication of them. It is not possible to date with any certainty the composition of these sermons. The matter and manner of them suggests that they were preached to clergy who had been recently inducted, in fact during the first two or three years of Taylor's episcopacy, when he had lately replaced, with Anglicans, the disposed presbyterians who could not acknowledge the rights of a bishop. Mr. Robert Gathorne-Hardy possesses an unpublished letter, with no date, written by Taylor to Lord Conway in Ireland; in it he says, "... I am (if the weather holds faire) going to visit the churches in Antrim up as farre as Colerane and so about to Glenarme and Caricfergus; to put all perfectly right, and to dispose the churches in order to execution of the act of Union and

Division of parishes, and towards our Quire at Lisburne." Lord Conway left Ireland during the late summer of 1664; the intended cathedral at Lisburne, which is mentioned in the letter, had not then been long proposed. It is fairly safe, therefore, to date this letter, with its allusion to the doubtful weather, in the late summer of 1663. The particular journey alluded to was one of Taylor's first after he had finally settled in the diocese, and it seems quite probable that the two sermons were preached during that season. As we have noted before, Taylor was, at this time, becoming diffident about the publication of his works, and this probably accounts for why they were not published until this late.

All internal titles are dated 1666, showing that the whole work was probably printed in that year. Since Taylor is not described as "late Lord Bishop" it was almost certainly published, or at any rate the printing was completed, before his death in August of 1667.

This volume is almost invariably found with the third edition of *Eniautos*, 1668 (No. 20 C). The NC copy is the only observed copy in an untouched contemporary binding.

Copies: BM, Bod, CUL, NC; Cla, I, RU, US.

44 B.   Second Edition. 1673. Wing T309.

ΔΕΚᾺΣ ᾿ΕΜΒΟΛΙΜᾶΙΟΣ . . . Eleven Sermons . . . Printed for R. Royston . . . . 1673. Fol.

Copy H, alone in a contemporary binding, has the integral internal title-page to Rust's *Funeral Sermon*. This is followed by the separate third edition of that sermon, complete with its title-page. It has advertisements on the verso of the last leaf; these are carelessly copied from the second and first editions of the work, and include ῾Εβδομάσ ᾿Εμβολιμᾶιοσ, the superseded *Seven Sermons*. Normally there are no advertisements in *Eleven Sermons*.

Although this is described in English on the title-page as "Eleven Sermons," the Greek title, becoming inaccurate, remains the same as in *Ten Sermons*.

This is essentially a reprint of the first edition, with the addition of the *Gunpowder Sermon* (No. 1). This sermon is added as sermon IX, making *The Whole Duty of the Clergy* sermons X and XI.

Clerus Domini, 1672 (No. 13 D) is also included at the end of the sermons and before *Rules and Advices*. At the end of *Rules and Advices* there normally follows Rust's *Funeral Sermon* (No. T 12). It continues consistently the paging begun afresh with *Clerus Domini,* that is, with the part of the book that does not contain sermons by Taylor.

Copies: H; I, US.

44 C.   Third Edition. 1678. No Wing number.

ΔΕΚᾺΣ ᾿ΕΜΒΟΛΙΜᾶΙΟΣ . . . Eleven Sermons . . . Printed by R. Norton for R. Royston . . . . 1678. Fol.

This, like the second edition, is normally found with *Eniautos* (No. 20 E) of that year.

Copies: [See "Copies" for No. 20 E.]

45 A. *Second Part of the Dissuasive from Popery*. First Edition. 1667. Wing T390.

Title: [all within double rules] The Second Part | OF THE | DISSUASIVE | FROM | POPERY: | In Vindication of | THE FIRST PART, | And Further | REPROOF and CONVICTION | OF THE | ROMAN ERRORS. | [rule] | By *Jer. Taylor* Chaplain in Ordinary to King *CHARLES* | the First, and late Lord Bishop of *Downe* and *Conner*. | [rule] | *Curavimus Babylonem & non est Sanata.* | [rule] | *LONDON*, | Printed for *R. Royston*, Bookseller to the Kings most | Excellent Majesty, at the Angel in S. *Bartholomew's* | Hospital, MDCLXVII.

Coll: Quarto: Π^2 $A\text{-}I^4$ K^2 A-2O⁴, ²A-²V⁴, 264 leaves. Paged A1ʳ-2O4ʳ: pp. 1-295; ²A1ʳ-²V4ʳ: pp. 1-159.

Contents: Π1ʳ, title-page (verso blank); Π2ʳ, contents; Π2ᵛ, imprimatur; A1ʳ-K2ʳ, introduction; K2ᵛ, blank; A1ʳ-2O4ʳ, text of Book I; 2O4ᵛ, blank; ²A1ʳ-²V4ʳ, text of Book II; ²V4ᵛ, blank.

Variants: Copy CCC is a large paper copy. This edition is bound up with large paper copies of the third edition of the first part of *Dissuasive* (No. 42 D) and Rust's *Funeral Sermon* (No. T 12). The leaves measure 9⅞ × 7¼ inches (a normal cut copy measures about 8 × 6¼). It has folded in as a frontispiece the Lombart portrait in its fourth state.

Notes: Although the title refers to Taylor as dead, the imprimatur is dated June 29, 1667, some six weeks before his rather sudden death. The book was entered in the Stationers' Register on the same day.

In all observed copies, the half-sheets Π and K are on thicker paper than is used in the rest of the preliminaries. They were clearly printed on a single whole sheet.

Sometimes the Hertochs print of the royal arms is found as a frontispiece, but not often enough to demonstrate that it was ever intended to be part of the work.

This work is very ofen found bound with the third edition of the first part of the *Dissuasive* (No. 42 D) and sometimes with the Dublin edition (No. 42 A).

In his *Funeral Sermon* Rust mentions Taylor's "*Disswasive from Popery . . .* and a *Vindication* of it (now in the Press) from some impertinent Cavillers, that pretend to answer Books, when there is nothing towards it, more than the very *Title-Page.*" We know of four writings by "impertinent Cavillers," and they will be found in the "Tayloriana" section of this bibliography. They are the anonymous *Letter to a Friend* (No. T20); *Diaphanta* (No. T21), whose author was probably J. V. Cane; Edward Worsley's *Truth Will Out* (No. T19); and John Sergeant's *Fourth Appendix to Sure-footing* (No. T22).

Taylor alludes in his text to "M. S."—presumably Sergeant, to "E. W."—

Worsley, and to "A. L."—perhaps the author of *Letter to a Friend*. Having completed the book, Taylor evidently decided that Sergeant needed a fuller answer, and this he provides in the "Introduction."

It would seem likely that the whole book was printed during Taylor's lifetime, and that he had corrected proofs of it. The reasons for this conjecture will be found in the *Notes* to the second printing below.

Copies: CCC, CM, LS; Cla, I, NW, PU, US, Y.

45 B. Second Printing. 1674.

See *Polemical Discourses,* 1674 (No. 28 B).

As with most other works printed in this volume, a number of errata are listed at the end. Several correct accidental misprintings. One of these is interesting. From a passage in the first edition, "infinite" is misprinted "infinitive"; this alone, being corrected in the errata, suggests that the text was carefully collated with the first edition. Far more significant are other corrections. Three amend in sense misprints present in the first edition; there are also two such corrections of original errors in Latin, and one in Greek.

In analyzing the errata leaf occasionally to be found with *Twenty-Eight Sermons* (No. 14 A), it was pointed out that their irregular arrangement suggests a series of corrections arriving in successive, separate lists from the author. It is extremely unlikely that Taylor could have seen the last printed sheets of the first edition. We would suggest that perhaps more than one set of proofs was sent out to him. After he had returned the corrected sheets, he discovered further errors in those which he had kept, and amendments to these were sent off too late to be used. The text of the 1674 *Polemical Discourses* strongly suggests that Royston had a set of Taylor's works with corrections, and that these were used for printing that volume.

46 A. *Christ's Yoke.* First Edition. 1675. Wing T295.

Title: [all within double rules] CHRIST'S YOKE | AN | EASY YOKE, | And yet the | *Gate* to *Heaven* a *Strait Gate.* | In two excellent | SERMONS, | Well worthy the serious perusal of | the strictest Professors. | [rule] | [all in black letter] By a Learned and Re- | [all in black letter] verend Divine. | [rule] | HEB. 11. 4. | *Who being dead, yet speaketh.* | [rule] | *LONDON*: | Printed for *F. Smith,* at the Eliphant and Castle | near the Royal Exehange in *Cornhil.* 1675.

Stet: Exehange

Coll: 8vo: A⁴ B-G⁸, 52 leaves. Paged B1ʳ-G4ʳ: pp. 1-87.

Contents: A1ʳ, blank; A1ᵛ, engraved portrait; A2ʳ, title-page (verso blank); A3ʳ-A4ʳ, "To the Reader"; A4ᵛ, blank; B1ʳ-G4ʳ, text; G4ᵛ-G6ᵛ, contents; G7-G8, blank.

Variants: Copies H and R have the preliminary half-sheet A reset. On the title-page lines four and five read: "An yet, | The Gate . . . ." Two advertisements are printed on the verso of A4, which profess to repudiate accusations, no doubt justifiable, of piracy.

Also in this variant state two words "doubt not" are spelled correctly whereas they are normally spelled "dout nobt."

Notes: This edition was advertised in the Hilary Term Catalogue for 1674/5.

The engraved portrait is a clumsy copy of that portrait which appeared in many of Taylor's works. Around the top of the oval frame is engraved "Dr IER TAYLOR OBIIT AVG. 13. 1667. [orn.]" The plate is signed "F. H. Van Houe." At the bottom of the page is the text "Wee Speak not great things, | But Live them. | Variety in Opinion & unity | In affection are not | Inconsistent. | Printed for F. Smith at ye Elephant & Castle in Cornhil."

It is generally accepted that these are indeed two of Taylor's early sermons. They were both used in *The Great Exemplar*. The first makes up rather more than half of Discourse XV in Part III. At the beginning, the subject is divided into five headings. In this book the work ends with the exposition of the third heading; the discourse in *The Great Exemplar* is complete, and it is clear that the manuscript used in this printing of 1675 was imperfect.

One passage in the 1675 printing was not used with the rest in 1649. On pp. 201-2 is a passage which deals with the repose of virtue and the miseries of ambition; this, in *The Great Exemplar,* was mosaicked into paragraph six of Additional Section VI, in Part I, where it is used to illustrate the turbulence of Herod's mind. Apart from this shifting of a passage, only one or two verbal differences from the text as it was printed in *The Great Exemplar* have been noticed. One of these readings in the first edition of 1649 is "Content . . . by stooping down makes the highest equal." In the second edition of 1653 it is "makes the lowest equal." In *Christ's Yoke* this is "makes the heights equal." This is no doubt a misreading for "highest"; however, it is strong evidence that the text was printed from a manuscript. Had this been in the nature of a fraud, the text would almost certainly have been taken from the latest edition. The third and fourth editions of *The Great Exemplar* have "lowest."

The case of the second sermon is very different. It is clearly, though short, a complete sermon in itself. But in this form it was never used in *The Great Exemplar*. Some half dozen or so passages from it, making about 50 lines in all, were inserted into a different composition, Section V of Part I, "Considerations concerning the Circumcision &c."

It is said in the preface that "By means of a Person of Honour yet living, they are now come into the Press for public use and benefit." Who that person was is beyond easy conjecture. The most probable answer is that the paper belonged to someone related, or connected, to the Earls of Northampton. Part II of *The Great Exemplar* was dedicated to Mary, Countess Dowager of Northampton. Here Taylor says, "I am now to present to your Honour part of that production . . . which was partly designed to satisfy [your] great appetites to vertue . . . Your Honour best knowes in what soyle the first designes of these papers grew, and but that that excellent personage who was their first roote is transplanted for a time . . . I am confident you would have received the fruits of his abode, to more excellent purposes. But because he was pleased to leave the managing of this to me, I hope your Honour will for his sake entertaine what that rare person *conceived,* though I was left to the paines and dangers of bringing forth."

It has been reasonably supposed that the "rare person" was the dead Earl of Northampton. If *The Great Exemplar,* containing, as it evidently does, many sermons of Taylor's was composed according to a plan suggested by that nobleman, it is far from unlikely that he possessed copies of many of those sermons as they were first delivered.

Copies: BM, Bod, CUL, DW, H, R; Col.

47 A. *On the Reverence Due to the Altar.* First Edition. Oxford and London, 1848.

Title: [all within single rules] On | The Reverence | Due to the Altar, | By | Jeremy Taylor, D. D., | Formerly Bishop of Down and Connor. | Now first printed from the original manuscript in the library of | Queen's College, Oxford. | Edited by the | Rev. John Barrow, M. A., | Fellow of Queen's College. | Oxford, | John Henry Parker; | and 377, Strand, London. | M DCCC XLVIII.

Coll: Quarto: a-b⁴, B-I⁴, 40 leaves; plates 1 (after I4). Paged a1ʳ-b4ᵛ: pp. i-xvi [pp. i-v and xvi unnumbered]; B1ʳ-I4ᵛ: pp. 1-64 [pp. 1, 54-57, and 64 unnumbered].

Contents: a1ʳ, half-title (verso blank); a2ʳ, title-page; a2ᵛ, imprint; a3ʳ-b4ʳ, preface; b4ᵛ, blank; B1ʳ-H3ʳ, text; H3ᵛ, blank; H4ʳ-I4ʳ, appendix; I4ᵛ, blank.

Notes: The plate is a lithographical facsimile of one page of the manuscript.

The volume was issued cut, in cloth. The spine is blank. On the front board is stamped in gold "On Reverence for the Altar. By Bp. Jeremy Taylor."

Charles Page Eden introduced this work into volume V of his revision of Heber's collected edition. At the beginning of the volume he says of this work, "Now first printed." However, the date on his title-page is 1849, and although it is possible that each version was set up independently from a different transcript, it can safely be taken for granted that the separate edition was published first.

This is the latest of Taylor's works to appear on its own, and it was quite possibly the earliest work written of those that have survived. The manuscript is among a collection left to Queen's College by Thomas Barlow, Bishop of Lincoln, the recipient of Sanderson's scandalized letter about Taylor's opinions on original sin (see under *Unum Necessarium,* No. 23). The work is in the form of a letter, and, like *Prayer Ex Tempore,* was probably left behind when

Taylor went away from the city forever, during the civil war. There is internal evidence that it was written before any troubles between King and Parliament, and before the system of episcopacy was violently challenged. In fact, it was probably composed about the same time as the *Gunpowder Sermon,* but whether a little later or a little earlier there are no means of deciding.
Copies: BM [copies are not scarce].

II

Works to Which Taylor Contributed

C 1. Wing N1110.

"The Copy of A Letter Written by a Divine, A Friend of the Author," An Apology for the Discipline of the Ancient Church . . . . By William Nicholson, Archdeacon of Brecon . . . . Printed for William Leake at the Crown in Fleet-street, betwixt the two Temple-gates. 1659.

Coll: Quarto: A⁴, *² 2*², B-2H⁴ 2I², 130 leaves.

Notes: This work was entered in the Stationers' Register July 17, 1658. Thomason's copy is dated November 4, and the year on the title-page is altered to 1658.

William Nicholson who, at the Restoration, became Bishop of Gloucester, was the third partner with Wyat and Taylor in their school at Newton Hall at Llanfihangel-Aberbythych, for which was composed *A New and Easie Institution of Grammar,* 1647 (No. 5 A). His monument is in Gloucester Cathedral.

Taylor's contribution to this work, the introductory letter, is signed "J. T." In concluding the letter, the author, who had evidently seen the book before publication, asks his correspondent "to send me a Copie into the farre distant place of my retirement." The style is Taylor's; two quotations will suffice. "First, the Apostles preached Jesus Christ and him Crucified, and every day winning souls to Christ did adopt them into his Body, and signed them to that Head; and there they had life and nourishment." "Now this Independant or Congregational way seems to me the *compendium* of humouring and pleas-ing all those little fellowes that love not, that endure not to be subject to their betters; for by this means a little Kingdome and a Royal Priesthood is provided for every one of them; a Kingdom of *Yvetot.*"

In the text of the book Taylor is mentioned in a marginal note on page 135, and on page 185, under the heading "The Communion-book-praying," Nichol-son says, "I refer you . . . especially to Dr. *Taylours* Preface before his Collec-tion of Offices; least I should draw a line after *Apelles.*"

Except for the passage just given, we are not aware that any of the Taylor material in this book has ever been reprinted.
Copies: Bod, Th; US.

C 2. Wing S5373.

"Epistle," ΘΑΝΑΤΑΛΟΓΙΑ, seu de Morte Dissertatio . . . . Authore Johanne Stearne, Medicinae Doctore . . . . Dublinii, Typis Gulielmi Bladen, & prostat venalis apud Georgium Sawbridg, sub signo Bibliorum, justa Fleetbridg, Londini, MDCLIX.
Coll: 8vo: (a)⁸, A-S⁸ T⁴, 156 leaves.
Notes: This work was not entered in the Stationers' Register. Thomason's copy is dated April.

Bladen, a Dublin printer, had printed Taylor's *Consecration Sermon* (No. 34), the first work he published in Ireland.

Sterne, or Stearne, was a grand-nephew of Archbishop Ussher; he founded the Irish College of Physicians. After the Restoration, when Taylor was re-organizing Trinity College, he recommended Sterne for a fellowship, in a letter dated December 19, 1660, to the Marquess of Ormonde, the Viceroy, asking for dispensation on the grounds that Sterne was married: "Dr. Stearne, whose great learning, and skill in the college affairs, we cannot want; and therefore though he was a married man, and lives in a house of the college very near it, yet we thought it fit to present him to your excellence, and the provost earnestly desires he may be admitted (at least till the affairs be quite settled) to this capacity of serving the college, and doing honour to it, in our great want of able men."

Taylor's introductory letter to this book, though not of much importance in itself, is interesting as one of the few surviving pieces of Latin written by him.
Copies: Bod, CD, CUL, E, ML, TCD, Th; Har.

C 3. Wing P4203.

"A Prayer before Sermon and A Prayer after Sermon," Pulpit Sparks, or Choice Forms of Prayer, By Several Reverend and Godly Divines, Used by Them, both Before and After Sermon . . . . Printed for W. Gilbertson at the Bible in Giltspur-street, 1659.
Coll: 12mo: [A]² (-[A]1) B-S¹² T¹ (=[A]1), (r)⁸, V¹² χ¹, 227 leaves.
Notes: This work was entered, to John Stafford, on February 7, 1654. Stafford's place of business was in George-Yard, near Fleet-bridge.

Heber, in 1822, printed Taylor's two prayers (Vol. XV, pp. 690-95), saying that they came from a copy of this book in the British Museum; this copy has since disappeared. Eden, in his new edition of Taylor's works, reprinted the prayers but gave the date as 1651, and this error has been blindly followed by most Taylor scholars.

Copies: TCC; Har.

C 4. Wing J504 and J508.

"Certaine Letters of Henry Jeanes, Minister of Gods Word at Chedzoy, and Dr. Jeremy Taylor, Concerning a Passage of his, in his Further Explication of Originall Sin," A Second Part of The Mixture of Scholastical Divinity . . . . by Henry Jeanes, Minister of Gods Word at Chedzoy in Somersetshire. Whereunto are Annexed, Several Letters of the Same Author, and Dr. Jeremy Taylor, Concerning Originall Sin . . . . Oxford, Printed by H. Hall, Printer to the University, for Thomas Robinson. 1660.

Coll: Quarto: a-b⁴, B-3H⁴, ²A-²K⁴ ²L⁴ (²L2+²L3'+²L3) ²M-²N⁴, 296 leaves.

Notes: Thomason's copy is dated March 26.

A brief passage of *A Further Explication* (No. 24) is quoted on 3C3ᵛ. This passage was the beginning of the controversy. There follows an undated letter from Jeanes to Mr. T. C., the mutual friend who brought the two divines into conflict. Next, a letter from Taylor to T. C., dated from London, July 4, 1657, followed by a letter from Jeanes to T. C., dated from Chedzoy, August 31, 1657. In this letter Jeanes says "I have heard that the Dr hath printed a very good Grammar, if he will also publish a Logicke . . . . I will very diligently peruse it." This letter was passed on to Taylor and, in Jeanes's words, "begat a very angry letter from him." The angry letter, which was addressed to Jeanes, follows, dated August 15, 1657. The rest of the tract is taken up by Jeanes anatomizing of the letter. Taylor signs himself "Sir, your affectionate Friend and Servant in the blessed Lord and Saviour Jesus." Jeanes, with less apparent charity, writes "In Christ Jesus your humble servant."

It has been suggested that Jeanes betrayed some malice in waiting to publish this prickly correspondence until early in 1660, when the Restoration had become probable. The conjecture is not an improbable one; such an attack on Taylor would have been more timely in 1657. Indeed, the collation itself smells of malice. The attack on Hammond, with which the second series of signatures begins, looks like an afterthought; the same may well be true of the correspondence with Taylor, coming as it does, rather irrelevantly, at the end of the main body of the book. And both of these high Anglicans are mentioned conspicuously on the title-page. Conforming ministers had become anxious, no doubt, to attack as soon as they could, and as openly as possible, important upholders of episcopacy.

The correspondence was reprinted by Heber in 1822, but Eden's revision

omitted Jeanes's last letter. Heber identified Mr. T. C. as Thomas Cartwright, but his grounds for this are not given.
Copies: Bod, Con (2), DC, TCD, Th; FU, Har, US (2).

C 5. Wing L1162 [Wing gives 1600, not 1660, as the date.]
"A Letter," A Discourse of Praying with the Spirit, and with the Understanding . . . . by Henry Leslie (maugre all Antichristian opposition) Bishop of Down and Connor . . . . Whereunto is annexed a Letter of Jer. Taylor, D. D. . . . London. Printed for John Crooke . . . . 1660.
Coll: Quarto: a⁴, A-E⁴, 24 leaves.
Notes: Thomason's copy is dated August 30, but this must have been some time after publication, for the book was clearly printed before the King's return in May, 1660.

This item is interesting partly for its early informal connection of Taylor with the See of Down and Connor. Henry Leslie was the author of a sermon called *The Martyrdom of King Charles,* preached and printed in the Hague in 1649 (Wing L1163). Lowndes rather wildly attributes this sermon to Taylor.
Copies: Th, TCD.

C 6. Wing R1354.
"A Friendly Letter," Abstracts of Some Letters Written by Mr. Robert Rich . . . . Together with a Friendly Letter of Dr. Jer. Taylor, to the said R. R. in Answer to One of His. Published by . . . . J. P. . . . London. Printed for Benjamin Billingsley . . . . 1680.
Coll: Quarto: A-C⁴ D², 14 leaves.
Notes: Rich was apparently a broad-minded merchant, resident of Barbadoes, who, to illustrate his charity of mind, gave sums of money for needy members of very different sects and churches. He chose Taylor as his agent for the Anglicans in the time of their greatest tribulation. Taylor's acknowledgement, which, with Rich's letter, is printed on A2ᵛ-A3ʳ (pp. 4-5), is dated February 13, 1657/8. After the fire of London, Rich made similar distributions, recorded in another tract, *Love without Dissimulation* (Wing R1361). The money, 30 pounds for each, was for the "Seven Churches of London," Roman, Anglican, Presbyterian, Independent, Anabaptist, Quaker, and Church of the First-born.

The "editor" was probably John Pennyman, since several of the copies are bound up with other tracts written or edited by him. Copy CUL is inscribed inside the back cover, "1706 March 29, dat mihi F. C. per J. P. ye author."
Copies: BM, Bod, CUL, FL; Cla, Har, Hav, SC.

C 7. Wing G822.

"Relation XXVI of Part II," Saducismus Triumphatus: or Full and Plain Evidence Concerning Witches and Apparitions . . . . By Joseph Glanvil . . . . London: Printed for J. Collins . . . . 1681.

Coll: 8vo: A⁴ B-R⁸ 2A-2Z⁸, 3A⁴, 310 leaves.

Notes: This work was entered on December 3, 1681, and was advertised in the Term Catalogue for Easter, 1681.

On page 276 of Part II (2Z5ᵛ) is Relation XXVI. This recounts the haunting of Francis Taverner by the ghost of James Haddock. These exciting events took place in Ireland, in Taylor's diocese. Taylor, in the company of Lady Conway, examined the tormented Taverner, and gave him a series of questions to put to the ghost. These, undoubtedly a composition of Taylor's, are printed in Glanvill's book. They produced no useful result, for when they were propounded to the ghost by its victim, "it gave him no answer, but crawled on its Hands and Feet over the Wall again, and so vanisht in white, with a most melodious Harmony." The ghostly catechism has been reprinted in modern times by more than one writer on Taylor.

Some writers have abused Taylor for the absurd credulity of these questions, and even for the impropriety of them. It has been suggested, on the other hand, that they implied a healthy common sense on his part, since they called in question the importance, and thus the existence, of the ghost. Being in the presence of his fantastic, mystical, credulous, and learned patroness, discretion and good manners alike would have forbidden his too obviously ridiculing the story. His questions read rather like a parody of a papist series of questions approved for exorcists in cases of possession; this diabolic catechism Taylor quotes with much humor in *A Dissuasive from Popery.*

This story was sent to Glanvill, through Henry More, by Thomas Alcock, who says that Taylor "commanded me, who was then Secretary to him, to write for *Taverner* to meet him." The following story, Relation XXVII, also given by Alcock, narrates the haunting by an old woman of David Hunter, a neat-herd employed by Taylor. Alcock supplied as well a third excellent story, the story of Mr. John Bourne, but it has no Taylorian associations.

Copies: BM, Bod, CUL, E, TCC; Har, HH, NL, PU, Tex, US, Y.

C 8. Wing P2436.

"Job's Curse," Harmonia Sacra; or, Divine Hymns and Dialogues: with a Thorow-Bass for the Theorbo-Lute, Bass-viol, Harpsichord, or Organ . . . . Printed . . . for Henry Playford . . . . MDCLXXXVIII.

Coll: Fol.: Π^2 a^2, B-X^2, 42 leaves.

Notes: There is a list of musical errata at the foot of a2^r. Five of these relate to Taylor's poem "Job's Curse."

The music in this work was edited by Purcell, who wrote most of it himself. On D1^v is "Job's Curse" set by Purcell. The heading is *"Words Translated by* Dr. Taylor, *Bishop of* Down *in* Ireland." This is the first printing of Taylor's paraphrase.

The two "Penitential Hymns" from the *Golden Grove* (No. 22) also appear in this volume, the first set by Pelham Humphryes, and the second by Purcell.

A good many of the poems out of *Harmonia Sacra* were reprinted in an anthology called *Miscellanea Sacra,* edited by Nahum Tate, and published by Playford in 1696 (Wing T195). In the preface, Tate says of the poems included, *"Some of 'em carry their Sanctions in the Names of their Authors; such as* Dr. Jeremy Taylor, Dr. Fuller, *Earl of* Roscommon, *and Others."* Taylor's poems in Tate's edition are the first penitential hymn and "Job's Curse."

This work has "Vol. I." on the title-page, but there was no second volume; the sheets were re-issued as the second edition, with additions at the end and a cancel title-page, in 1698 (Wing T196).

"Job's Curse" was reprinted in Willmott's biography (1848), and in Grosart's edition of Taylor's poems (1870).

This poem has no ascertainable history to explain how it got into Purcell's hands. However, there is a clue in the book itself. Four of the poems in *Harmonia* are by William Fuller, "late Lord Bishop of Lincoln." Fuller was a petty canon of Christ Church, Oxford, when Taylor was at All Souls' College; in the 1650s, being in great poverty, he kept a school at Twickenham, assisted by William Wyat, Taylor's old partner. At the Restoration he was made Dean of St. Patrick's, Dublin, and wrote them for that remarkable service when many bishops were consecrated, and Taylor preached. In 1662 he became Chancellor of Dromore, where Taylor was bishop. It is easy to imagine his possessing a copy of the poems, and Purcell probably received the text from Fuller, or his executors.

Copies: BM, Bod, H, MO, TCC; Cla, Har, HH, I, PU.

III

Printings of Taylor's Letters

L 1. An History of the Life of James Duke of Ormonde, From his Birth in 1610, to his death in 1688 . . . . In Two Volumes . . . . By Thomas Carte, M. A. . . . London, 1735.

Fragments of two letters appear in Volume II.

P. 208. Carte describes Taylor's capable re-establishment of the university at Trinity College. For this Carte relied on two letters written by Taylor to Ormonde on October 3, and December 19, 1660. Carte not only paraphrases these, but inserts, into his narrative, phrases and whole sentences exactly as Taylor wrote them. These letters were printed in full by Eden in 1854.

L 2. The life of . . . . Jeremy Taylor, D. D. By the Rev. Henry Kaye Bonney, M. A. . . . London, 1815.

Two letters by Taylor, and a fragment of a third, were first printed in this book.

Pp. 15-16. Letter from Taylor to his brother-in-law Dr. Langsdale. Bonney dates it November 24, 1643; C. J. Stranks (*Life and Writings of Jeremy Taylor,* 1952) says that it is dated 1653.

Loc: BM.

Pp. 253-55. Letter to unnamed recipient, probably Evelyn, dated February 22, 1656/7.

Loc: BM.

Pp. 275-76. Fragment of a letter to Sheldon. Printed in full by Heber.

L 3. Memoirs Illustrative of the Life and Writings of John Evelyn . . . . and a selection of his familiar letters . . . . The whole now first published, from the original MSS. In two Volumes. Edited by William Bray . . . . London, 1818.

Five letters from Taylor to Evelyn were first published in Volume II.

P. 151. Dated November 21, 1655.

P. 164. Dated April 16, 1656. Bray inaccurately dates it April 26.

    Loc: RB.

P. 172. Dated May 15, 1657.

P. 174. Dated June 9, 1657. A sentence is omitted from the middle of the letter; Heber followed this, and the letter was first printed in full by Eden.

P. 176 Dated February 17, 1657/8.

In the same volume there are also, on pages 148, 149, 166, 171, and 173, five letters written by Evelyn to Taylor. On page 157 is a letter written by Evelyn on Taylor's behalf to the Lieutenant of the Tower.

L 4. The Whole Works of the Right Rev. Jeremy Taylor, D. D. . . . . With a life of the Author . . . . by Reginald Heber, A. M. . . . . In Fifteen Volumes . . . . London, 1822.

Volume I of the collected edition contains Heber's biography of Taylor and the following letters were first published in this volume.

Pp. xliii-xliv. To Warner, from Mandinam, dated November 17, 1655.

Pp. xlvii-xlix. To Evelyn, dated St. Paul's Conversion, 1655/6.

Pp. xlix-l. To Sheldon. A sentence from this letter had already been published by Bonney (No. L 2).

    Loc: BM.

Pp. liii-liv. To Evelyn, dated July 19, 1656.

    Loc: RB.

Pp. lv-lvi. To Evelyn, dated August 23, 1656.

Pp. lvi-lvii. To Evelyn, dated November 15, 1656.

    Loc: GK.

Pp. lxviii-lxxi. To Evelyn, dated May 12, 1658. This letter is incomplete at the end.

Pp. lxxxiv-lxxxvi. To Evelyn, from Lisnegarvey, dated April 9, 1659.

    Loc: H.

Pp. lxxxvii-lxxxix. To Evelyn, from Portmore, dated June 4, 1659.

    Loc: PH.

Pp. xcii-xciii. To Evelyn, from Portmore, dated November 3, 1659.

Pp. xciv-xcv. To Evelyn, from Portmore, dated February 10, 1659/60.

P. cix. To Evelyn, from Dublin, dated November 16, 1661.

These further letters to Evelyn were eventually added to later editions of his diary.

L 5. The Life, Diary, and Correspondence of Sir William Dugdale . . . . Edited by William Hamper . . . . London, 1827.

Two letters from Taylor were first printed in this book.

Pp. 250-51. From Golden Grove, dated April 1, 1651. This letter is a fragment, being in a state described by the editor, exaggeratedly, as dimidiated; a strip has evidently gone from the left-hand side of the original.

P. 317. Dated November 22, 1656. The original was endorsed by Dugdale "Doctor Taylor's letter 22 November on receipt of my Booke of Warwickshire."

L 6. Memorials of the Great Civil War in England, from 1646 to 1652. Edited . . . . by Henry Cary, M. A. . . . London, 1842.

One letter by Taylor is first printed in Volume II of this book.

Pp. 75-100. To Dr. Richard Bayley, dated "The Vigils of Christmas, 1648." This is a private dissertation rather than a letter on the right of the King to alienate church lands. It is to be classed with *Prayer Ex Tempore* (No. 4), *Clerus Domini* (No. 13), and *On Reverence due to the Altar* (No. 47).

Loc: Bod.

L 7. Todd, J. H. "An Original Letter of Bishop Jeremy Taylor on Theological Studies." *The Irish Ecclesiastical Journal.* CII (January, 1849). 198-99.

Letter to Mr. Graham, fellow of Trinity College, Dublin. It was taken from a transcript in the commonplace book of Bishop Dopping in the library of Trinity College, Dublin.

L 8. The Whole Works of the Right Rev. Jeremy Taylor, D. D. . . . by the Right Rev. Reginald Heber, D. D. . . . Revised and corrected by the Rev. Charles Page Eden, M. A. . . . In Ten Volumes . . . . London, 1854.

In his revision Eden added a number of letters, which all appear in footnotes in Volume I.

P. xxxviii. To Sheldon, dated April 11, 1653.

Loc: Bod.

P. lvi. To Sheldon, dated January 19, 1655/6.

Pp. lxv-lxvi. To Evelyn, dated June 9, 1657. Five and a half lines are added in

this printing of the letter which had first appeared in print in 1818 (No. L 3).
P. lxvi. To an unnamed recipient, dated June 2, 1657.
    Loc: Bod.
P. lxxii. To Sheldon, dated December 19, 1657.
    Loc: Bod.
P. lxxvi. To an unnamed recipient, from Ivy Lane, dated March 21, 1657/8.
    Loc: Bod.
Pp. xciv-xcvi. Two letters to the Duke of Ormonde, from Dublin, dated October 3 and December 19, 1660. These letters had been paraphrased by Carte (No. L 1).
    Loc: Bod.
Pp. xcix-c. To the Duke of Ormonde, from Hillsborough, dated March 28, 1661.
    Loc: Bod.
Pp. ci-civ. Four letters, the first to the Duke of Ormonde, from Dublin, dated December 19; the second, with the same place and date, to Ormonde's secretary, Sir George Lane; the third to Ormonde, from Portmore, dated June 11, 1663; and the fourth to Ormonde, from Lisburne, dated "S. Stephen," probably 1666.
    Loc: Bod.
P. cvii. To the Duke of Ormonde, dated November 20, 1661.
    Loc: Bod.
Pp. cxix-cxx. To Sheldon, from Portmore, dated May 25, 1664.

L 9. Memorials of the Montgomeries, Earls of Eglinton. By William Fraser. Edinburgh, 1859.
    One letter by Taylor is printed in Volume II.
Pp. 313-14. To Hugh, 7th Earl of Eglinton, dated December 7, 1663.

L 10. *The Quarterly Review.* CXXXI (July, 1871). 60-77.
    One letter and brief extracts from eight others, all from the Murray transcripts and all addressed to Lord Conway, were first printed here.
P. 62. Dated April 17, 1658.
P. 63. Extract dated February 26, 1658/9.
    Extract dated April 9, 1659.
P. 64. Extract dated March 2, 1660/1.
    Extract dated January 2, 1660/1.
P. 65. Extract dated January 28, 1664/5.
P. 66. Extract dated April 9, 1659. cf. p. 63 *supra*

Extract dated February 26, 1658/9. cf. p. 63 *supra*
P. 67. Extract from undated letter.

L 11. Correspondence of the Family of Hatton, edited by Sir Edward Maunde Thompson. 2 vols. London, 1878.
    One letter was printed in Volume I.
Pp. 26-27. To Christopher, Lord Hatton, from Dublin, dated November 23, 1661. The letter is also briefly mentioned and extracted in the Appendix to the *First Report of the Historical Manuscripts Commission*, 1874, p. 20.
    Loc: BM.

L 12. Historical Manuscripts Commission, The Manuscripts of . . . the Duke of Rutland . . . . London, 1889.
    One letter by Taylor is printed in Volume II.
P. 5. To the Countess of Rutland, from Annesley, dated June 21, 1658.
    Loc: Belvoir Castle.

L 13. An Ulster Parish: being a History of Domaghcloney (Waringstown). By Edward Dupré Atkinson. Dublin, 1898.
P. 28. To William Warren, dated June 16, 1662.
    Loc: Dro.

L 14. Lawlor, H. J. "Two Letters of Jeremy Taylor," *Church of Ireland Gazette*. XLIII (June 14, 1901). 482-83.
    Two letters are printed in this article.
To Captain Charles Twig, from Hillsborough, dated October 22, 1660.
    Loc: H.
To Hugh, Viscount Montgomery, from Hillsborough, dated October 27, 1660.
    Loc: Bod.

L 15. English Literary Autographs. Ed. W. W. Greg. Oxford, 1932.
Item XC. To Christopher, Lord Hatton.
    Loc: BM.

L 16. The Life and Writings of Jeremy Taylor by C. J. Stranks . . . . London, 1952.

In this book were first published a number of extracts from the Murray transcripts, first publicly mentioned in *The Quarterly Review* (No. L 10).

Pp. 182-83. Dated April 17, 1658.

Pp. 186-87. Extracts from a letter dated April 24, 1658.

Pp. 191-92. Extracts from a letter dated February 26, 1658/9.

Pp. 192-93. Extracts from a letter dated March 10, 1658/9.

Pp. 193-95. Dated April 9, 1659.

Pp. 225-26. Extracts from a letter dated January 2, 1660/1.

Pp. 233-34. Extracts from a letter dated March 2, 1660/1.

P. 234. Extract from an undated letter.

P. 249. Extracts from a letter dated June 18, 1662. Stranks erroneously dates it January.

Pp. 258-59. Extracts from a letter dated January 28, 1664/5.

P. 269. Extracts from an undated letter.

P. 270. Extracts from a letter, from Portmore, dated Lammas, 1666.

IV

Tayloriana—Suppositious Works

T1. A Discourse of Auxiliary Beauty. Or Artificial Hansomeness . . . .
Printed for R. Royston . . . . 1656. 8vo. (Wing T1593).

This work was entered in the Stationers' Register on November 26, 1655.

The work is a moral dialogue about cosmetics between two ladies, one evidently of the cavalier party, and the other a puritan, who has the worst of it. The publisher's introduction begins, "This Discourse (of which, as I am certainly informed a Woman was not only the chief occasion, but the Author and Writer)—"; its attribution to Jeremy Taylor is among the prime oddities of the history of English letters. In the first edition of *Athenae Oxonienses,* the book is attributed impartially to Taylor and John Gauden. In the second edition, while still remaining among Gauden's works, it was removed, with two other falsely attributed works, from the list of Taylor's books.

The second edition of *Artificial Hansomeness* (1662), after first appearing separately, was bound up with a book called ΠΕΡΙΑΜΜΑ ΈΠΙΔΉΜΙῸΥ: *or Vulgar Errors in Practice Censored* (Wing W408), an imitation of Sir Thomas Browne. In the British Museum Catalogue, this is attributed to Obadiah Walker, an acquaintance of John Evelyn's, and long suspected, not without reason, of secret popery. This attribution was evidently made because the BM copy is bound up, with a general title, in the same volume as *Instruction concerning the Art of Oratory* (Wing W410) by Walker. A similar line of thought has led to the occasional attribution to Walker of *Artificial Hansomeness,* a temporary stable companion of *Vulgar Errors Censured.*

Gauden is still a possible author. The third edition (1692) has, for the first time, an "Epistle Dedicatory To All the Fair Sex"; this speaks of the author as "supposed to be a Learned Bishop," a statement which does not necessarily exclude Gauden. Indeed, in the British Museum there is a copy of this third edition, with a manuscript note assigning the "following Frothy Metaphorical Book" to Gauden.

A curious legend has helped to perpetuate the false association of this book with Taylor. In a copy of the fourth edition (1701), in the British Museum, there is a nineteenth-century manuscript note affirming that there is at Trinity College, Cambridge, a copy of the second edition, bearing on the title the initials "J. T. D. D." Although this tradition has been followed by Heber and many other Taylor scholars, there is no such volume in the Trinity College Library.

T 2. Christian Consolations Taught from Five Heads in Religion . . . . Written by a Learned Prelate . . . . London, Printed for R. Royston . . . . 1671. 12mo. (Wing C3943).

In the first, but not the second, edition of *Athenae Oxonienses,* this is listed among Taylor's works. In the Bodleian copy, a manuscript note on the title-page assigns it to Taylor. On the title-page of the Christ Church College copy, there has been written in a seventeenth-century hand, "Dr. Hackett. Bp. of Cov. & Litchfield." The Trinity College, Cambridge, copy is inscribed on the fly-leaf, in an old hand, "Written by Bishop Hackett," and "Bishop Hackett" is written on the title-page and corrected in pencil to "Jeremy Taylor." Heber included *Christian Consolations* in his collected edition, apparently only on the strength of the note in the Bodleian copy. He makes the suggestion, which has been repeated in modern times, that the book was written by Taylor especially for Lady Conway.

In 1848 there was issued a pamphlet, *A Letter to Joshua Watson, Esq. D. C. L. giving an account of a singular literary fraud practised on the memory of Bishop Jeremy Taylor* by Edward Churton, M. A. Archdeacon of Cleveland (the larger importance of this little work will be gone into more fully under the next heading, T 3, *Contemplations on the State of Man*). On page 4 is this sentence: " 'Christian Consolations' which had, as long ago as the year 1825, awakened the theological acumen of the memorable Alexander Knox, to reject it from the genuine productions of Taylor, has since been ascertained, by the diligence of a divine well-read in the theology of the seventeenth century, the Rev. James Brogden, to be the undoubted work of the worthy Bishop Hackett, the restorer of the cathedral of Litchfield." In the Bodleian Library this pamphlet has been bound up, under the title *Pseudo-Tayloriana,* with some manuscript notes on *Christian Consolations.* These show a number of quotations from the book in question, together with remarkable parallels from the acknowledged works of Hackett. Furthermore, Mr. Gathorne-Hardy has been lucky enough to discover external confirmation of Hackett's authorship by getting hold of a copy of Ralph Cudworth's *Intellectual System,* published by Royston in 1678 (Wing C 7471). At the end of his copy, two leaves of advertisements in proof have been bound in. Among the books listed is *Christian Consolations* "Written by the Right Reverend Father in God John Hackett, late Lord Bishop of *Leichfield* and *Coventry*." We do not know if these advertisements were ever published in this form.

The false attribution may come from a Thomas Hackett, of Trinity College, Dublin, who was made D. D. at Oxford in 1660, according to Wood. He afterwards became Bishop of Downe. The transfer of name and See would be an easy enough confusion.

T 3. Contemplations on the State of Man . . . . By Jeremy Taylor, D. D. . . . London: Printed for John Kidgell, and are to be sold by Dorman Newman, at the King's-Arms in the Poultry. 1684. 8vo.

This edition was advertised in the Hilary Term Catalogue for 1684. A second edition was issued in the same year.

For about a century and a half it never seems to have been doubted—at least not publicly—that this was an authentic and original work by Jeremy Taylor. The style of the work does bear an astonishing likeness to Taylor's, but the crude threatenings of a vivid hell are less in character. Heber accepted its authenticity but evidently read it with distaste.

In 1848, Churton published the pamphlet already noted in No. T 2. He showed that the book was not original, but a mosaic of passages translated from a Spanish devotional work, *De la Diferencia entre lo Temporal y Eterno* (1640), by the Jesuit Juan Eusebio Nieremberg. The book was very popular, being soon translated into several languages, and in Spain, to this day, is rarely out of print. Churton goes on to assert that, not only was *Contemplations* in substance a translation, but that it was put together from an English translation already in existence, namely *A Treatise of the Difference between the Temporal and Eternal....translated into English by Sir Vivian Mullineaux, knight* (Wing N1151). This version was published in 1672, some five years after Taylor's death. In developing his case, Churton, with excess indignation, showed, in almost the only quotations he gave, "how the forger mutilated and disguised his materials"; the verbal similarities given here are little more than could be due to a common origin. Other parallels are indicated, without quotations, with tables of page references.

Although Churton had proved that *Contemplations* was not original, he failed to establish that it was made up from Mullineaux's version. Accordingly, in 1930, Mr. Gathorne-Hardy expressed a tentative belief that *Contemplations* might well be Taylor's, or at least put together from a translation carried out by Taylor. Churton believed that Taylor could not read Spanish. But as was shown under *Deus Justificatus* (No. 26), not only did he quote Spanish but even corrected Spanish misprints in the errata. Henry Vaughan translated a short work by Nieremberg, and it is possible that Taylor was acquainted with Vaughan.

Comparison of *Contemplations* with the Spanish original shows many parallels to passages in Taylor's authentic writings, and many more parallels are to be found in the parts of the Spanish work which were not used in *Contemplations*. There is a strong possibility that Taylor had read *Diferencia*, and almost certainly in Spanish. The apparent influence is most evident in *Holy Dying* and the Golden Grove sermons. However, comparison of *Contemplations* with Mullineaux's translation very soon made it evident that Churton had been right. Long passages from Mullineaux are reproduced word for word in *Contemplations*. Such large identical readings could not possibly be due to a common foreign original, but are quite obviously parts of the same translation.

Contemplations appeared in further editions in 1692, 1699, 1702, 1707, and 1717. There was also a Welsh translation, *Ystyriaethau o Gyflwr Dyn . . . . O Waith y Gwir Barchedig Dad yn Nuw Jer. Taylor . . . . Printiedig, yng Nghaer-ileon, gan Roger Adams*, published in either 1724 or 1740; dating of the book differs widely.

T 4. A Form of Consecration or Dedication of Churches and Chappels . . . . Dublin, printed by John Crooke . . . . 1660. Quarto. (Wing F1566).

In Appendix A, Stranks (*Life and Writings of Jeremy Taylor*, 1952) says that *A Form of Consecration* was added to the quarto edition of the Irish Prayer Book, printed in Dublin in 1700, and it is included in modern editions of the Irish Prayer Book. He adds, "The authorship of the form, and the authority by which it was added to the Prayer Book, are both unknown." The Rev. F. R. Bolton, Vicar of East Markham, Nottinghamshire, has made an exhaustive examination of the Rite and is of the opinion, on stylistic and theological grounds, that it is the work of Jeremy Taylor (*The Caroline Tradition of the Church of Ireland*, 1958, pp. 251-297).

It is not at all impossible that Taylor should have written such a service. He was very active in restoring and building churches in his diocese. In the case of such a work as this it would be customary to publish the service anonymously; the absence of Taylor's name in the title is not, therefore, as it might be in other cases, a ground for rejecting his authorship. Contemporary silence seems a larger obstacle. Had Taylor composed the whole service it would surely have been mentioned by Rust in his funeral sermon. The fact that the prayers are consistent with Taylor's theological views carries little weight, since most Irish divines of this time had the same beliefs.

There remain the stylistic grounds, by which, in our opinion, the attribution must stand or fall. Even here there are more than ordinary difficulties. In the preface to *Ductor Dubitantium*, Taylor says, "the style that I here use is according as it happens, sometimes plain, sometimes closer . . . . I was here to speak to the Understanding, not to winne the affections, to convert, not to exhort." Although by "style" he probably meant something slightly different from what we do, he was speaking of the new style of the Restoration. The effect on his own writings was such that, with the exception of his funeral sermon on Bramhall, his Irish writings look forward to a future simplicity, rather than back to his old elaborate splendors. Now the latest prayers which he is certainly known to have written were published in *The Worthy Communicant,* a book in which his glories appear with a fainter light. And yet the prayers in it have a greater warmth and enthusiasm than any part of the work in question.

The prayers in *A Form of Consecration* fall very far short in beauty from those which are scattered through his works. Only two, the first and the last in the service, have the authentic ring. In the latter there significantly occurs "we beseech thee to take away from us all pride and prejudice." This expression was one of Taylor's favorites, and he was fond of repeating it in his writings (e.g., *Holy Dying* and *Liberty of Prophesying*). But even these two prayers lack the warmth and beauty of Taylor's best liturgical writings.

V

Tayloriana—Biographical and Critical

T 5. The Copies of Two Letters Written by two friends . . . . Concerning a pretended Dispute had betwixt Doctor Taylor . . . . and Master Alexander Henderson . . . . London, Printed Aprill 11. 1643. Quarto. (Wing T307).

This account, it may be imagined, did not favor the young doctor (other allusions to Taylor, and this encounter, are to be found in the periodical *Mercurius Aulicus* and also the rival *Mercurius Britannicus*), for it was written from the presbyterian side to put him in his place.

T 6. God Appearing to Parliament in Sundry Late Victories bestowed upon their Forces . . . . Printed at London for Edw. Husbands, March 10. 1644. Quarto (Wing G906).

This work mentions the capture of Taylor by parliamentarian forces in front of Cardigan Castle (see also *The True Informer*, No. 65, February 1-8, 1644/5). This is one of the few pieces of evidence about Taylor's life during the time after he left Oxford and before he became established in Wales. A curious piece of "evidence" about the lost years in Taylor's biography is found in Walter Money's *The First and Second Battles of Newbury*, Second Edition (London, 1884). Money says, "Dr. Jeremy Taylor . . . . is reported to have been present at the first engagement at Newbury . . . consoling the wounded . . . . He . . . is said to have 'laid the foundation' of several works in defence of Episcopacy during his service with the army." Unfortunately, Money cites no source for his information, and in his copy of the first edition, now in the Reading Public Library, prepared with manuscript additions for the second edition, this is the only addition for which he does not give a source.

One of the royalist officers at Newbury was Colonel Charles Gerard, who succeeded the Earl of Carbery as royalist commander in Wales in 1644. The deduction is almost irresistible that Taylor left Oxford, late in 1642, as a chaplain under Gerard and that it was by the transfer of Gerard to Wales that Taylor first made his way there.

T 7. Dr. Hollingsworth's Defence &c. . . . London: Printed for Samuel Eddowes . . . . 1692. Quarto. (Wing H2503).

This work is listed in what appears to be a violation of our chronological sequence because it deals with Taylor's participation in the production of ΕΙΚΩΝ ΒΑΣΙΛΙΚΝ. *The Portraiture of His Sacred Majesty* (1648/9). When, toward the end of the century, the authenticity of the King's Book was being questioned Hollingsworth was among those who defended it. In his *Defence* there is an affidavit signed by James Clifford. This tells that Royston was intending to call the book *The Royal Plea*, "but," it goes on, "Dr. Jeremiah Taylor, coming accidentally to Mr. Royston's shop . . . he told him that the Title would betray the book." Taylor, the account goes on, suggested the famous title, and wrote to the King for the approval which he gave.

T 8. The Church-history of Great Britain; from the Birth of Jesus Christ, Untill the Year M. DC. XLVIII. Endeavoured by Thomas Fuller. London, Printed for John Williams . . . . Anno. 1655. Fol. (Wing F2416).

In Book IV, p. 182, while treating of All Souls' College, Oxford, Fuller says, "Know Reader, I was promis'd by my respected friend, Dr. *Jeremy Taylor,* (late Fellow of this house) well known to the *world* by his worth, a Catalogue of the Eminent Scholars thereof; but it seems the *Press,* (like *Time* and *Tide*) staying for no man, I have not been so happy seasonably to receive it." Beyond this tantalizing sentence, nothing is known of the friendship between these two great writers and famous divines.

T 9. A Declaration of the Nobility and Gentry that adhered to the late King in and about the City of London. 1660. brs. (Wing D716).

The declaration is followed by a large number of signatures, among which is "Jeremiah Taylor, D. D."

T 10. The Proceedings observed In Order to, and in the Consecration of the Twelve Bishops at St. Patricks Church Dublin On Sunday the 27 of January

1660 . . . by Dudley Loftus . . . . London, Printed by J. C. for John Crook . . . .
1661 Quarto. (Wing L2826).

Dudley Loftus has already been mentioned, chiefly under *The Great Exemplar,* 1657 (No. 9 D). Since this pamphlet is scarce and obscure, we have reprinted here those passages which refer to Taylor.

> The Office of Common Prayer was then Celebrated by the Dean of the said
> Church . . . . which ended, Dr. *Jeremiah Taylor,* Lord Bishop Elect of *Down*
> designed to preach the *Concio ad Clerum* did ascend the Pulpit, during the
> singing of the *praeveni nobis.*

> After the said Bishop of *Down* had ended his Sermon he was conveyed by
> the Virger to his Stall.

> Upon his Lordships descent from the Pulpit an Anthem was sung.

> The Bishop of *Downe*'s Sermon was such as gave great and general Satisfaction, being elegantly, religiously, and prudently composed, and so convincingly satisfying the judgments of those who have opposed the order and
> jurisdiction of Episcopacy, as that the Lords, Justices, the Lord *Primate,* and
> the general Convention have all of them severally ordered and desired the
> speedy impression therof, which is the cause that no more shall be said in this
> place of Commendation, it being soon to appear in the lustre of its own
> excellency.

It is to be noted that a portion of the last paragraph was too optimistically
phrased. Too many in Taylor's own diocese were still to oppose the order and
jurisdiction of Episcopacy.

The words of the anthem were composed by William Fuller, then Dean of
St. Patrick's, of whom mention was made under *Harmonia Sacra* (No. C 8).

T 11.   A Pandarique Elegie Upon the death of the R. R. Father in God
Jeremy Late Lord Bishop of Downe, Connor, and Dromore. By Le. Mathews
. . . Dublin, Printed by John Crooke . . . . 1667. Quarto. (Wing M1289).

The author was Lemuel Mathews, Archdeacon of Down. The poem was
not adequate to the occasion, as can be seen from the last two lines:

> Bishop elect! there shortly shall be given
> To thee a Diocess in the large Hierarchy of Heaven.

T 12. A Funeral Sermon Preached at the Obsequies of the Right Reverend Father in God, Jeremy Lord Bishop of Down .... By Dr. George Rust, Dean of Connor. London, Printed by E. Tyler for Richard Royston .... 1668. Quarto. (Wing R2362).

Rust's *Funeral Sermon* was entered in the Stationers' Register on November 7, 1667, and was probably published about that time. It is evident from various of Taylor's works, that Royston often gave his winter publications the date of the coming year. The *Imprimatur,* signed "Tho. Tomkyns," is dated October 26, 1667.

A page of advertisement is devoted to Taylor's works (F2ᵛ). All but one are listed as he finally perfected them, except for *The Psalter of David* (No. 3) and the *Grammar* (No. 5) which are not listed. Even *The Worthy Communicant* (No. 33) is there, "Printed for J. Martin." The exception is *Seven Sermons* (No. 41), which is listed although it had been superseded by *Ten Sermons* (No. 44 A) in 1667. The second edition of *A Dissuasive from Popery* (No. 42 C) is advertised.

In this work Rust achieved what might well have been thought impossible; he preached a funeral sermon worthy of Jeremy Taylor. Modelling his work on his master's, he begins with a beautiful hortatory section; the biographical section which follows, in spite of requisite eulogistic qualities, remains at once an acute estimate of Taylor's work, and an accurately vivid picture of him.

Rust had been, while at Cambridge, a close friend of many of the Cambridge Platonists, particularly More. Taylor's choice and promotion of Rust was typical of his latitudinarian ways; Rust, like his associates Glanvill and Henry More, was inclined to believe in reincarnation, a tenet which, however piously held, hardly accords with the orthodox teaching of the Anglican Church.

There was a second edition in 1668, this time in folio.

T 13. Athenae Oxonienses .... London: Printed for Tho. Bennet .... MDCXCI-MDCXCII. Fol. (Wing W3383A).

In Volume II is to be found Wood's life of Taylor, containing some facts or assertions not to be found elsewhere. Wood supplied also a surprisingly complete list of Taylor's works, including some attacks on them, and four spurious writings. In the second edition of 1721, Wood omitted three of these works, namely *Artificial Hansomenesse, Christian Consolations,* and *Contemplations on the State of Man.* This correction has escaped the notice of many who were too much impressed by the evidence, such as it is, in favor of these apocryphal works.

VI

Tayloriana—Attacks on Taylor's Works

T 14. A Free Disputation Against pretended Liberty of Conscience . . . . By Samuel Rutherford . . . . London, Printed . . . . for Andrew Crook . . . . MDCIL. Quarto. (Wing R2379).

This book has already been mentioned under *Liberty of Prophesying* (No. 6). It has plausibly been asserted that Milton's "On the New Forcers of Conscience under the Long Parliament" was written on the publication in 1644 of Rutherford's *The Due Right of Presbytery* (Wing R2378). It seems possible, on the other hand, that, had this been the case, the sonnet would have been published in the 1645 edition of Milton's poems, whereas it did not appear until the second edition of 1673. It may also be doubted whether the term "long parliament" would have been used so early as 1644, though the title might have been added later. It seems as likely that Milton was referring to *A Free Disputation*. Heber referred to this work, no doubt with justice, as "perhaps the most elaborate defence of persecution which has ever appeared in a Christian country."

The title-page is usually a cancel. When it appears in its uncancelled state Taylor's name and degrees are given as "Dr. Jer. D. Taylor."

T 15. A Letter of Resolution to Six Quaeres . . . . By Henry Hammond, D. D. . . . Printed by J. Flesher for R. Royston . . . . 1653. 12mo. (Wing H545).

One section of this book is devoted to answering propositions propounded, although not preached and approved, by Taylor. The sixth "quaere" answered concerns the Anglican doctrine of the baptism of infants. In mentioning arguments against the orthodox position, Hammond says, "of these . . . the most diligent Collection I have met with, is that of my *worthy* friend, *Dr. Jer. Taylor,* in his *Book* of *Liberty* of *Prophesying,* where he hath so *impartially* inforced the *arguments* of his *adversaries,* that I know not where to furnish myself with so *exact* a *scheme,* and shall therefore upon that one account, choose to follow that *path* which he hath traced before me." As can be seen by this passage, the book was an attack in only a rhetorical sense. Taylor and Hammond had been good friends, and continued to be.

This part of the book was answered by the seemingly amiable Anabaptist, John Tombes, probably in the second part of his *Anti-paedo Baptism* in 1654 (Wing T1799). Hammond rejoindered with a quarto pamphlet, *The Baptizing of Infants Reviewed and Defended from the exceptions of Mr. Tombs,* published by Royston in 1655 (Wing H515A). The second chapter of this work is headed "The Doctor's pretended concessions examined"; the doctor is, of course, Taylor.

A Letter of Resolution has introduced a curious error into Taylor's biography. Charles I expressed a qualified disapproval of *Liberty of Prophesying;* Hammond was an intimate and trusted chaplain of the King's, whom he was allowed to attend in his closest imprisonment; Hammond, in the present work, answered Taylor's postulated defense of the anabaptists; and in the second printing of *Liberty of Prophesying,* 1657 (No. 6 D), Taylor added a long modification of these postulations. From these four facts several students, Gosse among them, have conceived the idea that the King ordered Hammond to answer Taylor's work as a plea for religious toleration. There is no evidence for this at all, either in Hammond's works or among the known facts of his life. Furthermore, the answer by Hammond seems to have been carried out with Taylor's affectionate approval. In the preface to *A Discourse of Baptism,* 1652 (No. 17 A), it is said that Taylor had considered a separate publication of that work unnecessary "because he hath understood that his very worthy friend Dr. *H: Hammond* hath in his charity and humility descended to answer that Collection; and hopes, that both their hands being so fast clasped in a mutual complication, will do some help and assistance to this Question, by which the Ark of the Church is so violently shaken."

T 16. An Antidote against Anabaptism . . . . by Jo. Reading, B. D. and sometimes student of Magdalen Hall in Oxford . . . . Printed by Tho. Newcomb, for Simon York, and Richard Barkey, dwelling in Dover, 1654. Quarto. (Wing R444).

John Reading, born in Buckinghamshire in 1588, came, according to Wood, of "sufficient parents." He was ordained in 1614. He was chaplain to Lord Zouch, Lord Warden of the Cinque Ports, and governor of Dover Castle. At the request of many citizens he was given the ministry of St. Mary's in that town, and he later became one of the King's Chaplains. Though puritan in his tenets, he was loyal to the King. On the discovery of a royalist plot to capture Dover Castle, he was seized at night, and hurried off to imprisonment in Leeds. After a long imprisonment his goods, but not his benefices, were restored to him. No doubt his Calvinistic leanings were helpful, and he was commissioned by the Assembly of Divines to help in the preparation of a commentary on the New Testament (not going to press until 1666, the commentary was lost in the Great Fire of London). In 1650 he publicly disputed against an anabaptist named Fisher in the church at Folkstone. Fisher drew many of his arguments from *Liberty of Prophesying*. After the debate, Wood tells us, "Reading thought himself obliged to answer several passages in the said book of Dr. Taylor, which gave too great a seeming advantage to Fanaticism and Enthusiasm." The result was *An Antidote*.

When Charles II landed in 1660, Reading delivered a short speech of welcome, and presented him, on behalf of the corporation of Dover, a large Bible with gold clasps. He died in 1667.

A second issue of *An Antidote* appeared in 1655 (Wing R443).

T 17. Sapientia Justificata . . . . by John Gaule . . . . printed for N. Paris and Tho. Dring . . . . 1657. 12mo. (Wing G378).

John Gaule was an unlearned ranter, according to the *DNB*, who courted both royalist and commonwealth authorities in turn hoping for preferment. However, a little charity must be allowed in that he says of Taylor, "he hath erred learnedly, far unlike the many sensless and scurrilous Hereticks and Schismaticks of this our exulcerated age."

T 18. Vindiciae Fundamenti: Or a threefold defence of the Doctrine of Original Sin . . . . by Nathaniel Stephens, Minister of Fenny-Drayton in Leicestershire . . . . Printed by T. R. and E. M. for Edmund Paxton . . . . 1658. Quarto. (Wing S5452).

Thomason's copy is dated April 24.

A note on the errata leaf (bound in between a3 and a4) apparently apologizes for discussing Taylor last in the book: "I have not followed so much the order of persons, as the order of time." For all this implicit deference, Stephens is not too charitable to Taylor. "Many," he says, "are likely to be taken with the purity and elegancy of his style, that probably are not able to judge of the foulenesse and impurity of his Doctrine."

T 19. Truth Will out: or, A Discovery of some Untruths Smoothly told by Dr. Jeremy Taylor In his Disswasive from Popery . . . . By his Friendly Adversary E. W. . . . Printed, in the Year, 1665. Quarto. (Wing W3618).

The author was an English Jesuit named Edward Worsley. He was born in 1605 and entered the Society of Jesus in 1620. He became rector of the English College at Liege in 1652, and died in 1672. *Truth Will Out* appears to have been his first published work. In the preface, he apologizes for some faults, among them, "no little want of English; but this I hope dear Reader you will easily Pardon; I am sure you would did you but know how long I have been a Stranger to my Country."

It has been thought that this book was published at Liege. Worsley's connection with that town, together with his implication that this book was written abroad, make the supposition a not unlikely one.

T 20. A Letter to a Friend, touching Dr. Jeremy Taylor's Dissuasive from Popery . . . . Printed in the Year, 1665. Quarto. (Wing L1655A).

The author of this book is unknown, but he may be the A. L. alluded to by Taylor in the *Second Dissuasive* (No. 45).

T 21. Diaphanta: Or Three Attendants on Fiat Lux . . . . 1665. 8vo. (Wing C427).

There was a second issue of these sheets in 1671.

The letter against Taylor begins on page 217, and is preceded by its "Occasion" (all the letters in this work have "Occasions" before them). The first epistle was written to an adversary, the second to a friend, the third (concerning Taylor) to one who had begun to think more moderately of Catholic religion but returned after reading Taylor's *Dissuasive*.

The author was a certain Vincent Canes. He was born into an Anglican family in Nottinghamshire, but in 1640 he was converted to Roman Catholicism and became a Franciscan in Douai. In 1648 he returned to England, spending some of his time in Lancashire, but mostly in London. *Fiat Lux* (Wing C429), to which *Diaphanta* forms a sort of appendix, was published, probably at Douai, in 1662.

T 22. Sure-Footing in Christianity . . . . with Three Appendixes . . . . Second Edition. Adding a Fourth, Subverting Fundamentally and Manifoldly my Ld. of Down's Dissuasive . . . . By J. S. . . . London. Printed in the Year MDCLXV. 8vo. (Wing S2596).

The first edition of *Sure-Footing* was published in 1665 (Wing S2595). The new material in the second edition, the attack on Taylor, begins on R4^r. In

1675 the sheets of the Fourth Appendix (concerning Taylor) were issued again (Wing S2564).

The author was John Sergeant (or Sargeant). He was born at Barrow-upon-Humber, Lincolnshire, in 1622. He spent three or four successful years at Cambridge and then became secretary to Thomas Morton, Bishop of Durham. His research in ecclesiastical history induced him to join the Church of Rome. He was at the English College at Lisbon, and was ordained priest. He attacked all the great Protestant writers of his time. Aside from Taylor, in England he attacked Bramhall and Hammond. It is a curiosity of his life and/or character that such a man was said to be on friendly terms with Thomas Hobbes. He died in 1707.

The part of *Sure-Footing* which concerns Whitby was answered in ΔΌΣ ΠΌΤΣΤΩ. *Or, An Answer to Sure Footing, so far as Mr. Whitby is concerned in it* . . . . Oxford, 1666 (Wing W1725). This volume contains, as an integral part of it, another work, on page 52 of which *Ductor Dubitantium* is mentioned; there are no other allusions to Taylor. The work was probably written in answer to the first edition of *Sure-Footing*.

Index

NOTE: Only the titles of Taylor's works, both canonical and supposed, have been indexed.

Gathorne-Hardy, Robert, 15, 24, 28, 110, 136, 138
Gauden, John, 81, 135
Gaule, John, 151
Gerard, Charles, 143-144
Gilbertson, William, 120
Glanville, Joseph, 123, 146
Golden Grove, The, 15, 39, 54, *63-69*, 78, 79, 84, 94, 124
Gosse, Edmund, 4, 15, 24, 25, 45, 71, 88, 150
Graham, Mr., 129
Great Exemplar, The, 21, *22-33*, 34, 35, 47, 48-49, 55, 62, 65, 77: *Antiquitates Christianae*, 31-33, 87, 96, 114-115, 145
Greg, W. W., 131
Gregory, F., 15
Grismond, John, 83, 99, 104
Grosart, Alexander B., 26, 65, 124
Groves, J., 68
Gunpowder Sermon, *3-5*, 15, 20, 34, 78, 79, 116

H., R. (printer), 95
Hackett, John, 136-137
Hackett, Thomas, 137
Haddock, James, 123
Hales, John, 17
Hall, H., 121
Hall, Joseph, 6
Hammond, Henry, 18, 88, 121, 149-150, 153
Hamper, William, 129
Harmonia Sacra, 64
Hatton, Christopher, 5, 8, 10, 15, 16, 23, 25, 27, 28, 30, 78, 79, 131
Hatton, Christopher (the younger), 15
Heber, Reginald, 15, 30, 89, 115, 120-121, 127, 128, 129, 136, 137, 149
Henderson, Alexander, 143
Heptinstall, John, 43, 53, 54, 69, 93
Hertochs (engraver), 70, 81, 89, 93, 106, 107, 108, 112
Heylyn, Peter, 5
Hobbes, Thomas, 153
Hollar, Wenceslaus, 39, 63, 64, 65
Hollingsworth, Richard, 144
Holt, R., 11
Holy Dying, 24, 27, 39, 40, 42, *48-54*, 55, 94, 107, 138, 139

Holy Living, 8, 24, 27, *34-43*, 49, 51, 53, 65, 70, 87
Hooker, Richard, 103
Humphryes, Pelham, 64, 124
Hunter, David, 123
Husbands, Edward, 143

James I, 49
James, M. R.: "The Mezzotint," 53
Jeanes, Henry, 73-74, 121-122
"Job's Curse," 123-124
Johnson, Thomas, 108
Juxon, William, 88

Knox, Alexander, 136

L., A., 152
Lane, George, 130
Langley, John, 15
Langsdale, Dr., 127
Laud, William, 3, 16
Lawlor, H. J., 131
Leake, William, 119
Leslie, Henry, 122
"A Letter," 122
Lewis, Mr., 19
Liberty of Prophesying, The, 14, *16-20*, 21, 23, 27, 34, 47, 78, 79, 81, 82, 139, 149, 150, 151
Lindsay, J. W., 92
Litchfield, Leonard, 3, 5, 7, 14, 17
Lloyd, David, 18, 103
Lloyd, Lodowick, 28
Loftus, Adam, 29
Loftus, Dudley, 29, 30, 77, 96, 145
Lombart, Peter, 26, 51, 70; Lombart Portrait, 32-33, 39-40, 49, 67, 81, 90, 92, 112
Lowndes, William T., 17, 45, 81, 122
Lyford, William, 65

M., E. (printer), 151
Macock, John, 11, 32, 61, 68
Macock, T., 61
Madan, Falconer: *Oxford Books*, 11
Magee, Brian, 91
Marriage Ring, The, 57
Marshall, William, 16, 66
Marten, Edward, 48, 54
Martin, John, 88, 89, 93, 94, 95, 103
Mathews, Lemuel, 145